ROAD BIKING™
Virginia

Jim Homerosky

FALCON®

Guilford, Connecticut
An imprint of The Globe Pequot Press

A FALCON GUIDE ®

All photos by author unless otherwise noted.
Text design by Lesley Weissman-Cook
Maps by Trailhead Graphics © The Globe Pequot Press

Library of Congress Cataloging-in-Publication Data
Homerosky, Jim.
  Road biking Virginia / Jim Homerosky. — 1st ed.
    p. cm. — (A Falcon guide) (Road biking series)
  ISBN 0-7627-1194-9
    1. Cycling—Virginia—Guidebooks. 2. Virginia—Guidebooks. I. Title.
  II. Series. III. Series: Road biking series

  GV 1045.5.V8 H66 2002
  917.5504'44—dc21   2002019654

Manufactured in the United States of America
First Edition/Second Printing

To Wendy,
for all her love, support, and friendship

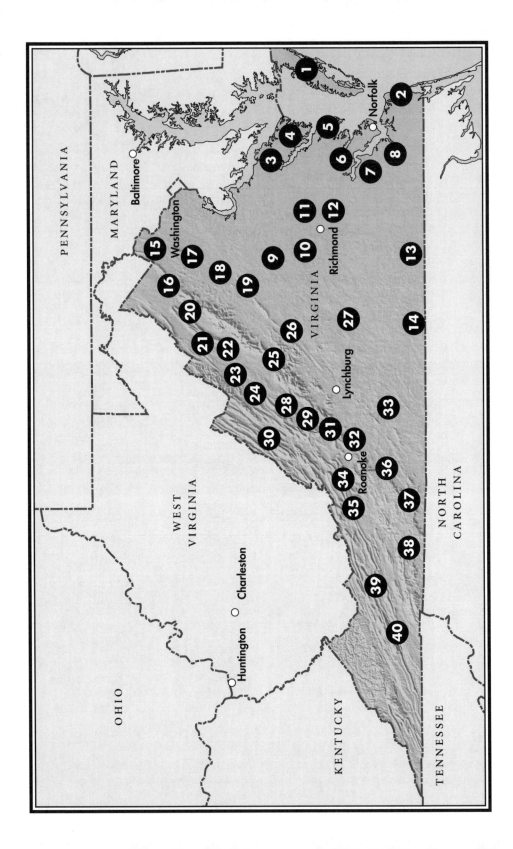

Contents

Preface

It wasn't easy choosing forty rides that best represent Virginia. One could easily argue that all forty could be located in the Shenandoah Valley, and the book would still be superior to most other states' bike ride books. The challenge was selecting the forty that best present the variety of scenery, history, and biking conditions that Virginia offers.

Starting locations for all rides were chosen for the presence of free and adequate parking, proximity to provisions and visitor's centers, and, most of all, safety. Routes were designed to strike a fine balance of secondary road riding with scenic and historic highlights along or near the route. Of course, terrain, traffic volume, and road conditions played a significant role. Most rides in the book are extremely rural. I intentionally avoided major population areas and found suitable routes through the few cities that the rides do pass. As you move farther west in Virginia, the mountainous terrain and rural nature of the region result in fewer options for route development, and occasional compromises had to be made.

My research was made easier by using Virginia Department of Transportation county maps and commercial mapping software. But even the latest technology would not have enabled successful completion without the help of many wonderful people and organizations. First, my thanks to the many bike shops and clubs that offered help and recommendations.

My deep gratitude goes to Carole Taylor, past president of the Tidewater Bicycling Association and board member of the Virginia Bicycling Federation; Bud Vye, ride captain for the Richmond Area Bicycling Association; Louise Hirsch of the Potomac Pedalers Touring Club; Reed Nester, president of the Williamsburg Area Bicyclists; Ron Hafer, vice president of the Peninsula Bicycling Association; Tom and Carol Bussey of the Franklin Freewheelers Bicycle Club; Bobby Wrenn, organizer of the Great Peanut Ride; Lindsay and Scott Vincent and Katy Rosemond; Tom King and T&M Photography for artwork; Sandy Butler for artwork; Jay Follansbee and Mike Williamson for help with editing; the many fine ladies and gentlemen of practically every visitor's center in the state; the many establishments that supplied information and tours; the American Automobile Association for the countless county maps and patience; my mother for her encouragement and support; and especially Jeff Serena of The Globe Pequot Press for taking a chance with this first-timer.

But most of all, thanks to my dear wife, Wendy, who helped in every phase of this project. I could not and would not have done it without her.

Help Us Keep This Guide Up to Date

Every effort has been made by the author and editors to make this guide as accurate and useful as possible. However, many things can change after a guide is published—trails are rerouted, regulations change, techniques evolve, facilities come under new management, etc.

We would love to hear from you concerning your experiences with this guide and how you feel it could be improved and kept up to date. While we may not be able to respond to all comments and suggestions, we'll take them to heart and we'll also make certain to share them with the author. Please send your comments and suggestions to the following address:

The Globe Pequot Press
Reader Response/Editorial Department
P.O. Box 480
Guilford, CT 06437

Or you may e-mail us at:

editorial@globe-pequot.com

Thanks for your input, and happy travels!

Introduction

From the Tidewater coastal plains to the peaks of the Blue Ridge Mountains, Virginia has so much to offer the cyclist. Add in the rolling hills of the Piedmont and the fabled Shenandoah Valley, and you have a state unmatched in scenic beauty, history, and cycling opportunities.

Virginia has three principal geographic regions. The Tidewater, or coastal plain, comprises the eastern coast and the areas surrounding the four mighty rivers that empty into the Chesapeake Bay—the Potomac, Rappahannock, York, and James. The Tidewater terrain is extremely mild and within the capability of any cyclist. While much of the land is agricultural, the region is rich in history, particularly in the historic triangle of Williamsburg, Jamestown, and Yorktown, one of the country's most visited areas.

From Charlottesville and Richmond to the horse-and-hunt country of northern Virginia are the rolling hills of the Piedmont. Cyclists face slightly more challenge in this region, riding past grand homes of former presidents, Civil War battlefields, and countless horse farms bounded by attractive split-rail fences and aged stone walls.

The Piedmont rises to the Blue Ridge Mountains, extending nearly the length of the state. West of the Blue Ridge and east of the Allegheny mountains lies a succession of beautiful valleys, including the legendary Shenandoah. The region contains some of Virginia's best scenery but also the most challenging cycling. Many of the rides in this region were designed as valley rides and turn just before difficult climbing would begin, thereby offering the casual cyclist more opportunities to cycle this wonderful area.

Although Virginia enjoys four distinct seasons, many residents bicycle

Along Duke of Gloucester Street in Colonial Williamsburg.

year-round. Cold winter conditions are usually confined to northern Virginia and the mountain regions. Tidewater and many Piedmont rides can be enjoyed throughout the winter months. However, expect high temperatures and humidity in the Tidewater region during the summer months. Plan to ride early in the day, and carry sufficient water.

Autumn may be the perfect time to bicycle Virginia. However, for many of the rides in the western mountains, throngs of tourists clog the Blue Ridge and Allegheny mountains during the foliage season. Take this into consideration when planning these rides, particularly if they follow the Skyline Drive and Blue Ridge Parkway.

Springtime remains a wonderful time to cycle Virginia. Crowds are down, and so are prices. With pleasant spring temperatures, Virginia's natural beauty is augmented by its full bloom of azaleas, dogwoods, and wildflowers. After a winter slowdown, there is no better way to be renewed than a bike ride in the Virginia springtime.

The forty Virginia rides presented here offer a cross section like no other. You can challenge some of the toughest mountains in the eastern United States or leisurely cruise the pancake-flat coastal plain. Cycle through fields full of tobacco, corn, cotton, and peanuts and past tranquil farms of horses, cows, and even llamas. Plan on visiting Civil War forts and battlefields, or tour a historic home of a past president or statesman. You will have an opportunity to explore several caverns and other geological wonders that remind you that Virginia's beauty is evident not only above but also below the ground.

Water will be your companion on many of Virginia's bike rides—from small farm ponds and mountain streams to recreational lakes and expansive rivers. And let's not forget the Chesapeake Bay, one of the world's largest estuaries, and, of course, the mighty Atlantic Ocean. You can cycle through sleepy fishing villages that time seemed to have forgotten, through meticulously preserved villages that seemed to have jumped out of England's countryside, and through some of America's best university towns and cities.

Make your bike ride a two-day outing, and spend the night in a cozy country inn or at a world-class resort hotel. Enjoy conversation with your inn's gracious hosts, or soak your weary muscles in a resort's rejuvenating thermal springs. Cycle through the Shenandoah National Park, as well as many state parks and national forests. Bike through the state's longest covered bridge or along Virginia's prized rails-to-trails. Stop and sample the wares of Virginia's many wineries, or learn about the inner workings of a gristmill. Challenge yourself to a century ride—English or metric. Take a break from cycling, and acquaint yourself with the local people and history by stopping in a coffee shop or by visiting a local museum. Discover that Virginia has a lot to offer, and Virginians even more so.

ROAD AND TRAFFIC CONDITIONS

Virginia is indeed a fabulous state in which to cycle. Unfortunately, the state's bicycling facilities still lag behind other regions of the country. There are several communities, such as Alexandria, Charlottesville, and Williamsburg, that constantly strive to improve conditions for cyclists. However, don't expect much in terms of bike lanes and wide shoulders once you leave the city limits.

The lack of bike lanes and shoulders is offset, however, by an extraordinary network of county and secondary roads. These roads are mostly numbered 600 and higher and comprise most of the routes in this book. Though also lacking shoulders, the 600 and 700 designated roads are generally very rural, making them suitable, safe, and very pleasant to cycle. Occasionally, a ride will use a primary road when no suitable alternate route is available. Exercise caution on these roads, and remember to follow safe cycling practices.

Rides that are located in tourist areas will naturally have heavier summer traffic. Also, take into consideration the fall foliage season when planning rides on the Skyline Drive and Blue Ridge Parkway. Motorists are twisting their necks to look for that perfect photo and not looking out for the cyclist.

The rides in the west and southwest regions of Virginia will involve considerable mountain climbing. Remember that what goes up, must come down. In this case, you'll be coming down a lot faster than going up. Unfortunately, nearly every ride in this region will involve negotiating "switchbacks" or tight turns on its descent. Keep your speed under control, and by all means, be sure your brakes are working properly before your ride. Pay particular attention to the Terrain and Traffic and hazards sections in The Basics in each chapter for more detailed safety instruction.

SAFETY AND COMFORT ON THE ROAD

Virginia laws governing bicycling are similar to most other states. Bicyclists must ride with the traffic on the right side of the road, as close as practical to the right edge of the roadway. Bicyclists may ride on road shoulders but are not permitted to ride on interstate highways and other controlled-access highways in Virginia.

Every bicycle ridden between sunset and sunrise must have proper lighting. Bicycles ridden on roadways must have brakes that will skid the wheels on dry, level, clean pavement (consider this before attempting some of the mountain rides in the book). Virginia law also requires cyclists to ride single file and to properly signal intentions to stop or turn.

Most of all, ride defensively. Stop at all stop signs and red lights, and keep an eye out for motorists making illegal turns into your path. Use your rearview mirror, or listen for vehicles approaching you from behind. Anticipate cars

Beautiful Mabry Mill just off the Blue Ridge Parkway.

continuing their progress as though no cyclist was present. Even though they may be in the wrong, you'll never win in a collision with one.

Several jurisdictions require helmet use for bicyclists fourteen years of age or younger. Instead of researching which ones do, just simply play it safe and *always* wear a helmet. Remember that it is not a matter of *if* you will fall but *when*. Today's helmets are lightweight and come in bright, visible colors. Hey, they even look cool! Your local bike shop can make sure that your helmet is properly fitted.

Consider wearing padded cycling gloves. They help buffer road shock that can lead to hand numbness commonly experienced by the bicyclist. Long-term riding this way can indeed increase the risk of nerve damage. Gloves will also help to minimize abrasions should you happen to fall.

Use a rearview mirror to monitor traffic behind you. Various styles are available that will mount to the handlebars, eyeglasses, or helmet. Experiment with the different styles until you find one that you can use safely and comfortably.

Note in the Ride Information section of each ride the availability of bike shops. You will not find a shop in most rural areas of Virginia. Therefore, at least pack the tools necessary to repair a flat tire. This would include a patch kit (or spare tube), tire levers, and a pump. I recommend that every cyclist also carry a multitool. This tool usually includes Allen wrenches, a spoke wrench, tire levers, and screwdrivers—enough to solve most roadside problems. Of course, the tool is worthless if you don't know how to use it.

Cycle clothing can also help increase comfort while in the saddle. Not only do bike jerseys provide increased visibility, but their fabric helps wick perspiration and keep you dry. They usually are equipped with convenient rear pockets to carry supplies and a longer cut in back to provide adequate cover in the stretched-out position. Padded shorts may look funny and invite stares, but they definitely reduce saddle soreness and protect your inner thighs from chafing. Biking shorts are one item on which you never want to compromise.

Nothing can ruin a ride or trip faster than saddle sores and blisters. Invest in the best you can afford.

All the rides in this book are suitable for cyclists with road, hybrid, or mountain bikes. The one exception is the New River Valley Trail. Here, 1¼-inch width tires or greater are recommended. Cycling this unpaved trail for nearly 50 miles with skinny road tires would be uncomfortable, unpleasant, and unsafe. Two other rides include very short sections on unpaved roads. Seeing that these segments are both under 1 mile, cyclists with road bikes can easily deal with these short stretches using a little caution.

Finally, always carry with you at least one water bottle. A good rule of thumb is to drink one water bottle for every hour of cycling. Most bikes are equipped to carry two bottles, and hydration systems that cyclists can strap to their back are widely available and becoming extremely popular. It's a good idea to carry a few Fig Newtons or energy bars with you on any ride. Review the Miles and Directions section of a ride before you head out to know before-hand if stores are available and where they are located. Bonking is no fun. Be prepared and bike smart.

HOW TO USE THIS BOOK

The forty routes in *Road Biking Virginia* are divided into four categories according to degree of difficulty. These classifications are subjective, taking into account the combination of distance, road grade, and bike-handling skills necessary to negotiate the full tour. Each route's name indicates its relative degree of difficulty.

♦ *Rambles* are the easiest and shortest rides in the book, accessible to almost all riders, and should be easily completed in one day. They are usually less than 35 miles long and are generally on flat to slightly rolling terrain.

♦ *Cruises* are intermediate in difficulty and distance. They are generally 25 to 50 miles long and may include some moderate climbs. Cruises generally will be completed easily by an experienced rider in one day, but inexperienced or out-of-shape riders may want to take two days with an overnight stop.

♦ *Challenges* are difficult, designed especially for experienced riders in good condition. They are usually 40 to 60 miles long and may include some steep climbs. They should be a challenge even for fairly fit riders attempting to complete them in one day. Less experienced or fit riders should expect to take two days.

♦ *Classics* are long and hard. They are more than 60 miles and may be more than 100. They can include steep climbs and high-speed descents. Even fit and experienced riders will want to take two days. These rides are not recommended for less fit and experienced riders unless they are done in shorter stages.

Remember that terrain is as much a factor as distance in determining a rides category. The 54-mile Farmville Cruise is actually a lot easier than the shorter 33-mile Mountain Lake Challenge. Examining the elevation profile of a ride together with the distance will enable you to select rides most appropriate for your ability level. (Note that only rides with an elevation change of 250 or more feet feature elevation profiles.)

Don't let the distance of a longer tour dissuade you from trying a ride in an attractive area. Out-and-back rides along portions of a route provide options that may be well suited to your schedule and other commitments. Likewise, don't automatically dismiss a shorter ride in an interesting area.

Directions in the route narrative for each ride include the cumulative mileage to each turn and to significant landmarks along the way. It's possible that your mileage may differ slightly. Over enough miles, differences in odometer calibration, tire pressure, and the line you follow can have a significant effect on the measurement of distance. Use the cumulative mileage in connection with your route descriptions and maps.

The selection of these routes is the result of extensive reading and research, suggestions from bike shops, cycling clubs, friends, and local experts, and a lot of bicycling. Some of the routes are well-known cycling venues; others are less frequently ridden. Taken as a whole, the routes in this book are intended to offer a cross section of the best riding locations in the state, indicative of the wide variety of roads and terrain Virginia has to offer.

To the greatest extent possible, each route has been designed with specific criteria in mind, although not all of them could be addressed in every instance. Starting points are normally easy to find, with convenient parking and reasonable access to provisions. Roads should be moderately traveled, be in good repair, and have adequate shoulders where traffic volume requires. I've also made an effort to guide the reader to interesting places along the way.

To fashion the most useful routes, some worthwhile features were bypassed for practical considerations. As a result, you might find it appropriate to use these routes as starting points or suggestions in designing your own routes. Rides can begin at any point along the course described in the route directions. You can always leave the route to explore interesting side roads and create your own routes.

Construction, development, improvements, and other changes are commonplace on Virginia roadways. As a result, the route descriptions and maps in this book may only be records of conditions as they once were; they may not always describe conditions as you find them. Comments, updates, and corrections from interested and critical readers are always appreciated, and can be sent to the author in care of the publisher.

Eastern Shore Ramble

*S*eparating the Atlantic Ocean and the Chesapeake Bay is the 70-mile-long peninsula known as Virginia's Eastern Shore. Countless waterways, small towns and villages, abundant wildlife, and miles of prime bicycling roads comprise this tranquil region. Starting in quaint and sophisticated Onancock, the ramble takes the cyclist through a marvelous network of flat country roads past small farms of tomatoes, peppers, and sweet potatoes. Stop in the fishing village of Wachapreague for a seafood lunch overlooking the marshes and barrier islands. End the ride in picturesque Onancock, and spend the night in one of its many bed-and-breakfasts. Plan on a cruise through the Chesapeake to remote Tangier Island, where the Elizabethan English accent can still be heard.

If coming to the Eastern Shore from the south, you will need to cross the Chesapeake Bay Bridge-Tunnel. An engineering marvel, the bridge-tunnel complex is 17.6 miles long and one of the world's largest. The trip across will set you back $10 for the toll, but the views of the Chesapeake Bay and the Atlantic Ocean are worth it. Leaving the frenzy of Virginia Beach behind, the bridge-tunnel delivers you to a completely different world.

Before you head out, stop in at the Hopkins & Bro. General Store. Built in 1842, this store has just about anything you would need and more, including bicycle rentals. Turn right out of the wharf onto Market Street and into Onancock. Agriculture, trading, and its convenient stopping point for ferries and ships that once sailed between Baltimore and Norfolk turned Onancock into a wealthy town. It's a pleasure cycling by the many historic churches, homes, and unique shops.

Start: From the Onancock Wharf parking lot.

Length: 35 miles

Terrain: Almost entirely flat, with just a few gentle rollers.

Traffic and hazards: Use caution on Route 13 Business when crossing Route 13 Bypass. All roads are paved and in good condition. Traffic picks up on way back to Onancock.

Getting there: Use Route 13 from the north or south. Follow Route 179 west toward Onancock for 2.4 miles (road changes to Market Street) to Onancock Wharf parking lot on the left. Free parking is available.

In just a few miles you'll roll into Accomac, one of the Eastern Shore's more charming colonial villages. I would recommend a detour here to explore this interesting and historic place. Guidebooks claim that there is more restored colonial architecture here than anywhere else in America, except for Williamsburg, of course. I'm not confirming that, but indeed, the town is enjoyable to stroll or cycle through. Be sure to check out the Debtor's Prison. Built in 1784, this jailors' residence later became a prison for debtors until legislation ended this practice in 1849. The building has remained virtually unchanged since its construction.

The next 14 miles or so will follow Route 605 as it runs south along the far eastern reaches of the Eastern Shore. Glimpses of the marshes and waterways occasionally present themselves, but dominating the views are the numerous farms lining both sides of this marvelous biking road. The primary crops are tomatoes, potatoes, peppers, corn, and snap beans. Regardless of what is planted, the rural nature and tranquillity of the region make cycling here special and worth the trip.

The ramble will detour off Route 605 a bit to take you into Wachapreague. Known as the "Flounder Capital of the World," this village is the home of the largest charter fishing fleet on the Eastern Shore. Home to fewer than 300 residents, Wachapreague has been spared the effects of tourism and remains a sleepy fishing village. Enjoy the fabulous views of the protected barrier islands from the Island House Restaurant, or pick up something to drink at Carpenter's Grocery in town. The town is laid out in a checkerboard fashion and is easy to cycle around without getting lost.

The rest of the ramble is more of the same—pleasant cycling along country roads, with plentiful farms and a handful of small villages. You never need to worry about running out of food or water on this ramble, as stores always seem to present themselves. Arriving back in Onancock, you'll now have the pleasure of cycling the length of the town on Market Street. It would help if you had a walking tour map of the town, as it would highlight more than thirty historic homes and churches. You'll pass Kerr Place, a 1799 Federal mansion that now houses the Eastern Shore of Virginia Historical Society. The museum contains an impressive collection of eighteenth- and nineteenth-century antiques and items relating to Eastern Shore history.

Back at the wharf, seek out the tours to Tangier Island. Home to 750 residents and about six and a half cars, this tiny remote island in the middle of the Chesapeake was discovered by Captain John Smith in 1608. Walking around the island and enjoying local seafood for lunch pretty much make up the entertainment on Tangier. But watching the local watermen go about crabbing, oystering, and raising softshell crabs and hearing the delightful Elizabethan accent passed on from their colonial ancestors are priceless. If you're considering taking your bike over, keep in mind that cycling every road on Tangier might get you 3 miles. I recommend leaving the bike back in Onancock.

LOCAL INFORMATION

♦ Eastern Shore of Virginia Tourism Commission, P.O. Box 460, Melfa, VA 23410, 757–787–2460.

LOCAL EVENTS/ATTRACTIONS

♦ Kerr Place, Eastern Shore of Virginia Historical Society/Museum, 69 Market St., Onancock, VA 23417, 757–787–8012. Open Tuesday to Saturday, 10:00 A.M. to 4:00 P.M. Admission is $4.00.

No cars allowed.

0.0 Turn right out of the wharf parking lot onto Market St.

0.3 Turn left on North St./Rt. 658 just past the Corner Bakery on the right. Outside of town, the road name changes to Town Rd.

2.1 Turn right at the stop sign on Merry Branch Rd./Rt. 657.

3.5 Turn left on Edgar Thomas Rd./Rt. 657.

4.2 Go straight at the stop sign on Rt. 657. Cross Greenbush Rd., then railroad tracks.

4.6 Turn left at the stop sign on Tasley Rd.

4.8 Go straight at the stoplight on Rt. 13 Business. Use caution at this intersection.

5.7 Turn right on Drummondtown Rd./Rt. 605 to stay on route. For a detour to Accomac, continue straight on Rt. 13 Business for 0.2 mile, then turn left on Courthouse Ave. Debtor's Prison is just ahead on the right. This will add about ½ mile to the ramble.

14.2 Turn left on Willis St.

14.9 Bear right on Rt. 180.

15.1 Turn left on Riverview Ave./Rt. 1710.

15.2 Turn right at the stop sign on Atlantic Ave. Go past Town Marina.

15.4 Turn right on Main St./Rt. 180. Just before turn, the Wachapreague Marina and the Island House Restaurant are on the left. In 0.1 mile, Carpenter's Grocery will be on your right. Closed Sundays.

15.9 Turn left on Bradford's Neck Rd./Rt. 605. Road name changes to Upshur's Neck Rd.

19.9 Turn right on Quinby Bridge Rd./Rt. 182.

23.6 Turn right on Main St. and cross railroad tracks. Go straight through the stoplight, using caution crossing Rt. 13. Immediately after crossing Rt. 13, turn right on Rt. 619 in front of Hickman Lumber Co. There is a Chevron Corner Market at this intersection.

26.2 Bear left at the stop sign on Rt. 180.

27.2 Turn right at the stop sign on Bobtown Rd./Rt. 178 North in Pungoteague. The Village General Store is on the left before the turn. In 2 miles, the route number changes to Rt. 718. Continue straight. In 2 more miles, the road name changes to Savageville Rd. Continue straight.

33.4 Turn right at the stop sign on Cashville Rd./Rt. 718. Road name changes to Hill St. when you enter Onancock.

34.5 Turn left on Market St. Chevron Station is on the right.

35.3 End the ride at the wharf parking lot on the left.

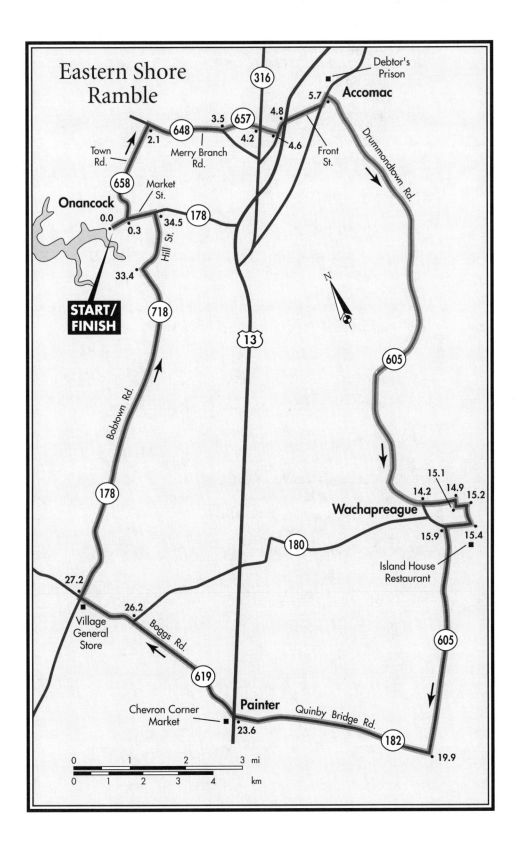

Eastern Shore Ramble

Onancock

Accomac

Debtor's Prison

Wachapreague

Painter

Village General Store

Chevron Corner Market

Island House Restaurant

START/FINISH

Town Rd.

Merry Branch Rd.

Front St.

Drummondtown Rd.

Market St.

Hill St.

Bobtown Rd.

Boggs Rd.

Quinby Bridge Rd.

316

657

648

658

178

178

718

13

605

605

180

619

182

0.0
0.3
2.1
3.5
4.2
4.6
4.8
5.7
34.5
33.4
14.2
14.9
15.1
15.2
15.4
15.9
27.2
26.2
23.6
19.9

N

0   1   2   3 mi

0   1   2   3   4 km

◆ Tangier-Onancock Cruises, 757–891–2240. Daily cruises from Memorial Day through October 15. Cost is $20 for adults, $10 for children. Leaves Onancock at 10:00 A.M.

RESTAURANTS

◆ Eastern Shore Steamboat Co. Restaurant, 2 Market St., Onancock, 757–787–3100. Located in the Hopkins & Bro. General Store. Seafood.
◆ Island House Restaurant, 17 Atlantic Ave., Wachapreague, 757–787–4242. Waterfront seafood restaurant.

ACCOMMODATIONS

◆ Spinning Wheel B&B, 31 North St., Onancock, VA 23417, 757–787–7311. An 1890 Victorian B&B with an antique spinning wheel in every room. Mid-range.
◆ Hart's Harbor House and Burton B&B, 9 Brooklyn Ave., Wachapreague, VA 23480, 757–787–4848. Adjacent Victorian B&Bs with access to the waterfront. Mid-range.

BIKE SHOP

◆ None in the area.

REST ROOMS

◆ At the start in the Hopkins & Bros. General Store
◆ Mile 0.3: at various locations in Onancock
◆ Mile 15.4: at Island House Restaurant and various places in Wachapreague
◆ Mile 23.6: at the Chevron Corner Market

MAP

◆ DeLorme *Virginia Atlas and Gazetteer* map 62

Ocean Ramble

W*ith all of Virginia's beautiful mountains, valleys, rivers, and bay, it's easy to forget that Virginia also has ocean-front. Situated within Virginia Beach city limits, the Ocean Ramble takes the cyclist through the more rural parts of the vast city to the quiet cottage community of Sandbridge Beach. Cycle through the laid-back coastal village and alongside its relatively unspoiled public beach. Detour to Back Bay National Wildlife Refuge and False Cape State Park to experience one of the last remaining undeveloped coastline areas on the Atlantic. At ride's end, pick up some fresh fruit and vegetables at the Farmer's Market, and stroll the variety of shops in the adjacent Countryside Shops.*

Don't be intimidated by the ramble's being within the city limits of Virginia Beach, Virginia's largest city. The route is surprisingly rural, and the ocean riding is at Sandbridge Beach, very different from the glitzy strip and high-rise hotels of downtown Virginia Beach to the north.

Carole Taylor, past president of the Tidewater Bicycling Association, graciously submitted this ramble and offered advice on the appropriate times to enjoy the ride. Summer, Carole claims, requires sharing narrow Sandbridge Road with many tourists vacationing at Sandbridge Beach. Avoid doing this ride during the high season. If you want to cycle Sandbridge during the summer, Carole recommends starting at the Sandbridge Seaside Market.

The ramble offers other variations. For a 28-miler, start at the Farmer's Market and turn around at the Sandbridge Seaside Market. To add on 3.4 miles to the advertised 36 miles, continue past Little Island Park and enter the Back Bay National Wildlife Refuge. Or, if you start at Sandbridge Seaside Market,

Start: From the Farmer's Market parking lot in Virginia Beach.

Length: 36 miles

Terrain: Flat. Beginner capability.

Traffic and hazards: Use caution when leaving the Farmer's Market on Dam Neck Road and when crossing Princess Anne Road. Sandbridge Road is very busy during the summer season; therefore, the ride should be attempted only during the off-season. It is safe, however, to bicycle Sandpiper and Sandfiddler Roads in Sandbridge Beach at any time. If starting the trip in Sandbridge Beach, park behind the Sandbridge Seaside Market at mile 14.1. Use caution on Sandfiddler Road, as sand is often covering portions of the pavement.

Getting there: From Virginia Beach, follow Pacific Avenue south, which turns into General Booth Boulevard. Turn right on Dam Neck Road and follow for 5.3 miles to the Farmer's Market on the right. It is located just before the intersection of Dam Neck Road and Princess Anne Road. Upon entering the market area, continue straight, and go past the circular-shaped Farmer's Market on the left. Park in the far rear parking lot. Plenty of free parking.

you can get nearly 13 miles biking to both ends of the long, narrow village. If you like the sand and ocean, the Ocean Ramble is your best opportunity in Virginia.

Expect a very flat and easy spin along the entire route. Several stores and restaurants pop up, as well as fresh seafood stands; sample their wares if you have the means to carry them. At the midpoint of the ride, you have an option to enter Back Bay Refuge.

Back Bay National Wildlife Refuge is an 8,000-acre mix of ocean, dunes, marshes, ponds, maritime forests, and barrier islands. Popular with bird-watchers and photographers, the refuge offers a number of nature trails for the hiker, as well as for the biker equipped to handle gravel surfaces. More than 300 species of birds have been observed in this beautiful coastal habitat, and mammals, such as deer, mink, fox, and river otter, also make their home here. There is a $2.00 fee if you want to enter the refuge.

Even more remote than Back Bay is False Cape State Park. There is no vehicle access to the park, so entry is by foot, bike, boat, or seasonal tram. More than 4,000 acres, False Cape is one of the last undeveloped areas along the Atlantic Ocean. Within the park, you can enjoy 6 miles of unspoiled beach and hike or bike the park's many trails in search of deer, wild horses, and boar. Camping is also permitted in the park if a permit is secured. An entrance fee is included with admission to Back Bay Refuge.

Heading back to Sandbridge, you'll surely enjoy biking along Sandfiddler Road. Don't expect a boardwalk, hotel, or T-shirt shop here. Separating you from the beach is simply a number of rental cottages, most built on stilts, offer-

Sandfiddler Road in Sandbridge Beach sometimes resembles a beach.

ing ocean views underneath and in between. The beach is narrow and literally a stone's throw from the road. Its close proximity often results in mini sand dunes that build up on Sandfiddler Road. Although caution should be used when biking over them, the fact that the road occasionally resembles a beach is part of the charm.

Sandbridge Beach has several restaurants and a market for a nice break or picnic lunch. Consider Sandbridge Restaurant and Raw Bar right next to the Sandbridge Seaside Market at mile 14.1 for lunch. For a picnic, consider Little Island Park at mile 17.8. The community park has picnic areas, a snack bar, outdoor grills, tennis and basketball courts, a fishing pier, rest rooms and bathhouse, a long public beach, and a seasonal tram to Back Bay Refuge. At the end of the ramble, allow some time to stroll the Farmer's Market. The market is a collection of shops featuring fruits and vegetables as well as local Virginia products and gifts. Next door is the Countryside Shops, offering even more interesting gifts and delicacies. Whatever your pleasure, you'll find it on the Ocean Ramble.

LOCAL INFORMATION

♦ Visitor Information Center, 2100 Parks Ave., Virginia Beach, VA 23451, 800–446–8038. Open daily from 9:00 A.M. to 5:00 P.M.

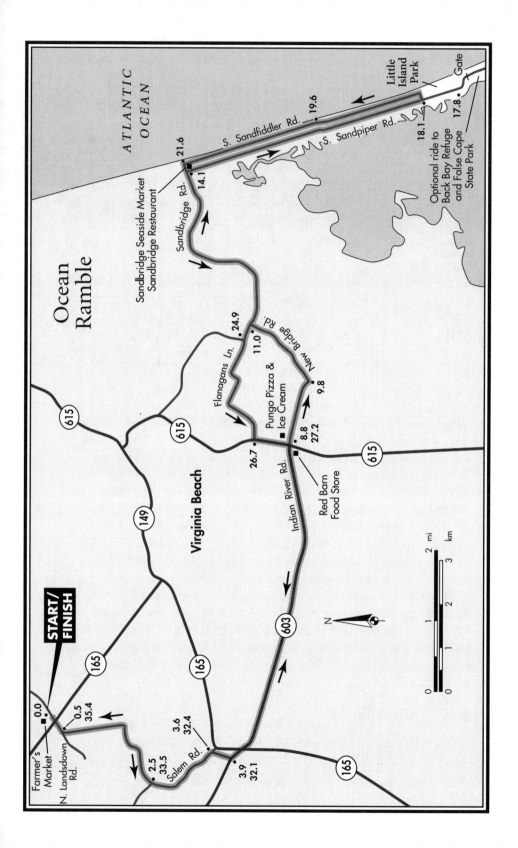

Ocean Ramble

ATLANTIC OCEAN

Virginia Beach

START/FINISH

Farmer's Market 0.0
N. Landsdown Rd. 0.5 35.4
2.5 33.5
Salem Rd. 3.6 32.4
3.9 32.1

Indian River Rd. 603

Red Barn Food Store

615

8.8 27.2

Pungo Pizza & Ice Cream

9.8

New bridge Rd.

11.0

26.7

Flanagans Ln.

615

24.9

Sandbridge Rd.

14.1

21.6

Sandbridge Seaside Market
Sandbridge Restaurant

S. Sandfiddler Rd. 19.6

S. Sandpiper Rd.

18.1

17.8

Gate

Little Island Park

Optional ride to Back Bay Refuge and False Cape State Park

615

149

165

165

165

N

2 mi
km
0   1   2
0   1   2   3

0.0 Turn right out of the Farmer's Market parking lot on Dam Neck Rd. Use caution biking up to the stoplight at Princess Anne Rd. Continue straight on Dam Neck Rd. at the light.

0.5 Turn left on Landstown Rd.

2.5 Turn left at the stop sign on Salem Rd.

3.6 Turn right on Winston Ave.

3.9 Turn left at the stop sign on Indian River Rd.

8.8 Continue straight at the stoplight on Indian River Rd., crossing Princess Anne Rd. On the right at the light is a Citgo/Red Barn Food Store.

9.8 Turn left on New Bridge Rd.

11.0 Turn right at the stop sign on Sandbridge Rd.

14.1 Turn right on Sandpiper Rd. Immediately on left is the Sandbridge Seaside Market and Sandbridge Restaurant and Raw Bar. Just past the market on the left is a parking lot for those wishing to begin the ramble here in Sandbridge.

17.6 The Baja Restaurant is on the right.

17.8 Turn left into Little Island Park. A snack bar and rest rooms are located here, as well as a public beach and fishing pier. Note: For those continuing to Back Bay National Wildlife Refuge or False Cape State Park, continue on Sandpiper Rd. another 0.5 mile to park entrance. Pay $2.00 fee. You can continue biking on a paved, park road for another 1.2 miles. There are rest rooms located at Back Bay. This option would add 3.4 miles to the ramble. Otherwise, after your rest stop at Little Island Park, turn right out of the park to head back on Sandpiper Rd. in the direction you came.

18.1 Turn right on White Cap Lane, then take the immediate left on Sandfiddler Rd. Be careful of windblown sand on the roadway.

19.6 Bear right to stay on Sandfiddler Rd.

21.6 Turn left on Sandbridge Rd. The Sandbridge Seaside Market will be on your left.

24.9 Turn left on Flanagans Lane.

26.7 Turn left at the stop sign on Princess Anne Rd.

27.2 Turn right at the stoplight on Indian River Rd. Just before this intersection, Pungo Pizza and Ice Cream will be on your left.

32.1 Turn right on Winston Ave.

32.4 Turn left at the stop sign on Salem Rd.

33.5 Turn right on Landstown Rd.

35.4 Turn right at the yield sign on Dam Neck Rd.

35.8 Continue straight at the stoplight on Dam Neck Rd., crossing Princess Anne Rd.

35.9 Turn left into the Farmer's Market. Caution making the turn against traffic.

LOCAL EVENTS/ATTRACTIONS

♦ Back Bay National Wildlife Refuge, 4005 Sandpiper Rd., Virginia Beach, VA 23456, 757–721–2412. Fee $5.00 vehicle, $2.00 bicyclist. This 8,000-acre refuge is popular for bird-watching, hiking, and photography.
♦ False Cape State Park, 4001 Sandpiper Rd., Virginia Beach, VA 23456, 757–426–7128. Isolated park offering primitive camping, beach, and hiking trails.

RESTAURANTS

♦ Sandbridge Restaurant and Raw Bar, 205 Sandbridge Rd., Sandbridge, 757–426–2193. Local seafood dining inside or out.
♦ The Baja, 3701 S. Sandpiper Rd., Sandbridge, 757–426–7748. Casual dining, with screened lounge area overlooking Back Bay.

ACCOMMODATIONS

♦ All accommodations in Sandbridge Beach are cottage rentals. Try Sandbridge Realty at 800–933–4800. For hotels, head north to Virginia Beach and its 11,000 hotel rooms.

BIKE SHOP

♦ Touring Cyclist Bike Shop, 1512 Princess Anne Rd., #1580, Virginia Beach, VA 23456, 757–467–6912.

REST ROOMS

♦ At the start in the Farmer's Market
♦ Mile 8.8: at the Citgo/Red Barn Food Store
♦ Mile 14.1: at the public rest rooms behind Sandbridge Seaside Market
♦ Mile 17.8: at Little Island Park
♦ Mile 17.8+: at the Back Bay Refuge (option)
♦ Mile 21.6: at the public rest rooms behind Sandbridge Seaside Market
♦ Mile 27.2: at the Citgo/Red Barn Food Store

MAP

♦ DeLorme *Virginia Atlas and Gazetteer* map 35

Northern Neck Cruise

The Northern Neck Cruise explores the quiet and picturesque peninsula nestled between the Potomac and Rappahannock rivers, two mighty tributaries of the Chesapeake Bay. Starting in the Westmoreland County seat of Montross, the cruise is an easy mix of flat to gentle rolling terrain and a delightful blend of natural beauty and historical interest. Cyclists can stop at the Westmoreland Berry Farm to pick or purchase fresh fruit, taste wines at the Ingleside Plantation Vineyards, tour Stratford Hall, one of America's great houses of history and the home of Robert E. Lee, and in between, cruise past countless meticulously kept farms of wheat, soybeans, and corn. Back in Montross, a just reward is dinner and overnight stay at the beautiful 1790 The Inn at Montross.

The name Northern Neck was given to this region because it is the most northern of the necks, or peninsulas, that are formed by Tidewater Virginia's mighty rivers. The Northern Neck's boundary to the north is the Potomac, or "River of Swans," while its southern boundary is the Rappahannock, or "Quick Rising Water." It is a region rich in history and charming in its simplistic beauty.

You'll start the cruise in the quiet and quaint town of Montross. If you find it rather small, well, it is, and it is also the only town on the route. So, if you're looking for solitude and excellent backroad bike riding, you've come to the right place. Just as you're heading out of town, you have a chance to pick up water or energy food at the Exxon Market.

The entire route is flat to gently rolling. Although there are no significant climbs, there are several short, steep hills. Don't expect to be physically challenged in the Northern Neck, however. The challenge you have is fitting in all the interesting stops along the way and getting back before dark.

What you will find amazing is the quantity of well-kept farms in the Northern Neck region. Corn, soybeans, wheat, barley, and even tree farms comprise the landscape. Just when you think you've identified every imaginable crop, along comes the Westmoreland Berry Farm.

The Westmoreland Berry Farm is just a mile and a quarter off the route, but I would highly recommend making the stop. Here, you can pick your own fruit or simply purchase small quantities of your favorites. Depending on the season, expect strawberries, cherries, black and fall red raspberries, blueberries, blackberries, peaches, and apples. There are rest rooms available, as well as a picnic area and snack bar with hot sandwiches and ice cream. The spectacular ride to the farm is along orchards and a dazzling field of sunflowers. It all adds up to one of the best rest stops in Virginia. Normally open daily from 8:00 A.M. to 7:00 P.M. in season, but call 804–224–9171 to confirm.

A few miles down the road, another temptation presents itself. Just a mile off the route is the Ingleside Plantation Vineyards. Built in 1834, this plantation has an interesting history, as it once was a boys' school, a Civil War garrison, a dairy, and a courthouse. Now it is one of just a few Virginia wineries producing sparkling wine. Perhaps its success is due to its climate, soil, and topography, which are similar to that of France's Bordeaux region. If you detour here, consider a tour or tasting and enjoy the winery's picnic areas.

Stopping to refuel. (Photo by Mary Turnbull)

If the Berry Farm and Vineyard haven't taken up all your day, consider a stop at the Westmoreland State Park. It will add about 3½ miles to your cruise, but it's worth the effort if you're interested in swimming, hiking, or picnicking. Otherwise, continue up the road to Stratford Hall Plantation for an enlightening history lesson.

Built in the late 1730s, Stratford Hall is an H-shaped manor house on 1,600 magnificent acres overlooking the Potomac River. Although its architectural style is noteworthy, Stratford Hall is renowned for the Lee family who lived there. Born in 1807, Robert E. Lee spent his boyhood years at Stratford before he was destined to become general of the Confederate Armies. After a short film, costumed guides will lead you on a thirty-minute tour of the house.

THE BASICS

Start: From Old Westmoreland Courthouse at King's Highway and Court Square.

Length: 44 miles

Terrain: Flat to gently rolling. No major climbs. A few short, steep hills.

Traffic and hazards: Use caution on Route 3, faster traffic (1.1 miles) at midpoint of ride. All roads are paved except for a 0.8-mile section on Route 625. This section is hard-packed and can be ridden with a road bike with caution. Use caution on Stratford Hall Road, as traffic is heavier and road is narrow.

Getting there: Route 3 (King's Highway) from the north or south will lead to Montross. In the heart of town facing Route 3 is the Old Courthouse. Court Square encircles the courthouse. Free and plentiful parking is available anywhere along Court Square.

Afterward, plan on additional time exploring the plantation's grounds, still operating as a working estate. If you didn't get a chance to stop at the Ingleside Plantation Vineyards, then plan on lunch in the rustic Plantation Dining Room at Stratford, where Ingleside's chardonnay and cabernet sauvignon wines are served.

If you find yourself behind schedule from all the stops, don't worry, as the ride back to Montross is a breeze. Once in town, consider a stop at the Westmoreland County Museum, which shares a building with the visitor's center. This small museum's exhibits detail 300 years of rural life in the Northern Neck. Next to the museum and visitor's center is The Inn at Montross. Built in 1790, this "new" inn and restaurant actually sits on a foundation that was originally John Minor's Pub, established in 1684. End your long day at the fireside bar, as others did more than 300 years ago.

LOCAL INFORMATION

♦ Montross Visitor Center, Court Square, Montross, VA 22520, 804–493–9623.

0.0 Leave Court Square and go out to Kings Hwy./Rt. 3. Turn right at the stop sign.

0.7 Turn left on Peach Grove Lane/Rt. 622. Just before the turn, Yesterday's Restaurant is on the left. Exxon Market is at this intersection.

1.9 Bear right on Snyder Rd./Rt. 622.

2.1 Go straight on China Hill Rd./Rt. 638.

4.2 Turn right on Newland Rd./Rt. 624.

5.9 Bear left on Ephesus Church Road in Foneswood.

6.2 Turn left at the stop sign on Horner's Mill Rd./Rt. 625.

10.6 Turn left at the stop sign on Layton Landing Rd./Rt. 640.

11.0 Turn right on Leedstown Rd./Rt. 637.

14.6 Turn left on Rappahannock Rd./Rt. 637.

16.6 Continue straight on Rt. 637 to stay on the route. Turn left to detour to West-moreland Berry Farm. It is 1.2 miles to the farm for a 2.4 mile add-on.

18.2 Turn right on Claymont Rd./Rt. 634.

18.6 Bear left to stay on Claymont Rd./Rt. 634.

19.4 Turn right on King's Hwy./Rt. 3. Caution, faster traffic.

20.5 Turn right on Leedstown Rd./Rt. 638. Shell Station Market at intersection.

21.9 Turn left on Twiford Rd./Rt. 625 to stay on route. For a detour to Ingleside Winery, continue straight on Rt. 638 for 1.0 mile, for a 2.0-mile total add-on.

23.9 Continue straight on Rt. 625 as the pavement ends. Hard-packed road ahead.

24.7 Turn left at the stop sign on Grant's Hill Church Rd./Rt. 640.

26.7 Bear left to stay on Grant's Hill Church Rd./Rt. 640.

27.2 Turn right at the stop sign on Flat Iron Rd./Rt. 624.

30.0 Turn left on Baynesville Rd./Rt. 642.

33.3 Turn right on King's Hwy./Rt. 3.

33.7 Continue straight on Rt. 3 to stay on route. For a detour to Westmoreland State Park, turn left here on State Park Rd./Rt. 347. There is a Chevron Food Mart at this intersection.

34.3 Turn left on Stratford Hall Rd./Rt. 214 East.

35.5 Continue straight to stay on route. To visit Stratford Hall, turn left here on Great House Rd.

36.2 Continue straight to stay on Stratford Hall Rd. at junction with Rt. 644. Route number changes to Rt. 609 soon after this junction.

39.3 Bear right to stay on Stratford Hall Rd./Rt. 622.

39.9 Turn right at the stop sign on Panorama Rd./Rt. 622. Road name changes to Polk St. near Montross.

43.5 Turn left on Court Square/Rt. 1201.

43.6 End the ride at the Old Courthouse on the right.

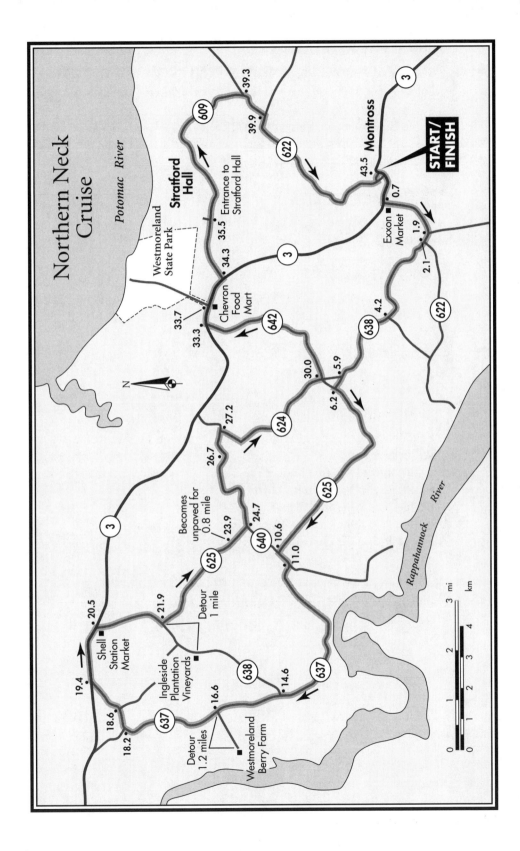

Northern Neck Cruise

Potomac River

Westmoreland State Park

Stratford Hall

Entrance to Stratford Hall

Montross

START/FINISH

Exxon Market

Chevron Food Mart

Shell Station Market

Ingleside Plantation Vineyards

Becomes unpaved for 0.8 mile

Detour 1 mile

Detour 1.2 miles

Westmoreland Berry Farm

Rappahannock River

N

39.3
39.9
43.5
0.7
1.9
2.1
35.5
34.3
33.7
33.3
4.2
5.9
30.0
6.2
27.2
26.7
24.7
23.9
10.6
11.0
21.9
20.5
19.4
18.6
18.2
16.6
14.6

609
622
3
622
638
642
624
625
640
625
637
638
637
3

km

mi

LOCAL EVENTS/ATTRACTIONS

♦ Stratford Hall Plantation, Stratford, VA 22558, 804–493–8038. Home of Robert E. Lee. Tours: $8.00 for adults, $4.00 for children. Open daily from 9:00 A.M. to 4:30 P.M.
♦ Ingleside Plantation Vineyards, 5872 Leedstown Rd., Oak Grove, VA 22443, 804–224–8687. Open Monday to Saturday from 10:00 A.M. to 5:00 P.M., Sunday from noon to 5:00 P.M.

RESTAURANTS

♦ The Inn at Montross, 21 Polk St., Montross, 804–493–0573. International and regional cuisine.

ACCOMMODATIONS

♦ The Inn at Montross, 21 Polk St., P. O. Box 908, Montross, VA 22520, 804–493–0573. Mid- to high-range 1790 colonial B&B.

BIKE SHOP

♦ None in the area.

REST ROOMS

♦ At the start in the Montross Visitor Center or various restaurants in Montross
♦ Mile 0.7: at the Exxon Market
♦ Mile 16.6: at Westmoreland Berry Farm (option)
♦ Mile 20.5: at the Shell Station and Market
♦ Mile 21.9: at the Ingleside Plantation Vineyards (option)
♦ Mile 33.7: at the Chevron

MAP

♦ DeLorme *Virginia Atlas and Gazetteer* map 71

Chesapeake Ramble

*T*he Chesapeake Ramble is an easy, delightful tour of the eastern reaches of the Northern Neck, the long peninsula bounded by the Rappahannock River to the south, the Potomac River to the north, and the Chesapeake Bay to the east. Starting in Kilmarnock, the ramble first takes in Historic Christ Church, one of the finest colonial churches in North America. Stop and shop in the unique stores in the villages of Irvington and White Stone. At the ride's midpoint, take a refreshing dip in the Chesapeake, and enjoy lunch at the popular Windmill Point Resort, located where the Rappahannock meets the Chesapeake. Finally, meander along tidal creeks back to Kilmarnock, the region's center of activity.

Kilmarnock is a small, pleasant town offering a small museum and several shops and restaurants. Most likely, however, you'll pick up what you need and head down the road, where quite a bit awaits you.

If you are looking for a good training ride, look elsewhere. The Chesapeake Ramble's gentle terrain lacks challenge, and its sights and scenery encourage a relaxed, touring pace. For those in search of a biking/sightsceing/lunch outing, this ramble is perfect. With several stops, the ramble can easily fill an entire day.

The route has you out of town in less than a mile, and after an uneventful, gently rolling 5 miles you'll pull into Historic Christ Church. Completed in 1735, Christ Church is one of the most beautiful and authentic colonial churches in North America. Cruciform in shape, Christ Church has been virtually unchanged since its completion and is both a Virginia and National Historic Landmark. Two unusual features of the church are its marvelous three-decker pulpit and its twenty-six original, individually enclosed pews. A small museum is located next door. Call 804–438–6855 to inquire about opening hours and services.

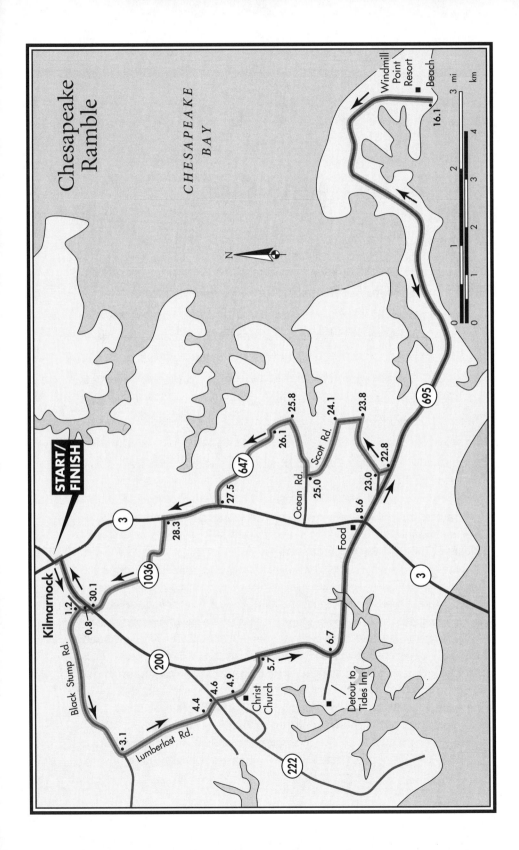

Chesapeake
Ramble

START/
FINISH

Kilmarnock

CHESAPEAKE
BAY

CHESAPEAKE
BAY

Windmill
Point
Resort

Beach

16.1

N

3 mi

km

4

3

2

3

2

1

1

0

0

695

25.8

26.1

24.1

23.8

647

22.8

Scott Rd.

27.5

25.0

23.0

Ocean Rd.

28.3

8.6

3

1036

30.1

Food

1.2

0.8

3

Black Stump Rd.

200

6.7

5.7

4.9

4.6

Christ
Church

Detour to
Tides Inn

3.1

4.4

Lumberlost Rd.

222

0.0 Turn right out of the public parking lot on unmarked Waverly Ave. Go a few yards, then turn left at the stop sign on Main St. Make the immediate right at the stoplight on Irvington Rd./Rt. 200 South. Caution, faster traffic on Rt. 200.

0.8 Turn right on James P. Jones Memorial Hwy./Rt. 675.

1.2 Turn left on Black Stump Rd./Rt. 675.

3.1 Turn left on Lumberlost Rd./Rt. 629.

4.4 Go straight on Lumberlost Rd./Rt. 630.

4.6 Go straight at the stop sign on Christ Church Rd./Rt. 646.

4.9 Turn right on Gaskins Rd./Rt. 709 to go to Christ Church. After your visit, return to Gaskins Rd., then turn right and go the short distance to the stop sign.

5.1 Turn right at the stop sign on Christ Church Rd./Rt. 646.

5.7 Turn right at the stop sign on Rt. 200 South. In 0.1 mile, Mom & Pop's Store is on the left.

6.7 Bear left at the stoplight to stay on Rt. 200 South. (At this intersection, turn right on Rt. 634 if you want to stop at The Tides Inn. It is ½ mile down Rt. 634.) Also, there is a Texaco Food Mart at this intersection on your left. Caution, faster traffic on Rt. 200.

8.6 Go straight at the stoplight on Rt. 695 in White Stone. Several shops and stores in town. The Buoy Food & Deli will be on the left at the light.

16.1 You will reach the end of the road at Windmill Point on your left. Follow the path at the end of Rt. 695 to the beach, or turn left on Windmill Lane into the Windmill Point Resort. Bear left once in the resort to go to the restaurant. After your stop, head back on Rt. 695 the way you came.

22.8 Turn right on Rt. 641.

23.0 Turn right at the stop sign on Rt. 642.

23.8 Bear left to stay on Rt. 642.

24.1 Turn left at the stop sign on Scott Rd./Rt. 643.

25.0 Turn right at the stop sign on Ocean Rd./Rt. 646.

25.8 Turn left on Rt. 647.

26.1 Bear left to stay on Rt. 647, in 0.1 mile, bear left again to stay on Rt. 647.

27.5 Turn right on Mary Ball Hwy./Rt. 3. Caution, fast traffic, but bike lane present.

28.3 Turn left on Rt. 1036.

30.1 Turn right on Irvington Rd./Rt. 200 North. Caution, traffic.

31.0 Turn left at the stoplight on Main St. Make immediate right on unmarked Waverly Ave. to the parking lot on the left.

Start: From the public parking lot on Waverly Avenue in Kilmarnock.

Length: 31 miles

Terrain: Mostly flat. Several gentle hills. Nothing that would challenge a beginner.

Traffic and hazards: Most of the roads on this trip have little traffic; however, the traffic can be fast. All roads are paved and in good shape but lack shoulders. Those who are uncomfortable riding under these conditions should not attempt this ramble. Use caution on the short (0.3 mile) stretch of Route 3, as traffic can be heavy and fast. There is a bike lane here, however.

Getting there: Route 3 from the north or south will take you directly through Kilmarnock. From the north, go past East Church Street (stoplight) ½ block, then turn left on unmarked Waverly Avenue. From the south, go past Irvington Avenue (stoplight) ½ block, then turn right on unmarked Waverly Avenue. Go another ½ block to the parking lot on the left. Parking is free.

In Irvington, consider a detour to The Tides Inn. The inn has been one of Virginia's top resorts for more than fifty years. Luxury-priced, the Tides may not be practical for your accommodation needs, but consider a stop here for lunch in one of its several restaurants. If you really want to pamper yourself, spend a night or two here and begin the ramble from the resort. It only adds a mile to the ride while offering numerous amenities such as golf, tennis, pool, yacht cruises, and sailing school.

A few miles down the road at the junction of Routes 200 and 3 is White Stone. The Buoy Food & Deli will be on your left at this intersection, while the River Market will be down Route 3 a few yards to the right. White Stone also has several unique shops, and a short stroll will take them all in while offering a short break from the saddle.

As you leave White Stone on Route 695, the terrain turns completely flat. Traffic is light (but fast), and the ride out to Windmill Point is a delight. The Rappahannock will begin to show itself on your right, while the Chesapeake appears on the left. The strip of land you're cycling will occasionally be as narrow as ¼ mile. Expect to be captivated by the region's peace, quiet, and beauty. There aren't many (safe) bike rides in Virginia where one can experience the Chesapeake Bay in such an intimate manner. This is one. Enjoy.

Halfway through the ramble, you'll reach Windmill Point and the end of the road. There is a small beach at the end of Route 695, where you can have a picnic or go for a dip. Take the path at the end of Route 695 for a few yards, then head to the left, away from the private condo beach area on the right. The areas to your left beyond the beach is the Windmill Point Conference and Yachting Center/Resort. Here you will find beachfront accommodations, golf, tennis, sailing, fishing, and a restaurant. Situated at the ramble's midpoint, the resort's restaurant serves up local seafood to refuel you for your return trip.

To avoid an out-and-back ride, the ramble branches off Route 695 and zigzags along several tidal creeks on the way back to Kilmarnock. The terrain remains mostly flat, while the roads turn extremely rural. This segment is mostly shady and provides a welcome and pleasant reprieve from the sun. Unfortunately, the Chesapeake coastline is irregular, and maintaining a network of similar rural roads is impossible. So you are dumped out on Highway 3. Don't be alarmed, however, as your ride on this four-laner is short and on a new bike lane. If you're in a rush, you can take Route 3 all the way in to Kilmarnock, but I recommend following the ramble's route for a little more peaceful ride.

LOCAL INFORMATION

♦ Town of Kilmarnock Visitor Information, 514 N. Main St., Kilmarnock, VA 22482, 804–435–1552.

LOCAL EVENTS/ATTRACTIONS

♦ Historic Christ Church, Route 646, Irvington, VA, 804–438–6855. Colonial church, from 1735. Free admission.
♦ The Kilmarnock Museum, 76 N. Main St., Kilmarnock, VA, 804–436–9100. Open every Thursday to Saturday. Free admission.

RESTAURANTS

♦ The Front Porch Restaurant at Windmill Point Resort, Route 695, Windmill Point, 804–435–1166. Local seafood.

ACCOMMODATIONS

♦ The Tides Inn, 480 King Carter Drive, Irvington, VA 22480, 800–843–3746. High-end waterfront resort.
♦ Windmill Point Resort, Route 695, Windmill Point, VA 22578, 804–435–1166. Mid- to high-end waterfront resort.

BIKE SHOP

♦ None in the area.

REST ROOMS

♦ At the start at various locations in Kilmarnock
♦ Mile 4.9: at Christ Church
♦ Mile 6.7: at the Texaco Station
♦ Mile 8.6: at the Buoy Food & Deli in White Stone
♦ Mile 16.1: at the Windmill Point Resort

MAP

♦ DeLorme *Virginia Atlas and Gazetteer* maps 60 and 61

Mathews Ramble

T he Mathews Ramble is an extremely flat and effortless tour of
Mathews County, situated at the far eastern reaches of
Virginia's Middle Peninsula. Extremely rural and rich in maritime history, Mathews is blessed with natural beach habitats, forested wetlands,
salt marshes, and a variety of marine and coastal plants and animals.
Stop at the Bethel Beach Natural Area Preserve to enjoy a dip in the
Chesapeake or to view the many bird species, or walk the observation
platform for a view of the historic New Point Comfort Lighthouse. After
this delightful tour on Mathews' fabulous biking roads, savor the local
seafood or chat with the friendly locals at the neighborhood Irish pub.

One of the smallest counties in Virginia, Mathews can boast some of the
best bike riding. The Tour de Chesapeake occurs here in late May and attracts
nearly 1,500 cyclists from throughout Virginia and neighboring states. With
only 9,000 residents in the entire county, Mathews offers many miles of low-
traveled country roads that are as well suited for family outings as they are for
race training.

Settled around 1650, Mathews became a major shipbuilding center in the
late 1700s. Its location on a narrow peninsula on the western shore of the
Chesapeake Bay led to the county's development as a port of entry and a commercial maritime center in the 1800s. Steamboats arriving and departing for
Baltimore and Norfolk were a daily occurrence. Today, Mathews is home to
farmers, fishermen, and many wealthy retirees, who are attracted to the region's
natural beauty and miles of shoreline.

The ramble starts in the heart of Mathews (the name of the principal town
as well as the county). Although small, the town offers some interesting sights

and is enjoyable to stroll. Pick up a walking tour map at the visitor's center, or simply browse the few blocks of town on your own. Mathews has a nice variety of stores and restaurants and several B&Bs if you desire to stay the weekend.

One thing you won't find on this ramble is a hill. If a challenge does arise, it will do so in the form of winds. Fortunately, many of Mathew County's country roads are sheltered by forests that provide welcome wind protection and summer shade. Traffic is extremely light, but caution must be exercised on Route 14, which runs north and south and serves as the spine of the county road system. Consider taking several of the dead-ends that branch off the main roads and lead to small marinas or quiet hamlets overlooking the East River or Chesapeake Bay.

Early on in the ramble, you'll arrive at Bethel Beach. This remains a favorite rest stop of cyclists, offering a sandy beach, magnificent Chesapeake views, and a chance to

THE BASICS

Start: From the municipal parking lot in downtown Mathews on Brickbat Road.

Length: 34 or 24 miles

Terrain: Almost entirely flat. Suitable for beginners.

Traffic and hazards: Use caution on Route 14 south of Mathews, particularly on the segment to New Point Comfort Lighthouse. Traffic, although light, can be fast. Roads are in very good condition. The small wooden bridge leading to Bethel Beach has openings between planks, where tires can get lodged. The last 0.2 mile leading to Bethel Beach is unpaved. Use caution if biking all the way to the beach.

Getting there: From Gloucester, take Route 14 East toward Mathews. Turn right on Route 14/198 at the T. Go 1.7 miles, then turn right on Main Street/Route 14 at Hardee's. Go 0.3 mile, then turn right on Brickbat Road (it's the first right after Church Street/Route 611). About 200 yards on the left is a free municipal parking lot.

spot some of the ninety species of birds that frequent this natural area preserve. Later, the ramble will take you to New Point Comfort, the windswept peninsula at the southernmost point of the county.

Standing guard on a tiny island hundreds of yards off the peninsula's southern tip is the New Point Comfort Lighthouse. Now a National Historic Landmark, the lighthouse served as a navigational beacon for 158 years before it was replaced with a more modern structure in 1963. The lighthouse was subsequently restored and now serves as a proud monument to the county's maritime heritage. An observation platform was built to view the lighthouse and to provide informational signs explaining the history of the lighthouse and surrounding areas. This is another rest stop that you won't want to miss.

Back in Mathews, be sure to stroll the courthouse green and take in Tompkins Cottage, the Courthouse, and the Debtors Jail. Walk over to Church

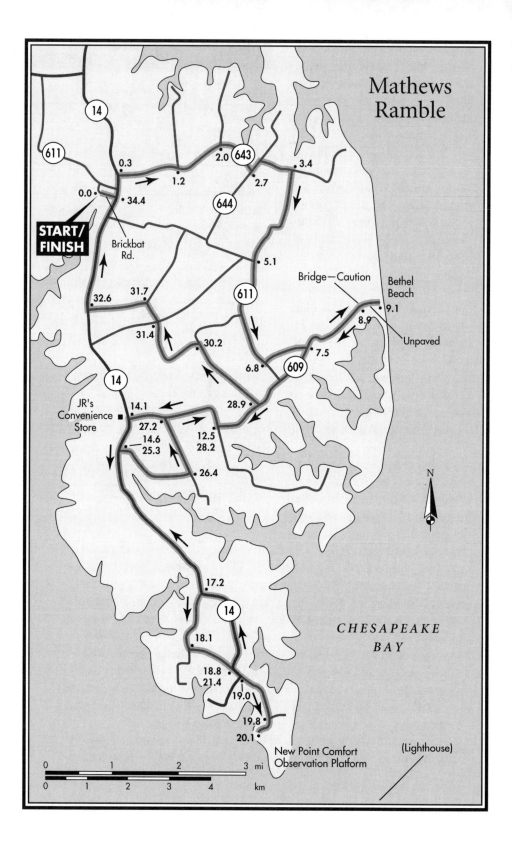

Mathews Ramble

14
611
14
643
644
611
609

0.3
1.2
2.0
2.7
3.4
34.4
0.0

**START/
FINISH**

Brickbat
Rd.

5.1

Bridge—Caution
Bethel
Beach
9.1
8.9
Unpaved
7.5
32.6
31.7
6.8
30.2
31.4
28.9

JR's
Convenience
Store
14.1
27.2
14.6
25.3
12.5
28.2
26.4

17.2
14

*CHESAPEAKE
BAY*

18.1

18.8
21.4
19.0
19.8
20.1

New Point Comfort
Observation Platform
(Lighthouse)

N

0   1   2   3 mi
0   1   2   3   4 km

0.0 Turn right out of the parking lot on Brickbat Rd. Go up to the stop sign and turn left on Main St./Rt. 14.

0.3 Turn right at the stop sign on Buckley Rd./Rt. 198. Hardee's is on the right.

1.2 Continue straight as the road becomes Rt. 642.

2.0 Bear right on Rt. 643.

2.7 Turn left on Rt. 643. In 0.2 mile, bear right to stay on Rt. 643.

3.4 Turn right on Knight Wood Rd./Rt. 613.

5.1 Bear left on Peniel Church Rd./Rt. 611.

6.8 Turn left on Rt. 677.

7.5 Turn left on Rt. 609.

8.9 Use caution crossing the old wooden bridge—gaps between the boards. Bear right after the bridge on the unpaved road to go to Bethel Beach.

9.1 Turn around at the beach and head back on Rt. 609.

12.5 Turn right on Hamburg Rd./Rt. 608.

14.1 Turn left on Rt. 14 at JR's Convenience Store. Ride with caution on Rt. 14.

14.6 Continue straight on Rt. 14. *Note:* To shorten the ramble by 10.7 miles, turn left here on Rt. 605. Go 1.1 mile, and pick up cue at mile 26.4.

17.2 Turn right on Rt. 600 at fire station.

18.1 Turn left to stay on Rt. 600.

18.8 Go straight on Rt. 14 at old post office.

19.0 Continue straight on Rt. 600 as Rt. 14 goes to the right.

19.8 Turn right to go to New Point Comfort.

20.1 After your stop at the lighthouse observation area, turn around and follow Rt. 600. When Rt. 14 joins from the left, continue straight.

21.4 Bear right on Rt. 14 at old post office.

25.3 Turn right on Rt. 605.

26.4 Turn left on Rt. 607.

27.2 Turn right on Rt. 608.

28.2 Turn left on Rt. 609.

28.9 Turn left on Rt. 614.

30.2 Turn left to stay on Rt. 614.

31.4 Continue straight at stop sign to stay on Rt. 614 at old trading post.

31.7 Bear left to stay on Rt. 614.

32.6 Turn right on Rt. 14. Caution, faster traffic.

34.4 Turn left on Brickbat Rd. to the parking lot on the left.

Cyclists take a break in Mathews County.

Street and stop in the visitor's center and some of the interesting gift shops. Turn the corner and head to my favorite hangout, The Irish Cottage. For providing such a wonderful ramble, buy me a beer. I'll be waiting for you.

LOCAL INFORMATION

♦ Mathews County Visitor and Information Center, Church Street, Mathews, VA 23109, 804–725–4229.

LOCAL EVENTS/ATTRACTIONS

♦ Mathews Market Days Street Festival, on the Courthouse Green, early September, local seafood, vendors, music, 804–725–4229.
♦ Bay Trail Outfitters, Onemo, 804–725–0626. Kayak rentals and guided tours of New Point Comfort Lighthouse and wetland areas.
♦ Annual Tour de Chesapeake, mid-May. Large bike ride around Mathews County, 802–897–8867.

RESTAURANTS

♦ The Irish Cottage, Main St., Mathews, 804–725–7900. Entertaining Irish pub.
♦ Southwinds Cafe, Church St., Mathews, 804–725–2766. Great clam chowder.

ACCOMMODATIONS

♦ Ravenwood Inn B&B, P.O. Box 1430, Mathews, VA 23109, 804–725–7272. A 1913 waterfront manor home. Mid-range.
♦ Buckley Hall Inn, P.O. Box 125, Mathews, VA 23109, 888–450–9145. Colonial-style 1880s inn. Mid-range.

BIKE SHOP

♦ None in the area.

REST ROOMS

♦ At the start in the public rest room across the street from parking lot.
♦ Mile 0.3: at Hardee's
♦ Mile 14.1: at JR's Convenience Store

MAP

♦ DeLorme *Virginia Atlas and Gazetteer* map 50

6

Colonial Cruise

T he Colonial Cruise is a gentle ride through one of the most historic areas in the United States. Starting in Jamestown, the cruise takes the cyclist through the woods and farms of Virginia's Lower Peninsula, a narrow strip of land bordered by the James and York rivers that witnessed the beginnings of colonial life in America. Take a detour down Duke of Gloucester Street, the heart of beautifully restored eighteenth-century Colonial Williamsburg. Ride on the Colonial Parkway, one of Virginia's most scenic bike routes. Then end the cruise back in Jamestown, where it all began nearly 400 years ago.

The Colonial Cruise is one of the most popular rides with the Williamsburg Area Bicyclists and other area clubs. Though mostly flat, the cruise does have several hills that will challenge beginners. The cruise also features considerable riding on bike lanes, a luxury not often found in Virginia.

The region's explosive expansion is evident in the early part of the cruise, as more and more housing developments sprout each year. But the route will branch off Centerville Road and follow the bicyclist-friendly Jolly Pond loop, a scenic and very popular route of recreational and racing crowds. Arriving at Richmond Road, you'll have an opportunity to refuel or make a pit stop at one of several establishments at this intersection.

At mile 15.7, you have a decision to make regarding the length of the cruise. Making a right will shave off about 9 miles and several hills, thereby turning the cruise into a ramble. Otherwise, stay straight and take in some of York County's fabulous country roads. At mile 22.1, you may want to detour to York River State Park for a little rest or to sample one of several off-road bike trails in the park. With great views of the York River, the park makes a perfect stop if you planned a picnic.

When you reach East Rochambeau Road, consider another detour to Pierce's Pit Bar-B-Que. It's about 1 mile to the right and somewhat of an institution here in town. Otherwise, continue along more bike lanes until you come to Route 132Y. A detour here will take you to the Colonial Williamsburg Visitor Center. Check it out only if you plan on spending considerable time exploring the historic area. If not, continue about ¾ mile to Duke of Gloucester Street and the heart of Colonial Williamsburg.

Mosquitoes. Unbelievably, it was this biting insect that plagued the early settlers at Jamestown and convinced them that a move inland from their James River site was necessary. Originally called Middle Plantation, Williamsburg thrived and soon became the center of government and commerce. The town played a prominent role in events leading up to the Revolutionary War, but it was after the war, in 1780, that the capital city was moved to Richmond, and Williamsburg's decline began.

THE BASICS

Start: From the VDOT commuter parking lot on Jamestown Road/Route 31 in Jamestown.

Length: 42 or 33 miles

Terrain: Mostly flat to gently rolling. Several short, steep hills will challenge beginners.

Traffic and hazards: All roads are paved. Traffic is heavier during the busier summer tourist season. The Colonial Parkway has exposed aggregate and is far from a smooth ride. Look out here also for open joints in the concrete. Many of the roads on this cruise have bike lanes.

Getting there: From Williamsburg, take Route 31 south toward Jamestown. After crossing Route 199, go 3.8 miles to the Jamestown Beach Campsites on the right. Continue straight on Route 31 toward the ferry for 0.1 mile to the VDOT commuter parking lot on the left. Plenty of free parking.

Williamsburg remained insignificant until the 1920s, when a man of vision, Dr. W. A. R. Goodwin teamed up with a man of money and determination, John D. Rockefeller, Jr. Restoration of the town began and the rest is, well, history (pun intended).

Even if you don't buy a ticket, it is easy and free to explore the colonial area by foot or bike. Pick up a map at the visitor's center on the corner, and wander down historic Duke of Gloucester Street. Looking is free; entering the buildings and museums will set you back a bit. Heading opposite of the colonial area will bring you to the magnificent campus of William and Mary. Pick up a walking tour map of the 1693 college, and check out the Wren Building and several other pre-Revolutionary structures. Head back to Merchant's Square, and try the Trellis Restaurant's famous "Death by Chocolate."

After your visit to CW, head down South Henry on another bike lane and turn onto the Colonial National Historical Parkway. The riding may be rough, but the experience is well worth it. The parkway makes up the backbone of the Colonial National Historical Park, which runs about 23 miles from Yorktown

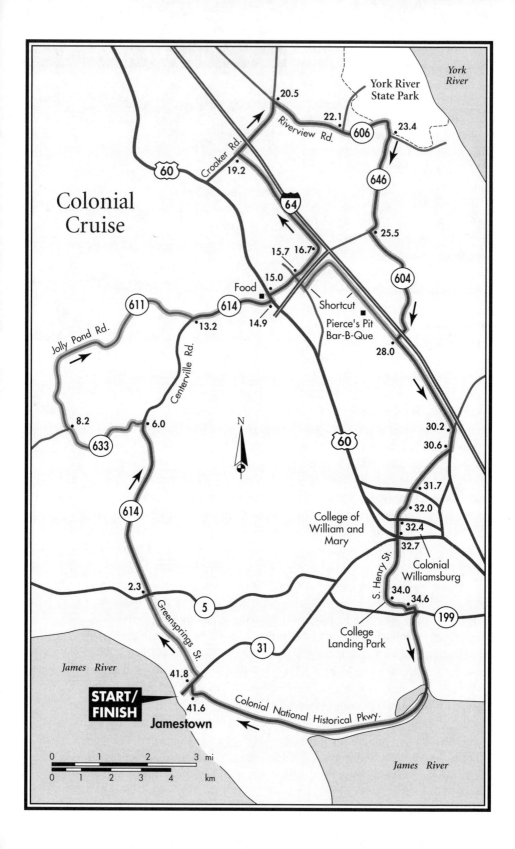

Colonial
Cruise

York
River

York River
State Park

20.5

Riverview Rd.

22.1

606

23.4

646

60

Croaker Rd.

19.2

64

25.5

604

15.7 16.7

15.0

Food

614

Shortcut

Pierce's Pit
Bar-B-Que

611

Jolly Pond Rd.

614

13.2

14.9

28.0

Centerville Rd.

8.2

6.0

N

30.2

60

30.6

633

31.7

614

32.0

32.4

32.7

College of
William and
Mary

Colonial
Williamsburg

S. Henry St.

2.3

5

Greensprings St.

31

College
Landing Park

34.0

34.6

199

James River

START/
FINISH

41.8

41.6

Jamestown

Colonial National Historical Pkwy.

0   1   2   3 mi
0   1   2   3   4 km

James River

0.0 Turn right on Jamestown Road/Route 31 out of the commuter lot. Go up about 0.1 mile to the Jamestown Beach Campground, and turn left on Route 614. As soon as you turn, make the immediate right to continue on Greensprings Rd./Rt. 614.

2.3 Turn right at the stop sign on John Tyler Hwy./Rt. 5. Caution, more traffic here. Make the immediate left on Centerville Rd./Rt. 614.

4.3 There is a small convenience store on the left.

6.0 Turn left on Jolly Pond Rd./Rt. 633.

8.2 Bear right on Jolly Pond Rd./Rt. 611.

13.2 Turn left at the stop sign on Centerville Rd./Rt. 614.

14.9 Turn left at the stoplight on Richmond Rd./Rt. 60. Caution, lots of traffic here, but there's an adequate shoulder. Miller's Neighborhood Market is located on the right, and the Williamsburg Outlet Mall is on the left. McDonald's is also on the left after the mall.

15.0 Turn right at the stoplight on Lightfoot Rd./Rt. 646.

15.7 Continue straight on Lightfoot Rd./Rt. F137. There is a Mobil Station Market on the right with a Subway. *Note:* To cut off 8.9 miles from the cruise, turn right here on Mooretown Rd./Rt. 646. Go 0.3 mile, then turn left on E. Rochambeau. Go another 2.1 miles, and Pierce's Pit Bar-B-Que will be on the right. Go another 1.0 mile to the junction with Barlow Rd. The longer route joins here. Continue straight on E. Rochambeau for 2.2 miles, and pick up with cue 30.2.

16.7 Continue straight as the road name changes to Rochambeau.

19.2 Turn right at the stop sign on Croaker Rd. In ½ mile, a 7-Eleven is on the left.

20.5 Turn right on Riverview Rd./Rt. 606. Garrett's Grocery Store is on the left before the turn.

22.1 Continue straight on Riverview Rd./Rt. 606. Detour left here if you want to enter York River State Park (4 miles round trip).

23.4 Turn right on Newman Rd./Rt. 646.

25.5 Turn left on Barlow Rd./Rt. 604.

28.0 Turn left at the stop sign on E. Rochambeau. This is where the shortcut reenters the cruise.

30.2 Turn right at the stoplight on Rt. 143 East.

30.6 Turn right at the stoplight on Rt. 132 South.

31.7 Continue straight at the stoplight on Rt. 132 South.

32.0 Continue straight on Rt. 132 South where Rt. 132Y goes left. Detour left here if you plan on going to the Colonial Williamsburg Visitor Center.

32.4 Continue straight at the stoplight on N. Henry/Rt. 132.

(continued)

32.7 Continue straight on N. Henry at Duke of Gloucester St. to stay on the route. Duke of Gloucester is the main street through Colonial Williamsburg. The historic area is to your left, while more Merchant Square shops and restaurants are to the right, as is the College of William and Mary. There is a small information and ticket center on the left at the corner of N. Henry and Duke of Gloucester St.

34.0 Continue straight on S. Henry. College Landing Park is on the right.

34.6 Turn left on the Colonial National Historical Parkway entrance ramp before the stoplight. Go up to the parkway, then turn right toward Jamestown. Ride with caution, as there are some open joints in the concrete surface.

36.4 The James River comes into view, and a nice beach is on the left.

41.6 Bear right on unmarked Rt. 359 toward Jamestown Settlement. *Note:* To visit Jamestown Island, continue straight on the parkway.

41.8 After passing Jamestown Settlement Park on your left, turn left at the stop sign on Jamestown Rd./Rt. 31.

41.9 End the ride at the commuter lot on the left.

to Jamestown via Williamsburg. Banned to commercial traffic, the parkway boasts spectacular scenery, particularly during the spring, when the dogwood and redbud trees are in bloom, and in the fall, when the oaks are in foliage. The mighty James River becomes your constant companion as you roll to Jamestown Island and Jamestown Settlement Park.

Jamestown Island features the original site of the early settlers. Some of the settlement's remains can be viewed, but the highlight of the park is a fascinating 5-mile loop road encircling the island. Popular with cyclists, the loop is indeed a wonderful ride, but recent "improvements" may require you to ride on gravelly surfaces. Inquire before you go.

As for Jamestown Settlement, this park includes replicas of the *Susan Constant, Godspeed,* and *Discovery.* You can board and explore all three of these ships that brought the original 104 colonists to the New World in 1607. The park also includes the re-created James Fort as well as the Powhatan Indian Village. Check it out, especially if your kids are along.

LOCAL INFORMATION

♦ Williamsburg Area Convention and Visitors Bureau, 421 N. Boundary, Williamsburg, VA 23185, 800–368–6511 or 757–253–0192.

LOCAL EVENTS/ATTRACTIONS

♦ Colonial Williamsburg Visitor Center located at Route 132Y. Restored eighteenth-century town including approximately eighty-eight buildings and several museums. No ticket required to walk or bike through the historic area. A one-day pass for entrance to buildings and museums runs $32 for adults, $16 for children. 800–HISTORY or 757–220–7645.

♦ Jamestown Island, at western terminus of Colonial National Historical Parkway, 757–898–2410. Fee: $5.00; free for children under sixteen. Site of actual 1607 colony. Artifact collection, ruins, archeology digs, guided tours.

♦ Jamestown Settlement, Colonial National Historical Parkway and Route 31, P.O. Box 1607, Williamsburg, VA 23187, 888–593–4682 or 757–253–4838. Fee: $10.75 for adults, $5.25 for children six to twelve. Restored ships, Indian village, James Fort, and museum galleries.

RESTAURANTS

♦ Christina Campbell's Tavern, Waller St., Williamsburg, 757–229–2141. George Washington was once a regular here. A Colonial Williamsburg-run establishment.

♦ Pierce's Pit Bar-B-Que, 447 Rochambeau Rd., Williamsburg, 757–565–2955. Local barbecue hangout.

♦ Paul's Deli, 761 Scotland St., Williamsburg, 757–229–8976. Casual pub with great sandwiches. The author is a regular here.

Bicyclists finish the Capitol to Capitol Ride from Richmond to Williamsburg.

ACCOMMODATIONS

♦ Williamsburg Lodge, S. England St., Williamsburg, VA 23185, 757–229–1000. Upscale Colonial Williamsburg-run hotel a block from the restored area.
♦ Holland's Lodge B&B, 601 Richmond Rd., Williamsburg, VA 23185, 757–253–6476. Mid-range, bicyclist-friendly B&B.

BIKE SHOP

♦ Bikebeat, Inc., 4640 Monticello, #9b, Williamsburg, VA 23188, 757–229–0096.

REST ROOMS

♦ At the start in Jamestown Settlement
♦ Mile 14.9: at various places on Richmond Road, Outlet Mall, McDonald's
♦ Mile 22.1: at York River State Park (option)
♦ Mile 28.0: detour to Pierce's Pit Bar-B-Que (and on the shortcut route)
♦ Mile 32.7: at various places in Merchant's Square

MAP

♦ DeLorme *Virginia Atlas and Gazetteer* maps 49 and 50

Surry Ramble

T he Surry Ramble is an easy ride through the quiet and rural landscape of Virginia's Southside. Take the free ferry (a destination in itself) across the James River to a land vastly different from Williamsburg and the Lower Peninsula. Cycle past miles of fields bursting with corn, soybeans, cotton, and peanuts. Stop at Chippokes Plantation State Park and Farm and Forestry Museum, where you can tour the manor houses and a farm that has been continuously worked for more than 370 years. Detour to Bacon's Castle, built in 1665 and documented as the oldest brick house in America. At the end of the ramble, make the obligatory stop at the Surrey House and enjoy southern cooking at its best.

Surry County riding is very popular with peninsula cyclists, including the two clubs to which I belong, the Williamsburg Area Bicyclists and the Peninsula Bicycling Association. The PBA holds the Surry Century in mid-September and attracts cyclists from several states. On any given weekend, you'll pass cyclists from all parts of Virginia, as Surry's gentle terrain and rural landscape attract a host of club and event rides.

Most visitors to Surry seem to come from Williamsburg and the peninsula's historic triangle. The route over the James River is on the Jamestown/ Scotland Ferry. This free ferry leaves every half hour and takes about twenty minutes. The scenic ferry ride is an enjoyable experience even for those of us who have made the trip numerous times. Check out the three restored ships of Jamestown Settlement as you approach the ferry on the Jamestown side. After the ferry, pick up what you need at the convenience store at the flashing light in Surry, as there are few opportunities on the route.

Bacon's Castle—the oldest brick house in North America.

The ramble follows low-traffic and flat country roads for the entire ride. In fact, there are many who claim that Surry County is lacking in scenic beauty and variety. Well, I agree. Although it is perhaps the least scenic ride in the book, however, cyclists still flock here to ride. Urban sprawl on the Lower Peninsula and in Hampton Roads has created a cycling haven on Virginia's Southside. For many, a little boredom is easier to manage than the frantic pace and confusion of the hoards of tourists on the peninsula.

About 7 miles into the ramble you'll enter Chippokes Plantation State Park. If you're just interested in cycling, then you'll simply breeze through here after making a pit stop. But consider a tour of the two nineteenth-century manor houses, formal gardens, and a working farm that has retained its original boundaries since 1619. There is also a small museum of antique farm and forestry equipment as well as hiking trails, campground, cottage rentals, and swimming pool. For the Park Visitor Center, call 757–294–3625; for the Farm and Forestry Museum, call 757–294–3439.

Down the road a way is the gem of Surry County, Bacon's Castle. Not exactly looking like a castle, the Jacobean-style house is believed to be the oldest brick structure still standing in North America. It was named for Nathaniel Bacon, who not only never lived in the house but probably never visited. Bacon was organizing rebellions against tyrannical English rule about 100 years before the Revolutionary War. It was one of Bacon's rebel forces who besieged the house and ruled Surry County for several months. Bacon's Castle's name is derived from the occupation. Guided tours of the house are available, but don't miss a stroll through the restored gardens, also one of the earliest in America.

At mile 19.2, you have a route choice to make. Turning left will lengthen the ramble but take you by Pons Store for a welcome pit stop. For the shorter ramble, continuing straight on White Marsh Road will shave off 6.6 miles. I recommend the longer route for the available rest stop and for several attractive farms along the way. The remainder of the ramble is more of the same—flat, traffic-free, and with peanut and cornfields dominating the quiet countryside.

Back in Surry, a stop at the Surrey House is a must. Operating since 1954, the Surrey House features local ham, pork, and seafood dishes, as well as the restaurant's famous peanut raisin pie. Get here early on the weekends, as this place is popular even with the noncycling crowd.

THE BASICS

Start: From the VDOT commuter parking lot behind the Surry County Government Center.

Length: 31 or 38 miles

Terrain: Almost entirely flat with just a few gentle rollers.

Traffic and hazards: Use caution for the short distance on Colonial Trail East/ Route 10, as traffic is faster. Use caution on the paved trail in Chippokes Park, as the trail is often covered with leaves or may be uneven. The route is very rural, paved, and has low traffic.

Getting there: From Route 10 coming west or Route 31 from the Jamestown/Scotland Ferry, follow to the flashing light in Surry. Continue on Route 31 South for 0.3 mile, then turn left on Route 1002. Go 0.1 mile to the VDOT commuter lot on the left behind the Government Center. From Route 10 coming east, follow to the junction with Route 31, then turn left. Go 0.7 mile and turn right on Route 1002. Go 0.1 mile to the parking lot on the left.

LOCAL INFORMATION

♦ Surry County Tourism Bureau, P.O. Box 387, Surry, VA 23883, 757–294–0066.

LOCAL EVENTS/ATTRACTIONS

♦ Bacon's Castle, 465 Bacon's Castle Trail, Surry, VA 23883, 757–357–5976. Fee: $6.00 for adults, $3.00 for children six to eighteen. Historic home. Closed Mondays.

♦ Pork, Peanut and Pine Festival, third full weekend in July, a celebration of the traditional agricultural products of Surry County. Food, entertainment, educational activities, 757–294–3625.

0.0 Turn left out of the commuter parking lot on Rt. 1002, and go to the stop sign. Turn right on Rt. 1001.

0.1 Turn left at the stop sign on Rt. 626.

1.4 Turn left on Brownsville Lane/Rt. 634.

2.8 Turn right on Colonial Trail East/Rt. 10, then make an immediate left on Alliance Rd./Rt. 634.

6.5 Turn left on Chippokes Park Rd./Rt. 665. Continue through park entrance. No admission fee for bicyclists.

7.2 Turn right at the end of Chippokes Park Rd. onto the park's bicycle path. Rest rooms are available just ahead before the turn.

7.9 Continue straight past the Chippokes Manor House and farm.

8.3 Turn right on Chippokes Farm Rd./Rt. 633. Use caution here when crossing the cattle grates.

9.8 Continue straight on Chippokes Farm Rd./Rt. 633/634.

10.0 Turn left on Highgate Rd./Rt. 634.

11.2 Turn left on Colonial Trail East/Rt. 10 Use caution, faster traffic.

11.9 Turn left on Bacon's Castle Trail/Rt. 617 to go to Bacon's Castle. If you want to skip the house, turn right here instead on White Marsh Rd./Rt. 617. You'll cut off 1 mile of the ramble. There is a small store at this intersection that is currently closed. It may reopen in the near future.

12.4 Bacon's Castle is on the left. After your stop, turn around and go back to the intersection with Rt. 10.

12.9 Continue straight on White Marsh Rd./Rt. 617.

19.2 Turn left on Bellvue Rd./Rt. 625. *Note:* To cut off 6.6 miles from the ramble, continue straight here and go 2.0 miles to the junction with Rt. 622 from the left. Continue straight on White Marsh Rd./Rt. 617 at that point, and pick up the next cue at mile 28.9.

22.0 Turn right at the stop sign on Mill Swamp Rd./Rt. 621. Pons Store is across the street.

24.8 Turn right on Sycamore Cross Rd./Rt. 622.

27.3 Bear left at the stop sign to stay on Rt. 622.

27.8 Turn left at the stop sign on White Marsh Rd./Rt. 617/622.

28.9 Turn right on Runnymede Rd./Rt. 622.

32.0 Turn right on Golden Hill Rd./Rt. 616.

33.9 Turn left at the stop sign on Beechland Rd./Rt. 626.

37.5 Turn right on Rt. 1001 just before fire department.

37.6 Turn left on Rt. 1002 to the commuter lot on the right.

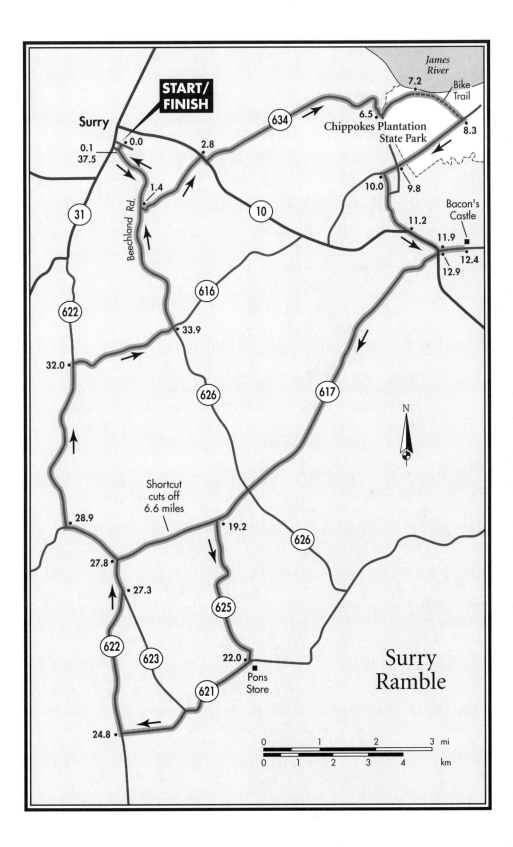

START/
FINISH

Surry

0.1
37.5

0.0

2.8

1.4

Beechland Rd.

634

31

10

616

626

617

622

33.9

32.0

Shortcut
cuts off
6.6 miles

28.9

19.2

27.8

27.3

625

622

623

626

621

22.0

Pons
Store

24.8

James
River

7.2

Bike
Trail

6.5

8.3

Chippokes Plantation
State Park

10.0

9.8

11.2

Bacon's
Castle

11.9

12.4

12.9

N

Surry
Ramble

0   1   2   3 mi

0   1   2   3   4   km

RESTAURANTS

♦ The Surrey House Restaurant, Routes 10 and 31, Surry, 757–294–3389. Breakfast, lunch, and dinner; open every day. Local specialties.

ACCOMMODATIONS

♦ The Surrey House Country Inn, Routes 10 and 31, Surry VA 23883, 757–294–3389. Low to mid-range.

BIKE SHOP

♦ Bikes Unlimited, 759 Scotland St., Williamsburg, VA 23185, 757–229–4620.

REST ROOMS

♦ At several locations in Surry at start of ride
♦ Mile 7.2: at Chippokes State Park
♦ Mile 12.4: at Bacon's Castle
♦ Mile 22.0: at the Pons Store

MAP

♦ DeLorme *Virginia Atlas and Gazetteer* maps 33 and 49

Smithfield Cruise

S mithfield, also known as the "ham capital of the world," is the base for this flat cruise around Isle of Wight County. The cruise winds through Virginia's Southside, the region south of the James River noted for its agriculture and slower pace of life. Popular with peninsula cyclists, the Smithfield Cruise is at its best in the fall, when the many cotton fields are in full bloom. Spend some time after the ride in the hospitable town of Smithfield, where its link to the past is reflected in its homes, landmarks, and food.

Known the world over for its hams, Smithfield's history of curing meats dates back over 200 years. Although you can't tour the processing plants, local restaurants and stores can most certainly offer their prized pork in any form or fashion. Remember, to carry the Smithfield name, hams must be cured within the town limits. So don't be fooled by those cheap imitations.

You can pick up anything you need at a variety of stores in Smithfield. The town itself is a real treasure, with numerous interesting shops, antiques stores, and fine restaurants and accommodations. Its architecture is an interesting mix of Colonial, Federal, and Victorian, which is thoroughly detailed on the town's walking tour map. A stop at the Isle of Wight County Museum located just a few steps from the visitor's center is also in order.

If you're looking for a good training ride, you found it here. Although Smithfield is full of interesting stops, the Smithfield Cruise quickly takes you out of town and past the many fields of corn, wheat, cotton, and peanuts. There are no museums, wineries, or presidents' homes on this cruise, just good, down-to-earth country road cycling.

If you need a break, consider stopping by one of several dams near the midpoint of the ride. After passing Lake Burnt Mills Dam, you'll cycle directly between Western Branch and Lake Prince dams. With refreshing water views on both sides, a stop here is a change of pace from the croplands that dominate the rest of the cruise. Watch for local sport fishermen plugging for bass around the many submerged stumps and along the shoreline.

The terrain in Isle of Wight County is primarily flat, so to be challenged, speed is in order. The lack of traffic, the gentle terrain, the lack of prominent rest stops, and the good pavement all add up to a perfect training opportunity. You may be distracted in the fall, however, for when the cotton is in bloom, the fields resemble a blanket of fresh snow. For those not accustomed to this beautiful sight, concentration on training becomes difficult to impossible while your ride is interrupted by photo ops.

Back in Smithfield, be sure to stop at the Smithfield Gourmet Bakery and Cafe for delicious sandwiches on homemade breads. It's just a block away from the visitor's center and popular with local cycling clubs. Staying the night? Consider The Smithfield Inn, which has provided lodging for George Washington and others since 1752. The Isle of Wight County Museum includes a reproduction of an old country store that will surely delight. Just 2 miles down the road on Route 10 east of Smithfield is St. Luke's Church. Not only is St. Luke's the only original Gothic church in the United States, it is the country's oldest existing church of English foundation. "Old Brick," as it's affectionately called, is believed to have been constructed around 1632. The church is absolutely beautiful, with its setting amid towering trees and the moss-covered headstones of its graveyard. This is a must stop on your visit to Smithfield.

LOCAL INFORMATION

♦ Isle of Wight Tourism Bureau, 130 Main St., Smithfield, VA 23431, 800–365–9339. Open daily from 9:00 A.M. to 5:00 P.M..

Curious onlookers.

LOCAL EVENTS/ATTRACTIONS

♦ Isle of Wight County Museum, 103 Main St., Smithfield, VA 23430, 757–357–7459. Closed Monday. Local history; free admission.
♦ St. Luke's Church, 14477 Benns Church Blvd., Smithfield, VA 23430, 757–357–3367. Circa 1632 Gothic church. Closed Monday; free admission.

RESTAURANTS

♦ Smithfield Gourmet Bakery and Cafe, 218 Main St., Smithfield, 757–357–0045. Local favorite for lunch, sandwiches, baked goods.
♦ Smithfield Station, 415 South Church St., Smithfield, 757–357–7700. Waterfront restaurant specializing in local seafood and pork.

ACCOMMODATIONS

♦ The Smithfield Inn, 112 Main St., Smithfield, VA 23430, 757–357–1752. Charming 1752 B&B. Mid-range.
♦ Smithfield Station, 415 South Church, Smithfield, VA 23430, 757–357–7700. Waterfront inn, with several lighthouse rooms. Mid-range.

BIKE SHOP

♦ Bike West, 1103 N. Main St., Suffolk, VA 23434, 757–539–1820.

0.0 Turn left out of the public lot onto Main St., away from the traffic light.

0.6 Go straight at the stoplight on Main St./Rt. 258 South. Cross the Rt. 10 bypass. Once through the intersection, make the immediate left on Great Springs Rd./Rt. 655. There is an Exxon Food Mart on the right after the turn.

3.5 Turn left at the stop sign on Scott's Factory Rd./Rt. 620.

5.0 Continue straight on Bowling Green Rd. at the junction with Rt. 644.

5.7 Turn left on Longview Dr./Rt. 602.

11.9 Turn right at the stop sign on Everets Rd./Rt. 603. Just before this intersection, there is a portable toilet out by the lake on the right.

12.6 Turn left on Lake Prince Dr./Rt. 604.

13.5 Turn left on Milners Rd./Rt. 605.

14.9 Bear right on Girl Scout Rd./Rt. 605.

16.8 Turn right at the stop sign on Lake Prince Dr./Rt. 604.

18.2 Turn left on Exeter Dr./Rt. 606.

20.6 At the stop sign and with Indika Farms on your left, take the second right onto Orbit Rd./Rt. 637.

23.4 Orbit Grocery is on your left.

23.9 Bear left to stay on Orbit Rd./Rt. 637 at Woodland United Methodist Church.

26.3 Bear right to stay on Orbit Rd./Rt. 637.

27.4 Turn left at the stop sign on Courthouse Hwy./Rt. 258 South.

27.6 Turn right on Trump Town Rd./Rt. 651.

31.0 Turn right on Foursquare Rd./Rt. 620.

31.9 Turn left on Comet Rd./Rt. 652.

33.3 Turn right on White House Rd./Rt. 682.

35.1 Turn left on Magnet Dr./Rt. 680.

35.4 Turn right on Waterworks Rd./Rt. 709.

38.2 Turn left at the stop sign on Courthouse Hwy./Rt. 258 North.

39.2 Go straight at the stoplight on Main St./Rt. 258 North Business.

39.8 End the ride at the public parking lot.

REST ROOMS

- At the start in various locations in Smithfield
- Mile 0.6: at the Exxon Station
- Mile 11.9: at a portable toilet by the lake

MAP

- DeLorme *Virginia Atlas and Gazetteer* map 34

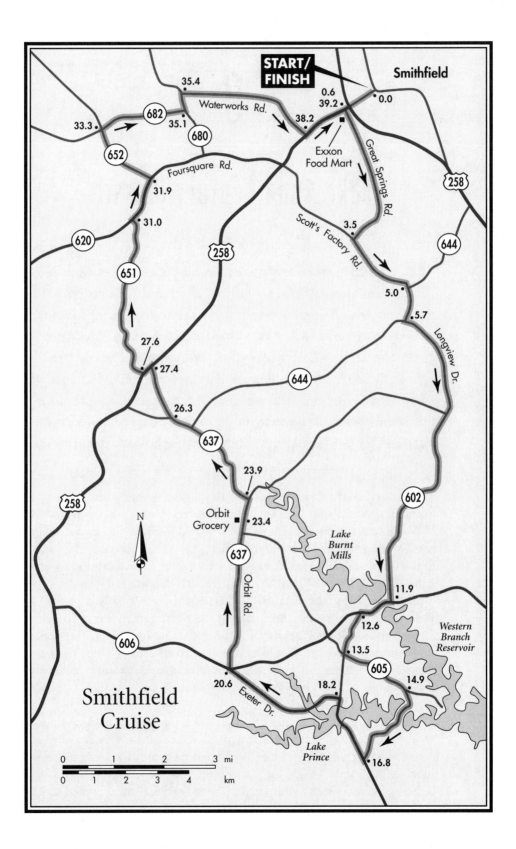

START/FINISH

Smithfield

35.4

682

33.3

35.1

680

652

Waterworks Rd.

38.2

0.6
39.2

0.0

Exxon
Food Mart

Great Springs Rd.

258

Foursquare Rd.

31.9

Scott's Factory Rd.

3.5

644

620

31.0

651

5.0

5.7

27.6

258

27.4

Longview Dr.

26.3

644

637

602

23.9

N

Orbit
Grocery

23.4

Lake
Burnt
Mills

637

258

Orbit Rd.

11.9

Western
Branch
Reservoir

12.6

606

13.5

605

14.9

20.6

Exeter Dr.

18.2

Smithfield
Cruise

16.8

Lake
Prince

0   1   2   3 mi

0   1   2   3   4 km

9

Lake Anna Century Classic

L *ocated in the heart of central Virginia, beautiful Lake Anna was created in 1972 for the purpose of providing cooling water for the North Anna Nuclear Power Station. The region is now a popular outdoor recreational facility for Richmond and northern Virginia residents. The Century Classic offers both an English and metric century around the scenic lake and through the quiet and rolling Piedmont of Spotsylvania, Orange, Louisa, and Hanover counties. Having no mountain climbs, traffic, or anything larger than a village to contend with, this classic is the perfect opportunity to satisfy any cyclist's century goals.*

When visiting Lake Anna, it won't take you long to realize that this area is a gold mine. Actually, the Lake Anna State Park region was once known as Gold Hill because it was the site of the Goodwin Gold Mine. Mining in the region began when gold was discovered in the late 1820s. The mine reached its peak in the 1880s, and the last gold was found during the 1940s. Little did anyone know then that the next "gold" discovery was to be lakeside real estate.

Lake Anna was created in 1972 as part of the Lake Anna Nuclear Power Plant construction project. By damming the North Anna River, a lake was formed to provide cooling water for the nuclear power facility. The scenic 13,000-acre lake with its 200 miles of shoreline has attracted not only avid outdoors enthusiasts but also numerous waterfront cottages, marinas, and housing communities. Don't be alarmed, however; the classic route rarely comes in contact with the lake's developments.

The classic starts in the small hamlet of Montpelier, only 25 miles northwest of Richmond. From Montpelier, you have the option of doing an English (102 miles) or metric (65 miles) century, with a few miles to spare. Using the same route for the first 28.8 miles, you'll have a few hours to see how you're feeling before you decide which century to do. The additional 37 miles of the English century takes in more of the gentle and tranquil countryside of Orange and Spotsylvania counties.

For those coming from northern Virginia, consider starting the classic from Todd's Tavern, the northernmost point of the route. Take Catharpin Road/Route 612 from Brock Road/Route 613 for 0.2 mile. Turn left on Mill Pond Road/Route 649, and you will enter the classic route at mile 53.5. You'll return on Catharpin Road, where you'll bear left at the Mill Pond intersection and go back to Brock Road and Todd's Tavern to the left.

There are several stores along the route, but occasionally there are long distances in between. Make a note of the stores' locations, and plan your stops accordingly. In addition, restaurants along the route are extremely limited. Chelsea Jo's is 1.6 miles off the route at mile 74.5, while J. L. Leonards Restaurant is on the English century route at mile 29.6. Metric century riders will need to detour 0.8 mile to reach this one. Apparently, some services in the area have yet to catch up with housing development.

You'll find the terrain on both centuries pleasantly mild. The route surrounds the lake at a slightly higher elevation, thereby creating small

THE BASICS

Start: From the Montpelier Center for Arts and Education in Montpelier.

Length: 102 or 65 miles

Terrain: Flat to gently rolling. Some long flat sections and some rolling, particularly around the many tributaries and inlets of the lake. Difficulty is due only to the ride's length. No major climbs.

Traffic and hazards: All roads on the classic are rural. Some do carry faster traffic and caution should be taken, especially on the short stretches of Routes 522 and 208. All roads are paved and in good condition.

Getting there: From the I–295 beltway around Richmond, take exit 49 and follow Route 33 toward Montpelier for approximately 13.5 miles. Turn left on Clazemont Road/Route 715. Go about 100 yards, and turn left on Sycamore Tavern Lane. Pass the library on the left, and park in the municipal lots across from the Ruritan Club. If coming from northern Virginia, consider starting the century from Todd's Tavern. There is a store located here, as well as parking at the Civil War historical marker. It is just 0.2 mile from the century route. From Route 1 in Fredericksburg, take Route 208 to Spotsylvania. Turn right on Brock Road/Route 613, and go approximately 5.8 miles to Todd's Tavern Market on the right and the Civil War site on the left.

dips down to the lake level at every crossing of its many tributaries. They are rarely steep, long, or challenging, but the cumulative effect will definitely provide validity to the century. Leaving the lake, the route enters Orange County, where some of the best cycling of the classic awaits you. Spotsylvania County is extremely rural, with a mix of croplands and pine tree farms.

Arriving back at the lake, you have an option of entering Lake Anna State Park. Although there is a $2.00 or $1.00 admission charge, depending on the season, the park boasts a beautiful and sandy swimming beach. There are changing facilities here, as well as a visitor's center, snack bar, and numerous picnic

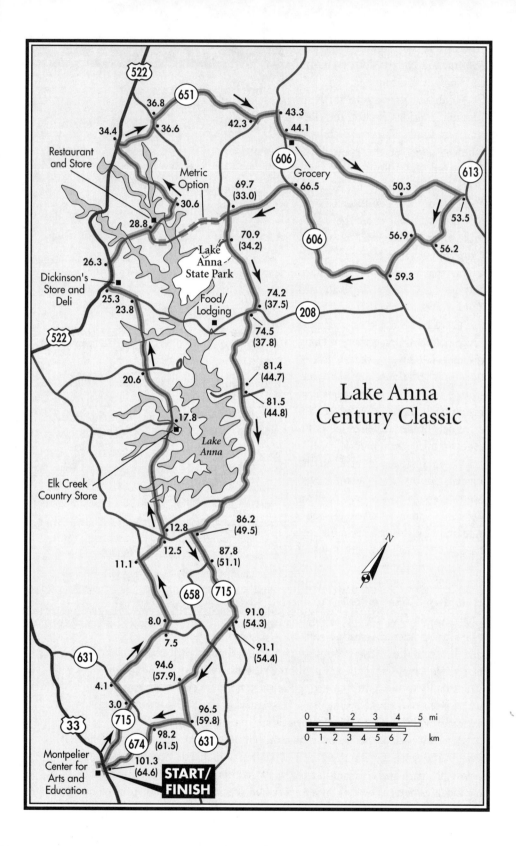

522

651

36.8
42.3
43.3
44.1

34.4
36.6

606 Grocery

Restaurant
and Store

50.3
613

Metric
Option

69.7
(33.0)

66.5

53.5

30.6

56.9
56.2

28.8

70.9
(34.2)

606

26.3

Lake
Anna
State Park

59.3

Dickinson's
Store and
Deli

25.3
23.8

Food/
Lodging

74.2
(37.5)

208

74.5
(37.8)

522

81.4
(44.7)

20.6

81.5
(44.8)

17.8

Lake
Anna

Lake Anna
Century Classic

Elk Creek
Country Store

86.2
(49.5)

12.8

N

12.5

11.1

87.8
(51.1)

658   715

91.0
(54.3)

8.0

7.5

91.1
(54.4)

631

94.6
(57.9)

4.1

3.0

96.5
(59.8)

33

715

0   1   2   3   4   5 mi

674

98.2
(61.5)

631

0 1 2 3 4 5 6 7 km

Montpelier
Center for
Arts and
Education

101.3
(64.6)

START/
FINISH

0.0 From the Montpelier Center for Arts and Education, head back out Sycamore Tavern Lane, then turn right on Clazemont Rd./Rt. 715.

0.1 Go straight at the stop sign to stay on Clazemont Rd./Rt. 715 (cross Rt. 33). There is a small sporting goods store that sells drinks and snacks at this intersection.

3.0 Turn left on Old Ridge Rd./Rt. 631 There is an Amoco Market at the turn.

4.1 Turn right on Shiloh Church Rd./Rt. 680.

7.5 Turn left on Woodson's Mill Rd./Rt. 680.

8.0 Turn left on Belsches Rd./Rt. 618. Ed's Convenience Store is 0.2 mile ahead on the right.

11.1 Turn right on Borden Rd./Rt. 701.

12.5 Go straight at the stop sign on Rt. 601, and cross the railroad tracks. In 0.1 mile, turn left on Rt. 701.

12.8 Continue straight on Kentucky Springs Rd./Rt. 652 where Rt. 701 goes right.

17.8 Elk Creek Country Store is on the right.

20.6 Continue straight at the flashing light on Rt. 652.

23.8 Turn left at the stop sign on New Bridge Rd./Rt. 208.

25.3 Turn right on Zachary Taylor Hwy./Rt. 522 North. Dickinson's Store and Deli is on the right at this intersection.

26.3 Turn right on Days Bridge Rd./Rt. 719.

28.7 Continue straight on Rt. 719 at the junction of Monrovia Rd./Rt. 612 from the left (west).

28.8 This is the point where the metric branches off from the English century. For the 102-mile route, bear left here on Belmont Rd./Rt. 719. For the 65-mile metric century, bear right here on Stubbs Bridge Rd./Rt. 612. At mile 29.1 (metric mileages are given in parentheses), bear left to stay on Stubbs Bridge Rd. At mile (32.5), Chanay's Grocery Store is on the left. At mile (33.0), you will turn right on Lawyers Rd./Rt. 601 and reenter the English century route. This (33.0) mile cue corresponds to mile 69.7 of the English century route. The next cue to follow is 70.9 (34.2).

29.6 On the left is Hunter's Landing Convenience Store and J. L. Leonards Lakeside Restaurant.

30.6 Turn left on Days Bridge Rd./Rt. 719.

34.4 Turn right at the stop sign on Zachary Taylor Hwy./Rt. 522. In 0.1 mile, turn right on Terry's Run Rd./Rt. 651.

36.6 Bear left at the stop sign on Orange Springs Rd./Rt. 651.

36.8 Turn right at the stop sign on Tatum Rd./Rt. 651.

42.3 Turn left at the stop sign on Lawyers Rd./Rt. 601.

43.3 Turn right at the stop sign on West Catharpin Rd./Rt. 608.

44.1 Bear left on West Catharpin Rd./Rt. 608. Keystone Grocery is at this corner.

(continued)

50.3 Bear left on Catharpin Rd./Rt. 612.

53.5 Turn right on Mill Pond Rd./Rt. 649. *Note:* This is the point at which you will enter the route if you start from Todd's Tavern.

56.2 Turn right at the stop sign on Robert E. Lee Dr./Rt. 608.

56.9 Turn left on Seays Rd./Rt. 649.

59.3 Turn right at the stop sign on Post Oak Rd./Rt. 606.

66.5 Turn left on Stubbs Bridge Rd./Rt. 612.

69.7 **(33.0)** Turn left at the stop sign on Lawyers Rd./Rt. 601. This is the reentry point for the metric century route, which comes from Stubbs Bridge Rd. in the opposite direction.

70.9 **(34.2)** Option to turn right to enter Lake Anna State Park. Otherwise, continue straight.

74.2 **(37.5)** Turn right on Courthouse Rd./Rt. 208.

74.5 **(37.8)** Turn left on Lewiston Rd./Rt. 601. Note: For food and lodging, continue straight on Rt. 208. In 1.6 miles, Lake Anna Lodge and Chelsea Jo's Restaurant will be on your right. In another 1.4 miles, Anna Point Marina Resort is on the right.

81.4 **(44.7)** Continue straight on Lewiston Rd./Rt. 601.

81.5 **(44.8)** Continue straight on Arritt Rd./Rt. 601.

86.2 **(49.5)** Turn left at the stop sign on Rt. 715.

87.8 **(51.1)** Continue straight at the stop sign on Beaver Dam Rd./Rt. 715

91.0 **(54.3)** There is an Amoco Market on the left.

91.1 **(54.4)** Turn right at the stop sign on Beaver Dam Rd./Rt. 715. Cross railroad tracks.

94.6 **(57.9)** Turn left on Parsons Rd./Rt. 608.

96.5 **(59.8)** Turn right at the stop sign on Old Ridge Rd./Rt. 631.

98.2 **(61.5)** Turn left on Woodman Hall Rd./Rt. 674.

101.3 **(64.6)** Turn right on Mountain Rd./Rt. 33.

101.6 **(64.9)** Turn left on Clazemont Rd. /Rt. 715.

101.7 **(65.0)** Turn left on Sycamore Tavern Lane to the parking lot on the right.

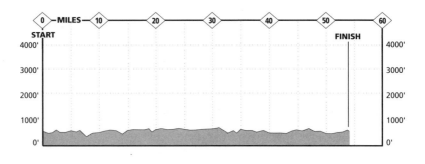

tables along the lake's northern shore. It's definitely worth a stop in season.

Hanover County always delights the cyclist, and this classic is no exception. Nestled between the more strenuous mountains to the west and the too-easy coastal plains to the east, Hanover County is home to about 24 miles of the classic. Cycle past horse pastures, hayfields, woodlands, and fields of tomatoes and pumpkins. What a wonderful way to start and end your century ride.

LOCAL INFORMATION

♦ Spotsylvania County Visitor Center, 4704 Southpoint Pkwy., Fredericksburg, VA 22407, 800–654–4118.

LOCAL EVENTS/ATTRACTIONS

♦ Lake Anna State Park, 6800 Lawyers Rd., Spotsylvania, VA 22553, 540–854–5503.
♦ North Anna Nuclear Power Station Visitor Center, P.O. Box 402, Mineral, VA 23117, 540–894–4394. Open Monday to Friday from 9:00 A.M. to 4:00 P.M.

RESTAURANTS

♦ J. L. Leonards Restaurant, Rt. 719, Mineral, 540–854–6113. Lakeside dining.
♦ Chelsea Jo's Restaurant, at the Lake Anna Lodge, 5152 Courthouse Rd., Spotsylvania, 540–895–5844. Closed Mondays.

ACCOMMODATIONS

♦ Lake Anna Lodge, 5152 Courthouse Rd., Spotsylvania, VA 22553, 540–895–5844. Mid-range.
♦ Anna Point Inn, 13721 Anna Point Lane, Mineral, VA 23117, 540–895–5900. Mid-range.

BIKE SHOP

♦ Bike Works, 104 William St., Fredericksburg, VA 22401, 540–373–8900.

REST ROOMS

♦ At the start in the Montpelier Library
♦ Mile 3.0: at the Amoco Market
♦ Mile 25.3: at Dickinson's Store and Deli
♦ Mile 29.6: at the Hunter's Landing Convenience Store
♦ Mile 70.9 (34.2): at Lake Anna State Park (option)
♦ Mile 74.5 (37.8): at Chelsea Jo's Restaurant (option)
♦ Mile 91.0 (54.3): at the Amoco Station (portable toilet)

MAP

♦ DeLorme *Virginia Atlas and Gazetteer* maps 57 and 69

10

Ashland Ramble

The Ashland Ramble takes cyclists through the gently rolling farmlands of Hanover County. Riders must fuel up at the start in Ashland, as the ride is very rural and has no stores or restaurants along the route. Popular among Richmond cyclists, this ramble offers a pleasant mix of flat and rolling terrain, with several hills that will challenge the beginning cyclist. About halfway through the ride, the cyclist will pass Scotchtown, home of Patrick Henry and one of Virginia's oldest plantation houses. The ramble ends back in Ashland, a charming country town with a railroad that runs right down the middle of its main street.

Just 12 miles north of the bustling capital city of Richmond lies the charming and serene town of Ashland. Once a country resort built by a railroad company, Ashland's railroad roots are evident—the tracks run directly down the middle of its main street. Pick up a map at the visitor's center for a self-guided walking tour of the town, which offers a delightful mix of historic homes, Victorian architecture, shops, and restaurants.

The ride begins right at the visitor's center. Within 1 mile, you will find yourself out of town and among countless farms, most charming enough to have their names proudly displayed. After a very flat 7 miles, you will encounter some gently rolling terrain on your way to Scotchtown. Home of Patrick Henry, Scotchtown is a rather modest white clapboard house built in the early 1700s. Henry lived in this house during the 1770s while he was serving as governor of Virginia. Some of Henry's personal belongings are among the many eighteenth-century antiques on display. A one-hour tour of the house and parklike grounds offers a welcome break from cycling and a historic step back in time to eighteenth-century plantation life.

After Scotchtown, you will encounter more flat and gently rolling terrain as you cycle by even more horse and livestock farms. If you didn't take a break at Scotchtown, you will want to stop for a few minutes when you leave Scotchtown Road onto Rocketts Mill Road. Relax a bit and eat that sandwich you packed. The surrounding roads, farms, pond, and peace and quiet found here are what makes Virginia bicycling so special. Hydrate well, as the more challenging portion of the ramble awaits you.

You'll soon find yourself on Old Ridge Road and will notice some interesting road signs. Interstate Bike Routes 1 (north–south) and 76 (east–west) both use this section of Old Ridge Road. The sign placement and attractive backdrop make for a good photo opportunity.

Blunts Bridge Road will be your primary route back into Ashland. You'll experience several challenging hills along the way. Exercise caution on the descents, as several include sharp turns at or near the bottom.

As you near the ride's end, you'll cycle along Ashland's railroad lines and past Randolph-Macon College, the oldest Methodist college in the United States. With several buildings registered as historic Landmarks, this attractive campus is included in Ashland's 1-mile walking tour. After your ride, you can easily walk to many of Ashland's restaurants. For a great deli sandwich and tantalizing desserts, try Homemades by Suzanne, just a few steps from the visitor's center. You won't have any problem replenishing calories in this place. Those wishing to spend the night should consider The Henry Clay Inn. This attractive country inn, located just behind the visitor's center, offers a huge porch, where you can rest those sore muscles after your ride.

THE BASICS

Start: From the Ashland/Hanover Visitors Center and train station at 112 North Railroad Avenue.

Length: 26 miles

Terrain: Gently rolling. Some long, flat stretches and several hills that will challenge beginners. One of the most challenging rambles in the book.

Traffic and hazards: All roads on this route are low traffic and rural. Use caution on Ashcake and Old Ridge Roads, as traffic can be fast. Shoulders are narrow to nonexistent but not necessary on these pleasant country roads. Entire route is paved and in good condition. The only hazards are several sharp turns on some of the descents.

Getting there: From I–95, take exit 92 to Route 54 West. Go 1.2 miles to the center of Ashland. Make a right onto Railroad Avenue. The visitor's center is on the left across the railroad tracks. Parking is free and plentiful along Railroad Avenue and at the visitor's center.

LOCAL INFORMATION

♦ Ashland/Hanover Visitors Center, 112 N. Railroad Ave., Ashland, VA 23005, 800–897–1479.

0.0 Head south on Railroad Ave. The train tracks will be on your left.

0.1 Turn right at the stop sign on Thompson St., then immediately bear left onto Hanover Ave. You will see an England St. sign at Thompson—it goes to the left, so ignore it. Before the turn on Hanover Ave., Ashland Coffee and Tea is on the right and is a popular cyclists' stop.

1.1 Turn left on Elmont Rd./Rt. 626.

1.4 Turn right on Ashcake Rd./Rt. 657. Expect faster traffic on this stretch.

4.0 Bear right on Greenwood Church Rd./Rt. 657. Do not take the sharp right onto Blatton Rd. Traffic is light on Greenwood Church Rd.

9.9 Turn right on Scotchtown Rd./Rt. 671.

12.3 Go straight at the stop sign to stay on Scotchtown Rd. Cross Rt. 54.

12.5 Bear right to stay on Scotchtown Rd. Ebenezer Baptist Church is on your left after the turn.

13.7 Make a left onto Chiswell Ln. if you want to visit Scotchtown, home of Patrick Henry. Entrance is several hundred yards down Chiswell. Continue straight on Scotchtown Rd. to stay on route. Enjoy this easy, flat stretch of country road.

16.1 Turn left on Rocketts Mill Rd./Rt. 685. The farm pond on the right makes for a pleasant rest stop.

17.4 Turn right on Old Ridge Rd./Rt. 738 at The Fork Church. Be careful of faster traffic the next 2 miles.

19.3 Make the right onto Blunts Bridge Rd. and begin the hillier portion of the ramble. Use caution on the descents, as several include sharp turns.

22.6 Continue straight to stay on Blunts Bridge Rd. Don't be confused with Blunts Rd. to the right.

24.6 Continue straight. Road name changes to N. James St.

24.9 Bear left on W. Patrick St.

25.1 Turn right on N. Center St. immediately before railroad tracks. N. Center St. changes its name to Railroad Ave. close to the visitor's center.

25.5 End the ride at the visitor's center. The Henry Clay Inn is on your right. Homemades by Suzanne is a few yards past the visitor's center on the right.

LOCAL EVENTS/ATTRACTIONS

♦ Strawberry Faire, features arts and crafts and a salute to strawberries. At Randolph-Macon College, usually second Saturday in June. 804–798–8289.

♦ Scotchtown, 16120 Chiswell Lane, Beaverdam, VA 23015, 804–227–3500. Offers one-hour tours of Patrick Henry's home and grounds, which emphasize eighteenth-century plantation life. Admission: $6.00 for adults, $3.00 for children. Opening hours vary.

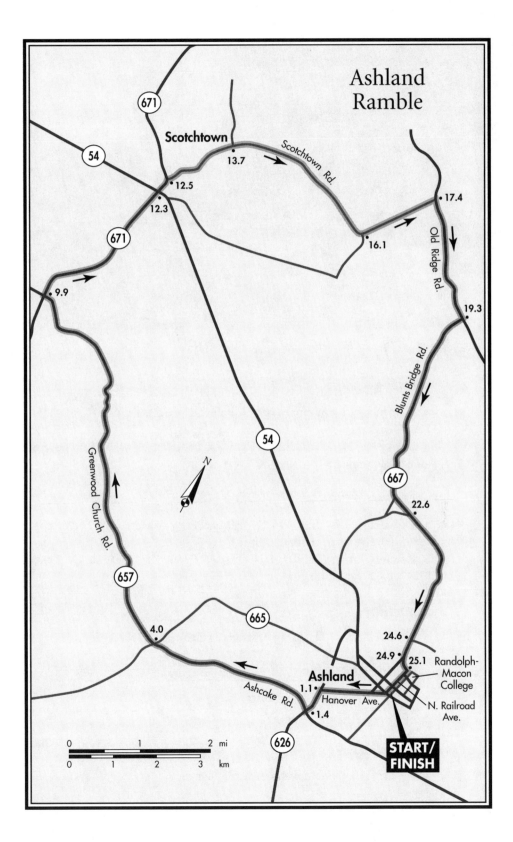

Ashland
Ramble

671

54

Scotchtown

671

Scotchtown Rd.

• 13.7

• 12.5

12.3

• 17.4

• 16.1

Old Ridge Rd.

• 19.3

• 9.9

Blunts Bridge Rd.

Greenwood Church Rd.

54

667

• 22.6

657

665

• 4.0

• 24.6

• 24.9

• 25.1 Randolph-
Macon
College

Ashland

• 1.1

Hanover Ave.

N. Railroad
Ave.

Ashcake Rd.

• 1.4

626

START/
FINISH

N

0   1   2 mi

0   1   2   3 km

Interstate Bike Routes 1 and 76 converge near Ashland.

RESTAURANTS

♦ Homemades by Suzanne, 102 N. Railroad Ave., Ashland, 804–798–8331. Lunch, desserts.

♦ Smoky Pig, 212 S. Washington Hwy., Ashland, 804–798–4590. Very popular local establishment.

ACCOMMODATIONS

♦ The Henry Clay Inn, 114 N. Railroad Ave., Ashland, VA 23005, 804–798–3100. Higher end country inn.

♦ Comfort Inn Ashland, 101 N. Cottage Green Dr., Ashland, VA 23005, 804–752–7777. Mid-range.

BIKE SHOP

♦ Cycles Ed, 12275 Maple St., Ashland, VA 23005, 804–798–7046.

REST ROOMS

♦ At the start in the visitor's center
♦ Mile 13.7: at Scotchtown

MAP

♦ DeLorme *Virginia Atlas and Gazetteer* map 58

Hanover Cruise

T he Hanover Cruise is a delightful tour through the heart of central Virginia. Starting in the small, historic town of Hanover, the cruise takes in parts of three counties: Hanover, Caroline, and King William. Popular with Richmond cyclists, the cruise is a pleasant mix of flat and gently rolling terrain—past horse farms and croplands and through shady woods and quiet countryside. After the cruise, explore Hanover with a tour of its Historic County Courthouse, Hanover Tavern, and Old Hanover Jail.

Bud Vye of the Richmond Area Bicyclists Association submitted the Hanover Cruise. Although there are a number of good rides in the Richmond area, Bud indicated that Richmond would not be well represented unless a ride in the Hanover area was included. Immediately upon leaving the Hanover Courthouse Complex parking lot, you'll agree with Bud.

Only 10 miles from Richmond's I–295 beltway, the Hanover Cruise is surprisingly rural. Besides the small town of Hanover, where the cruise starts and ends, you won't pass another town, stoplight, fast-food restaurant, or shopping center. Although Hanover has several historical sights, don't come here to sightsee or browse museums. The cruise's attraction is its lack of attractions—and distractions. Come to Hanover for a good ride.

The terrain is mild, with a mixture of some long, flat stretches and rolling hills. Several of the hills may challenge the beginner, but the average cyclist will not have any problem. Actually, the hills are spread out evenly throughout the cruise and offer a welcome variety. There are a couple of stores along the route early on. Take their location into consideration when deciding which direction to do the loop. In addition, there is an opportunity to shave off 5.6 miles at mile 26. There's nice scenery either way, so the decision is simply based on which distance you prefer.

Start: From the municipal parking lot at the Hanover County Courthouse Complex.

Length: 40 or 34 miles

Terrain: Mostly flat to gently rolling.

Traffic and hazards: All roads are paved and in good shape. Use caution on Route 301 in Hanover, which carries heavier traffic, and on the 1-mile stretch of Route 30, which has faster traffic.

Getting there: From exit 92 off I-95, take Route 54 east approximately 5.5 miles to Route 301. Turn right on Route 301 South and go 0.3 mile. Turn left on Library Drive and enter Hanover Courthouse/Government Complex. Park in any of the municipal lots in the courthouse complex.

The cruise is a good mix of woodlands and croplands. You'll find yourself riding miles in the shade and at other times past fields of corn, soybeans, tomatoes, and horses. Tomatoes are popular in these parts, and in early July, Hanover County stages a Tomato Festival celebrating its taste and heritage.

Hanover has several interesting sights in town. The Historic County Courthouse (1735), the Hanover Tavern (mid-1700s) and Old Hanover Jail (1830s) are all free to tour but appointments are necessary. Since you probably won't have an appointment, head to the Hanover Cafe or the nearby Houndstooth Cafe and celebrate with a cold beer. Appointments are not required.

LOCAL INFORMATION

♦ Ashland/Hanover Visitors Center, 112 N. Railroad Ave., Ashland, VA 23005, 800–897–1479.

LOCAL EVENTS/ATTRACTIONS

♦ Annual Hanover Tomato Festival and Heritage Fair, early July, Pole Green Park, 804–550–4705. Celebration honoring Hanover's finest fruit and its heritage. Tomato foods, crafts, and music.

RESTAURANTS

♦ Houndstooth Cafe, 13271 Hanover Courthouse Rd., Hanover, 804–537–5404. Closed Sunday and Monday.
♦ Hanover Cafe, 13185 Hanover Courthouse Rd., Hanover, 804–537–5290.

ACCOMMODATIONS

♦ Comfort Inn Ashland, 101 N. Cottage Green Drive, Ashland, VA 23005, 804–752–7777. Mid-range.

Late autumn in the Shenandoah Valley brings a moment of reflection.

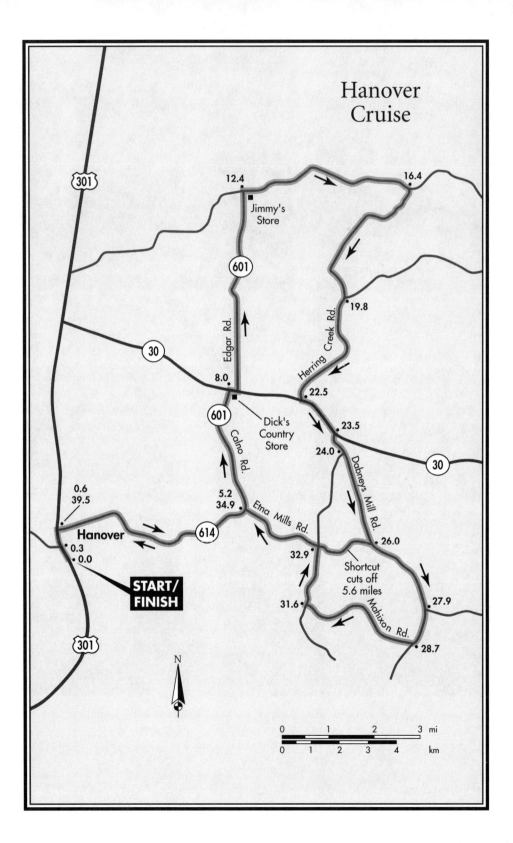

Hanover Cruise

301

12.4

Jimmy's Store

601

Edgar Rd.

30

8.0

601

Dick's Country Store

16.4

Herring Creek Rd.

19.8

22.5

23.5

24.0

Dabneys Mill Rd.

30

0.6
39.5

Hanover

0.3
0.0

START/
FINISH

301

N

Calno Rd.

5.2
34.9

Etna Mills Rd.

614

32.9

31.6

26.0

Shortcut cuts off 5.6 miles

27.9

Mahixon Rd.

28.7

0   1   2   3 mi

0   1   2   3   4 km

0.0 Leave the Courthouse Complex on Library Dr. Turn right on Rt. 301 North. Caution, heavier traffic on Rt. 301.

0.3 Houndstooth Cafe is on the left at the junction with Rt. 54. Continue straight.

0.6 Turn right on Normans Bridge Rd./Rt. 614. Before the turn, Kelley's Country Store is on the left.

5.2 Continue straight on Calno Rd./Rt. 601.

8.0 Turn right at the stop sign on King William Rd./Rt. 30. Dick's Country Store is on the right. After the store, make an immediate left on Edgar Rd./Rt. 601.

12.4 Turn right at the stop sign on Frog Level Rd./Rt. 600. Jimmy's Store is on the right.

16.4 Turn right on Herring Creek Rd./Rt. 604.

19.8 Turn right at the stop sign to stay on Herring Creek Rd./Rt. 604.

22.5 Turn left at the stop sign on King William Rd./Rt. 30. Caution, faster traffic.

23.5 Turn right on Rt. 604.

24.0 Bear left on Dabneys Mill Rd./Rt. 604.

26.0 Continue straight to stay on Dabneys Mill Rd./Rt. 604. *Note:* To cut off 5.6 miles, turn right here on Etna Mills Rd./Rt. 614. After 1.3 miles, go straight on Etna Mills Rd., then pick up the next cue at mile 34.9.

27.9 Turn right to stay on Dabneys Mill Rd./Rt. 604.

28.7 Turn right on Mahixon Rd./Rt. 652.

31.6 Turn right at the stop sign on Nelsons Bridge Rd./Rt. 615.

32.9 Turn left on Etna Mills Rd./Rt. 614.

34.9 Turn left at the stop sign to stay on Etna Mills Rd./Rt. 614.

39.5 Turn left at the stop sign on Hanover Courthouse Rd./Rt. 301.

40.1 Turn left on Library Dr. to parking lot and end of ride.

BIKE SHOP

♦ Cycles Ed, 12275 Maple St., Ashland, VA 23005, 804–798–7046.

REST ROOMS

♦ At the start in various government buildings in the Courthouse Complex
♦ Mile 8.0: at Dick's Country Store

MAP

♦ DeLorme *Virginia Atlas and Gazetteer* map 58

Richmond Battlefield Cruise

S ituated just 10 miles southeast of Richmond, the Richmond Battlefield Cruise takes the cyclist on a historic and moderately easy tour of several significant Civil War forts and battlegrounds. Beginning at Fort Harrison, the cruise rolls past Fort Hoke and through the now peaceful Richmond National Battlefield Park. Additional historic stops can be made at Malvern Hill Battlefield and Glendale Visitor Center and National Cemetery. A ride into Dory Park, with its scenic lake and picnic areas, offers a welcome rest stop and a chance to reflect on the significance of the forts and battlefields just witnessed.

Although Richmond has been Virginia's capital since 1780, the city served as the capital of the Confederate States of America in the early 1860s. For nearly four years, Union troops tried in vain to capture the city, while several key battles took place at Fort Harrison and Malvern Hill in Richmond's outskirts. An 80-mile car tour will take in most of the region's war activity, while this cruise offers a good portion in just 33 easy miles.

For a more thorough examination of Richmond's Civil War history, begin your day at the Civil War Visitor Center at the Tredegar Iron Works in Richmond. If you're skipping Richmond, settle for a brief introduction at the visitor's center at Fort Harrison. Leave the visitor's center going left on Battlefield Park Road. Just after you pass Fort Hoke, turn left on Hoke Brady Road for a delightful tour through Richmond National Battlefield Park. Look closely and you will see remnants of Battery IV, one union fortification of four that was constructed to connect Fort Harrison with Fort Brady to the south. When you reach Kingsland Road, a detour straight will take you to the well-preserved Fort Brady.

The cruise remains very rural, with a mix of woodlands and croplands as it makes its way to Malvern Hill. The battle here was the last of the historic Seven Days' Battles. The Union's position on high ground forced the Confederates to advance across open fields, with disastrous results. A trail leads to the steep slopes that protected the Union's position.

There are a few convenience stores on Darbytown Road as you approach Dory Park. If you are planning on a break or picnic at this fine community park, you can pick up a few things at these stores. Follow Dory Park Road all the way to the end to enjoy the lake and picnic areas. Ride with caution for the next 2 to 3 miles after you leave the park. Being only 3 miles from downtown Richmond, it is the only segment on the cruise that carries considerable traffic. In fact, if you're doing this cruise early on the weekend, consider reversing direction. You'll exit Darbytown Road before the traffic picks up.

THE BASICS

Start: From the Fort Harrison Visitor Center parking lot.

Length: 33 miles

Terrain: Mostly flat with some moderate hills. Suitable for beginners.

Traffic and hazards: Use caution on the two short segments on Route 5, as traffic can be fast. Use caution on Darbytown Road, as traffic can be heavy. This busier stretch of road categorizes the ride as a cruise and not a ramble.

Getting there: Take Route 5 east out of Richmond for approximately 7 miles. Turn right on Battlefield Park Road, then go 2.3 miles to the Fort Harrison Visitor Center on the left. lenty of free parking.

Civil War battlefield at Malvern Hill outside Richmond.

0.0 Turn left out of the Fort Harrison Visitor Center onto Battlefield Park Rd.

1.1 Fort Hoke is on the right. In 0.1 mile, turn left on Hoke Brady Rd.

3.0 Turn left at the stop sign on Kingsland Rd. *Note:* To detour to Fort Brady, continue straight on Hoke Brady Rd. for approximately 1.0 mile.

7.0 Turn right at the stop sign on New Market Rd./Rt. 5. Watch for faster traffic.

7.4 Turn left on Long Bridge Rd.

10.0 Turn right on Carters Mill Rd.

11.4 Turn right at the stop sign on Willis Church Rd.

11.6 Turn right into Malvern Hill Battlefield. Continue to the historical markers on the right. When leaving the park, turn left on Willis Church Rd.

12.0 Continue straight on Willis Church Rd. at the junction with Carters Mill Rd.

13.6 Glendale Visitor Center and National Cemetery are on the right.

14.3 Turn left at the stop sign on Darbytown Rd.

17.4 Grandpa's Store is on the right.

18.0 There is a Shell Station convenience store on the right.

20.6 Turn left on Dory Park Rd. to enter park. The rest rooms, picnic area, and lake are 1.0 mile into the park. When leaving the park, turn left on Darbytown Rd. at mile 22.6. Be cautious here, as the traffic picks up.

25.3 Turn left on Old Oakland Rd.

26.0 Turn left at the stop sign on Oakland Rd.

26.9 Turn left at the stop sign on Old Osborne Turnpike/Rt. 5. Expect faster traffic next ½ mile.

27.3 Bear right on Osborne Turnpike leaving Rt. 5. There is a 7-Eleven at this turn.

30.6 Turn left on Mill Rd.

31.4 Turn right on Battlefield Park Rd.

32.0 Fort Johnson is on the right.

32.6 Turn left into the Fort Harrison Visitor Center and end of ride.

Thanks to Reed Nester, a history buff and president of the Williamsburg Area Bicyclists, for submitting this ride and leading it as a club ride several times a year. Reed emphasizes some preparatory study on Richmond battles prior to your ride to enhance your experience here. Indeed, it is a good ride, but more so, it is a ride through the center stage of Virginia's history and an opportunity to further understand our country's most devastating conflict.

LOCAL INFORMATION

♦ Richmond Civil War Visitor Center, 470 Tredegar St., Richmond, VA 23219, 804–771–2145. Open daily from 9:00 A.M. to 5:00 P.M.

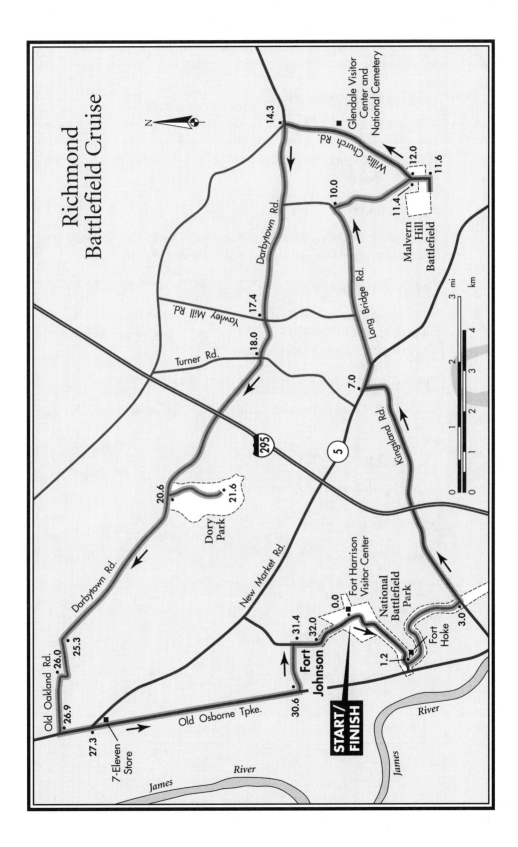

Richmond Battlefield Cruise

◆ Fort Harrison Visitor Center, Battlefield Park Rd., Richmond, VA 23219, 804–226–1981. Open daily from 9:00 A.M. to 5:00 P.M.

LOCAL EVENTS/ATTRACTIONS

◆ Special events at Fort Harrison are the Memorial Day ceremony at noon and the anniversary programs on September 29 and 30. Special programs and Ranger-guided tours are offered during these days. Contact the centers above for more information.

RESTAURANTS

◆ Indian Fields Tavern, 9220 John Tyler Hwy., Charles City, 804–829–5004. Charming restored farmhouse down Route 5 toward Williamsburg.

ACCOMMODATIONS

◆ There are thousands of hotel rooms available in Richmond. The closest to the route may be the Holiday Inn–Airport, 5203 Williamsburg Rd., Richmond, VA 23150, 804–222–6450. Mid-range.

BIKE SHOP

◆ Rowlett's Bicycles, 1904 Staples Mill Rd., Richmond, VA 23230, 804–353–4489.

REST ROOMS

◆ At the start in the Fort Harrison Visitor Center
◆ Mile 18.0: at the Shell Station
◆ Mile 21.6: at Dory Park

MAP

◆ DeLorme *Virginia Atlas and Gazetteer* map 48

Peanut Ride Ramble

*E*arly September in Virginia means it's time for the annual Great Peanut Ride. Cyclists en masse take over the country roads of southern Virginia and northern North Carolina for four days of wonderful cycling and eating. The Peanut Ride Ramble is a sampling of the many routes offered in the Great Peanut Ride. In fact, the ramble's figure-eight layout offers three rides in one: a 15-mile flat ramble, a 30-mile ramble with some gently rolling hills, and a combination of the two rambles for a 45-mile cruise. If you can't make it for the Great Peanut Ride, try one of these trips to see what you've been missing.

The very successful Great Peanut Ride is the result of the vision and hard work of Bobby Wrenn. A lifelong resident of the area and a cyclist himself, Bobby has transformed the ride into Virginia's best cycling event, attracting locals as well as riders from twenty-three other states. In addition to its pool of 400 dedicated volunteers, the ride's success is largely due to its wonderful rest stops: the cucumber stop, the tomato sandwich stop, the pickled watermelon rind stop, and, of course, peanuts everywhere in every imaginable form.

The Great Peanut Ride always takes place the Thursday to Sunday after Labor Day. The routes are superbly marked, and support is second to none. For about $50, you're entitled to take in the entire four-day weekend. It's a bargain; try it.

No matter which ramble you're doing, your starting point is The Good Earth Peanut Co. Housed in a pre–Civil War building, Good Earth is run by two wonderful people, Lindsay and Scott Vincent. Having grown up on peanut farms, their love for their homeland and for their homegrown products is quite evident. Pick out a gift basket (they deliver) or some apple butter or nuts to

THE BASICS

Start: From The Good Earth Peanut Co. parking lot in Skippers.

Length: 15, 30, or 45 miles

Terrain: Mostly flat, with a few gentle rollers. Suitable for beginners.

Traffic and hazards: Traffic is extremely light. Prime cycling roads and conditions.

Getting there: From I–95, exit 4, take Route 629 East toward Skippers for 1.0 mile to the junction with Route 301. The Good Earth Peanut Co. is just ahead on the left after you cross Route 301 and the railroad tracks. Park away from the building.

nibble on during the ride. Good Earth also serves up soft drinks and Gatorade. They've even offered the use of the picnic table outside for cyclists to use before or after the ride. Stop in and meet the down-to-earth folks at Good Earth.

There are two loop rides for this ramble: a very flat 15-miler that goes east and a 30-miler that heads west, which is mostly flat but has a few rollers. The scenery is about the same on both. It's a heavy agricultural region with cotton, soybean, corn, and peanut fields comprising the landscape. True, cycling in Greensville County will invoke a sense of sameness. But the region's solitude, friendliness, and magnificent roads make cycling here a real pleasure.

Virginia is the northernmost state to grow peanuts—its growing region basically confined to the area east of Richmond and south of the James River. There are several varieties of peanuts—Runners, Valencia, Virginia, and

Cyclists gather at The Good Earth Peanut Co. during the Great Peanut Ride.

EAST LOOP (15 MILES)

0.0 Turn left out of The Good Earth Peanut Co. parking lot on Zion Church Rd./ Rt. 629.

2.5 Turn right at the stop sign on Little Low Ground Rd./Rt. 622.

7.6 Turn right at the stop sign on Taylors Mill Rd./Rt. 625.

13.1 Turn right at the stop sign on Rolling Acres Rd./Rt. 628.

14.6 Go straight at the stop sign into The Good Earth Peanut Co. parking lot and end of ride.

WEST LOOP (30 MILES)

0.0 Turn right out of The Good Earth Peanut Co. parking lot on Zion Church Rd./ Rt. 629. Cross the railroad tracks and go straight on Rt. 629 at the stop sign (cross Rt. 301). If you need any other supplies, Moore's Grocery is a couple of hundred yards to the right on Rt. 301.

1.2 There is a Citgo Station convenience store on the left. Just past it is an Econo Lodge.

2.0 Continue straight on Moore's Ferry Rd./Rt. 629.

2.8 Bear left to stay on Moore's Ferry Rd./Rt. 629.

3.8 On the right is the Cattail Creek Campground—the base of operations for the Great Peanut Ride. There is a camp store that is open in season.

5.4 Turn right on Spring Church Rd./Rt. 631.

8.7 Turn right at the stop sign on Gaston Rd./Rt. 603. At the turn, look to your left to see that North Carolina is only about 100 feet away. In ¼ mile, there is a small convenience store on the left.

10.3 Turn right at the stop sign on Pine Log Rd./Rt. 633.

10.6 Turn left on Fish Rd./Rt. 603.

13.7 Turn left on Brink Rd./Rt. 627.

14.1 Turn right on Macedonia Rd./Rt. 603.

16.0 Turn right on Doyles Lake Rd./Rt. 604.

18.8 Turn right on Bowen Rd./Rt. 693.

20.3 Turn right at the stop sign on Independence Church Rd./Rt. 633.

23.1 Continue straight at the stop sign on Pine Log Rd./Rt. 633.

23.9 Turn left on Diamond Grove Rd./Rt. 621.

27.2 Turn right at the stop sign on Quarry Rd./Rt. 621.

27.7 Turn left at the stop sign on Moore's Ferry Rd./Rt. 629.

29.8 Turn left into The Good Earth Peanut Co. parking lot and end of ride.

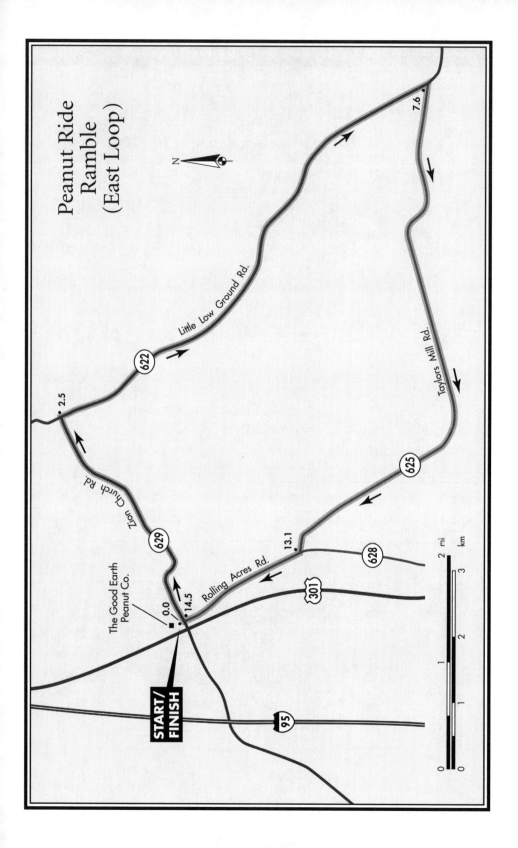

Peanut Ride
Ramble
(East Loop)

N

The Good Earth
Peanut Co.

START/
FINISH

Zion Church Rd.

Little Low Ground Rd.

Taylors Mill Rd.

Rolling Acres Rd.

622

629

625

628

301

95

2.5

7.6

13.1

14.5

0.0

2 mi

km

1

2

3

1

2

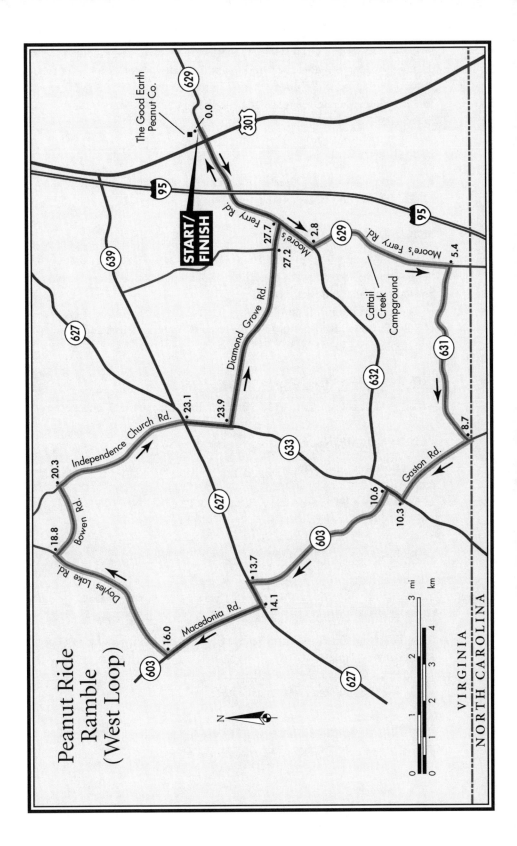

Peanut Ride Ramble (West Loop)

The Good Earth Peanut Co.

START/FINISH

0.0

2.8
5.4
8.7
10.3
10.6
13.7
14.1
16.0
18.8
20.3
23.1
23.9
27.2
27.7

Moore's Ferry Rd.
Moore's Ferry Rd.
Cattail Creek Campground
Diamond Grove Rd.
Independence Church Rd.
Bowen Rd.
Doyles Lake Rd.
Macedonia Rd.
Gaston Rd.

301
95
95
629
629
639
627
627
627
603
603
631
632
633

N

3 mi
km

VIRGINIA
NORTH CAROLINA

Spanish—but it's the Virginia variety that is grown here. The Virginia type is distinguished by its reddish brown skin and large oval shape. Known for their outstanding flavor and crunchy texture, these are the largest peanuts grown and are frequently referred to as "gourmet." And that pretty much sums it up, in a nutshell.

LOCAL INFORMATION

♦ Emporia–Greensville Chamber of Commerce, 400 Halifax St., Emporia, VA 23847, 804–634–9441.

LOCAL EVENTS/ATTRACTIONS

♦ Virginia Peanut Festival, mid-September, 804–348–3378. A celebration of the prominence of the peanut in Virginia's culture. Food, concerts, carnival, fireworks, parade, and classic car show.

♦ The Great Peanut Ride, Thursday to Sunday after Labor Day, 800–449–BIKE. Large bike ride through Greensville County's farms and country-side emphasizing food.

RESTAURANTS

♦ Squire House Restaurant, 632 S. Main St., Emporia, 804–634–0046.

ACCOMMODATIONS

♦ Comfort Inn, 1411 Skippers Rd., Emporia, VA 23847, 804–348–3282. Mid-range.

♦ Econo Lodge, I–95 and Route 629, Skippers, VA 23879, 804–634–6124. Low-end.

BIKE SHOP

♦ None in the area.

REST ROOMS

♦ At the start in The Good Earth Peanut Co., the only facility on the East Loop
♦ On the West Loop:
   Mile 1.2: at the Citgo Station
   Mile 8.9: at the small convenience store

MAP

♦ DeLorme *Virginia Atlas and Gazetteer* maps 31 and 32

Buggs Island Lake Ramble

S traddling the Virginia–North Carolina border lies the 50,000-acre John H. Kerr Dam and Reservoir. Kerr Dam is the official name, but most Virginians call it Buggs Island Lake, named after an early settler who lived on a small island just below the present-day dam. The U.S. Army Corps of Engineers manages this reservoir, which was built as one in a series of flood control dams along the Roanoke River. In addition to the reservoir's functioning as a hydroelectric power plant, this lake region is a recreational paradise. Of course, most activities involve the water, but this short and easy ramble is a must for your next outing there.

The Occonneechee Indians once roamed these parts of what is now called Southside Virginia's Lake Country. The twentieth-century need for hydroelectric power and a means of flood control led to the creation of the 50,000-acre John H. Kerr Dam and the 28,000-acre Lake Gaston. John H. Kerr was a North Carolina Congressman who supported the project, but the "unofficial" Buggs Island Lake is the preferred name for Virginians.

An early settler, Samuel Bugg, lived with his family on a small island in the Roanoke River. When the dam site was selected just north of this island, the project was simply called Buggs Island. Today, after nearly fifty years of operation, U.S. Army Corps of Engineers brochures and guides still have "also known as Buggs Island Lake" under the official name of John H. Kerr. You can see the small island from a wildlife-viewing platform in Tailrace Park.

Leaving Tailrace Park, the ramble takes you south on Route 4, which also happens to be Interstate Bike Route 1. Within a mile, you'll be crossing the dam, which, if you've never seen it before, will surely impress you. At 2,785 feet

Start: From Tailrace Park Picnic Area, just below the John H. Kerr Dam.

Length: 25 miles

Terrain: Flat with several gentle rollers.

Traffic and hazards: All roads on this route are low traffic and rural. Use caution on Route 4, where traffic, although light, can be fast.

Getting there: Heading west on Route 58 from South Hill, turn left onto Route 4 South. Go 5.4 miles, then turn left into the entrance for the John H. Kerr Dam and Reservoir Powerhouse. Go 0.3 mile, and turn left into entrance for Tailrace Park. Parking is free and plentiful in the park.

long and 144 feet tall, it doesn't quite measure up to Hoover Dam, but the structure does dam up the Roanoke River for 39 miles and has created more than 800 miles of shoreline. What's great about this dam, however, is that the gentle terrain around the lake makes accessibility extremely easy. Stop along the dam for some great views and photo ops of the lake and tailrace area, but use caution as traffic can be fast along Route 4.

The loop on the south end of the ramble is very flat and offers pleasant country cycling. Midway through the south loop, Lake Country Dairy Bar and Grill on your right should have something to cool you off. If not, turn left at mile 8.8 and head to Palmer Point Park. There is a $1.00 entrance fee to the park, which has a splendid sandy beach, along with swimming and picnic areas.

After you go back across the dam, you'll now bear left and begin the northern loop of the ramble. Before you do, however, make a stop at the Visitor Assistance Center to learn more about the Buggs Island Project.

In addition to flood control, power generation, and recreation, the Virginia Department of Game and Inland Fisheries and the North Carolina Wildlife Resources Commission jointly coordinate fish and wildlife management in and around the lake area. Exhibits at the visitor's center showcase these efforts. Other exhibits along with the staff will surely answer all your questions about the dam's construction, flood control, and the countless recreational opportunities at the lake. You actually leave here with a higher appreciation for government projects such as this and knowing that your tax dollar is well spent.

Shortly after the visitor's area, you'll pass North Bend Park on your left. In addition to swimming, fishing, and picnicking, this park offers one of the major camping areas for the lake. Two miles past the park, the route makes a left on Phillis Road/Route 707. If you desire a shorter ramble, turn right to cut off about 8 miles. Otherwise, continue left to complete the northern loop. The terrain in this portion is slightly rolling but still within a beginner's capability. The roads are rural, low traffic, and pleasant, but, I must add, lacking in scenic interest when you lose sight of the lake.

So when your travels bring you to these far reaches of southern Virginia, bring your bike with you. There's no better way to explore the John H. Kerr Dam (also known as Buggs Island Lake).

LOCAL INFORMATION

♦ South Hill Chamber of Commerce, 201 South Mecklenberg Ave., South Hill, VA 23970, 800–524–4347.
♦ John H. Kerr Visitor Assistance Center, 1930 Mays Chapel Road, Boydton, VA 23917, 804–738–6143.

LOCAL EVENTS/ATTRACTIONS

♦ Annual Virginia Lake Festival, mid-July, 800–374–2436. Antique and classic cars, water sports demonstrations, street festival with arts, crafts, and food, music.
♦ John H. Kerr Dam Powerhouse Tours, 804–738–6633. Summer months.

RESTAURANTS

♦ Pino's Pizza and Italian Restaurant, 6228 Buggs Island Rd., Boydton, VA 23917, 804–738–6999.

ACCOMMODATIONS

♦ The Kinderton Manor Inn, 850 Kinderton Rd., Clarksville, VA 23927, 804–374–4439. An 1830s classic Georgian manor home.

BIKE SHOP

♦ None in the area.

REST ROOMS

♦ At the start in Tailrace Park
♦ Mile 8.8: at Palmer Point Park (optional route)
♦ Mile 12.8: at the Visitor Assistance Center
♦ Mile 24.0: at Pino's Pizza and Italian Restaurant on the left

MAP

♦ DeLorme *Virginia Atlas and Gazetteer* map 30

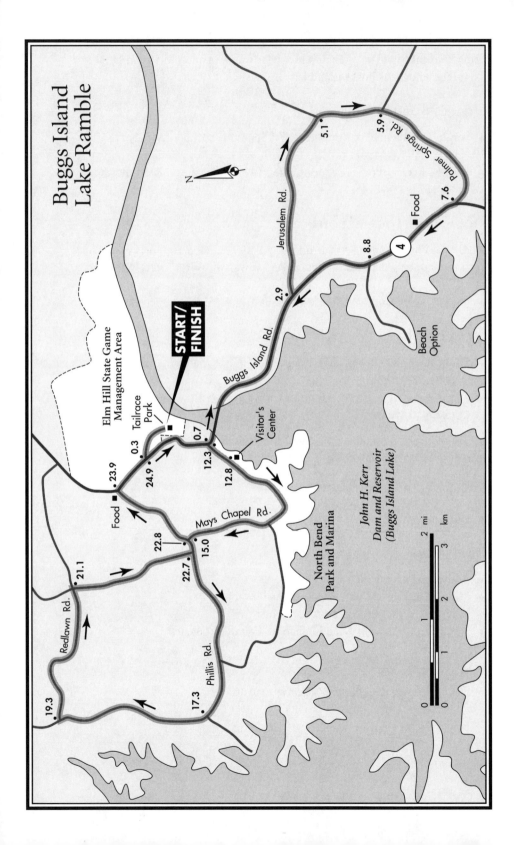

Buggs Island Lake Ramble

START/FINISH

Elm Hill State Game Management Area

Tailrace Park

0.3

23.9

24.9

0.7

Food

21.1

Redlawn Rd.

19.3

22.8

22.7

15.0

Phillis Rd.

17.3

Mays Chapel Rd.

12.3

12.8

Visitor's Center

North Bend Park and Marina

Buggs Island Rd.

2.9

Jerusalem Rd.

5.1

5.9

Palmer Springs Rd.

7.6

Food

8.8

4

Beach Option

John H. Kerr Dam and Reservoir (Buggs Island Lake)

N

2 mi

km

0   1   2   3

0.0 Exit Tailrace Park.

0.3 Turn left at the stop sign on Rt. 4 South. In 0.3 mile, you'll pass the Nature Center on the left.

0.7 Bear left at the Y on Rt. 4 South to cross the dam.

2.9 Turn left on Jerusalem Rd./Rt. 616. In 0.2 mile, continue straight on 616.

5.1 Turn right at the stop sign on Mineral Springs Rd./Rt. 711.

5.9 Turn right at the stop sign on Palmer Springs Rd./ Rt. 712.

7.6 Turn right at the stop sign on Buggs Island Rd./Rt. 4 North. In 0.3 mile, you'll come to Lake Country Dairy Bar and Grill on your right.

8.8 If you want to go to Palmer Point Park, make the left here on Palmer Point Rd./ Rt. 827. It's 2.6-mile round trip, with a $1.00 entrance fee. Enjoy the picnic areas, beach, and swimming. Otherwise, continue straight on Buggs Island Rd.

12.3 After you recross the dam, bear left at the Y on Mays Chapel Rd./Rt. 678.

12.8 Turn left into the Visitor Assistance Center. Exhibits and rest rooms are available. After your visit, go back out to Mays Chapel Rd., then turn left to continue the ramble.

15.0 Turn left at the stop sign on Phillis Rd./Rt. 707. *Note:* If you would like to short-en the ramble by 7.8 miles, turn right here on China Grove Rd./Rt. 707 instead of left. After 1.1 miles, pick up cue at mile 23.9.

17.3 Bear right to stay on Rt. 707.

19.3 Turn right on Redlawn Rd./Rt. 615.

21.1 Turn right at the stop sign on Antlers Rd./Rt. 678.

22.7 Turn left at the stop sign on Phillis Rd./Rt. 707.

22.8 Continue straight on China Grove Rd./Rt. 707.

23.9 Turn right at the stop sign on Buggs Island Rd./Rt. 4 South. In 0.1 mile, Pino's Pizza and Italian Restaurant will be on your left. On your right is Brame's Grocery.

24.9 Turn left into the John H. Kerr Dam and Reservoir Powerhouse.

25.2 Turn left into Tailrace Park and end of ride.

Waterford Cruise

The Waterford Cruise explores the gentle farmlands and villages of the Catoctin Valley. Starting in the town of Purcellville, the cruise takes in a few miles of the paved W&OD Trail, one of northern Virginia's great recreational resources. Then it's on to Waterford, considered to be the prettiest village in Virginia. Founded by a Pennsylvania Quaker, Waterford most resembles an Irish village and is now listed as a National Historic Landmark. Pass through several more Loudoun County villages on your way to the base of Short Hill Mountain, where you'll enjoy an easy and spectacular spin back to Purcellville.

Louise Hirsch of the Potomac Pedalers Touring Club (PPTC) graciously submitted the Waterford Cruise to me. Serving the metro Washington, D.C., area, the PPTC is one of the largest bike clubs in the country. The club sponsors more than a thousand rides each year and offers numerous weekend trips and adventures throughout the year. Definitely look them up if you plan to cycle in the Mid-Atlantic region.

Purcellville was first developed in the mid-1700s, along an old ox cart track that ventured west out of Leesburg. Although most of its original architecture was wiped out by a fire in the early 1900s, Purcellville remains a quiet and appealing town and serves as a business center for western Loudoun County. Now the town is becoming popular as the western terminus of the W&OD Trail.

The Washington and Old Dominion Railroad ran through Purcellville for nearly a century. After terminating service in 1968, the W&OD Railroad eventually gave way to the W&OD Trail, a 45-mile paved trail that runs east from Purcellville to Shirlington Village in Arlington. Well managed by the Northern Virginia Regional Park Authority, the trail has become one of the most popular and successful rails-to-trails in the United States.

Pick up your supplies at one of the many stores in Purcellville, then head out for the trail. Remember to stay to the right, as you'll be sharing the trail with many other bicyclists, walkers, joggers, and rollerbladers. You'll get to enjoy 4.7 vehicle-free miles of the trail before you exit at Simpson Circle. If you like trail riding and wish to explore more of the trail at another time, call the W&OD Regional Park at 703–729–0596.

You will enter the charming village of Waterford in just a few miles. Founded by a Pennsylvania Quaker in the 1730s, Waterford grew around Janney's Mill on the south fork of the Catoctin Creek. Originally called Janney's Mill, the town's present name supposedly was coined by Quaker Thomas Moore, whose forebears were from Waterford, Ireland.

By the mid-1840s, most of Waterford's buildings were in place.

When the railroad that was built several decades later bypassed the village, Waterford's pace slowed, preserving much of the town. Most of the Quakers moved out of the village (mainly to Ohio) in the early 1800s because of slavery issues. Today, metro Washington's affluent own most of these homes, which, fortunately, retain their pre–Civil War quaintness. It's a real pleasure strolling the village—you'll feel as though you were somehow transported thousands of miles across the Atlantic to one of Ireland's charming villages. Be sure to stop. The village of Waterford and its surrounding 1,420 acres were designated a National Historic Landmark in 1970.

Just a few miles after Waterford, you'll pull into Lovettsville, where you can pick up lunch at a pizza/sub restaurant at the center of town. Take this opportunity since the route turns very rural the rest of the cruise. There are some rollers as you make your way to Short Hill Mountain. Once you reach the mountain, turn south and cruise along its eastern base for a remarkably flat and scenic spin. When you reach Purcellville, turn left on the W&OD Trail for a quick ride back to the school. If you want to check out the historic Purcellville Train Station, turn right instead. The station is just down the trail and is a great photo opportunity.

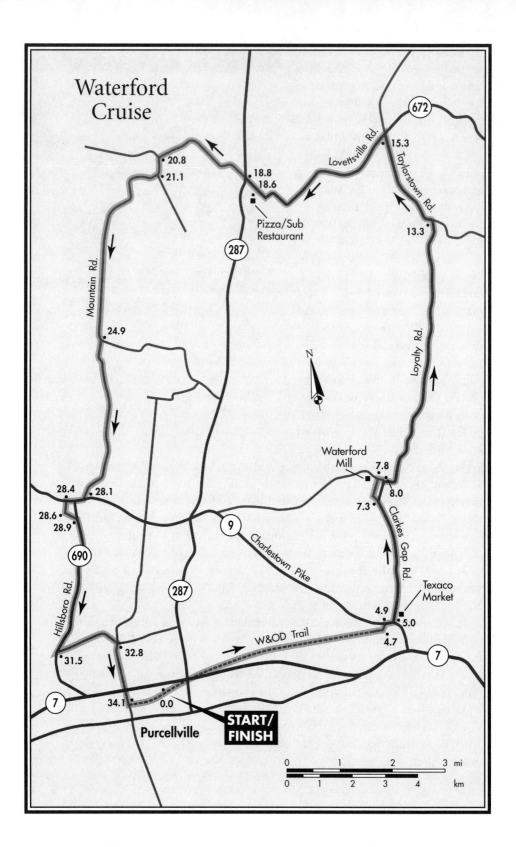

Waterford
Cruise

672

15.3

Lovettsville Rd.

Taylorstown Rd.

20.8
21.1

18.8
18.6

Pizza/Sub
Restaurant

13.3

287

Mountain Rd.

24.9

Loyalty Rd.

N

Waterford
Mill

7.8

8.0

7.3

Clarkes Gap Rd.

28.4
28.1

28.6
28.9

9

Charlestown Pike

Texaco
Market

690

287

4.9
5.0

4.7

Hillsboro Rd.

W&OD Trail

7

31.5

32.8

7

34.1

0.0

Purcellville

**START/
FINISH**

| 0 | | 1 | | 2 | | 3 | mi |

| 0 | 1 | 2 | 3 | 4 | km |

0.0 Turn right out of the Loudoun Valley High School parking lot on Rt. 722 and make an immediate right on the W&OD Trail.

4.7 Turn left off the trail on Simpson Circle/Rt. 662.

4.9 Turn right on Rt. 9. Caution, faster traffic.

5.0 Turn left on Clarkes Gap Rd./Rt. 662. There is a Texaco Market on the left.

7.3 Turn left on Factory St., which soon becomes Second St. Marvel at the old homes.

7.7 Waterford Market is on the left.

7.8 Turn right on Water St./Rt. 698. To see more of Waterford, detour here by turning left on Main St. and going 0.2 mile to the Waterford Mill. There are benches and picnic tables at the mill, which makes a perfect rest stop. After your stop, turn around and head back to Water St. to continue the cruise.

8.0 Bear left on Loyalty Rd./Rt. 665.

13.3 Turn left at the stop sign on Taylorstown Rd./Rt. 663.

15.3 Turn left at the T on Lovettsville Rd./Rt. 672.

18.6 Road becomes E. Broadway in Lovettsville. Also, the pizza/sub restaurant is on the left in town.

18.8 Go straight at the stop sign on W. Broadway/Rt. 673. A 7-Eleven is on the right at this intersection. Road eventually changes to Irish Corner Rd.

20.8 Bear left to stay on Irish Corner Rd.

21.1 Bear right on Mountain Rd./Rt. 690.

24.9 Turn right on Mountain Rd./Rt. 690.

28.1 Turn right at the stop sign on Charlestown Pike/Rt. 9.

28.4 Turn left on Gaver Mill Rd./Rt. 812.

28.6 Turn left to stay on Gaver Mill Rd./Rt. 812 at Rt. 718.

28.9 Turn right at the stop sign on Hillsboro Rd./Rt. 690.

31.5 Turn left on Allder School Rd./Rt. 711.

32.8 Turn right at the stop sign on Purcellville Rd./Rt. 611. Turns into Hatcher Rd.

34.1 Turn left onto W&OD Trail.

34.8 End the ride back at the school parking lot.

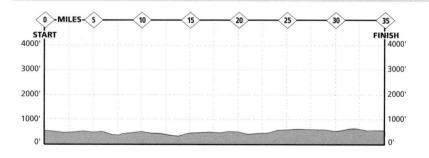

Cyclists break from a winter ride on the W&OD Trail. (Photo by Sandy Butler)

LOCAL INFORMATION

♦ Loudoun Convention and Visitors Association, 108-D South St., Leesburg, VA 20175, 800–752–6118. Open daily from 9:00 A.M. to 5:00 P.M.

LOCAL EVENTS/ATTRACTIONS

♦ Annual Waterford Homes Tour and Crafts Exhibit, first weekend in October, 540–882–3085. Features 144 juried heritage crafters, historic homes open for tour. Admission $12 for adults; children under twelve free.

RESTAURANTS

♦ Candelora's at the Purcellville Inn, 36855 West Main St., Purcellville, 540–338–2075. Italian restaurant in an old restored inn.

ACCOMMODATIONS

♦ Georges Mill Farm B&B, 11867 Georges Mill Rd., Lovettsville, VA 20180, 540–822–5224. Civil War–era stone home on 200-acre farm. Mid-range.

BIKE SHOP

♦ Trailside Bicycles, 201 N. 21st St., Purcellville, VA 20132, 540–338–4687.

REST ROOMS

♦ Mile 5.0: at the Texaco Station/Market
♦ Mile 18.6: at restaurants in Lovettsville

MAP

♦ DeLorme *Virginia Atlas and Gazetteer* maps 79 and 80

16

Shenandoah River Ramble

T his short ramble is a great beginner's ride that takes the cyclist along the pleasant country roads of Clarke and Warren counties. Although there are several short climbs, the terrain is mainly gently rolling and suitable for any cyclist. While the first half of the ride offers splendid views of the Blue Ridge, the second half winds along the Shenandoah River, tempting the cyclist to take a refreshing dip. The ride begins and ends in Millwood, a small village and home to the Burwell-Morgan Mill.

You may want to pay a visit to Berryville, the county seat, which is about 6 miles north of Millwood. A variety of restaurants, stores, and accommodations can be found here, as well as the Clarke County Visitor Center. Pick up any necessary supplies here, since very few facilities are found along the route.

Leaving Millwood, you will traverse the beautiful farmland of the river valley. You'll have a few ups and downs but nothing that a beginner can't handle. As you wind your way toward the river, great views of the Blue Ridge greet you at every turn. One terrific stretch of road offers a gradual downhill that bisects the beautifully manicured golf course of the Bowling Green Country Club.

As you approach the Shenandoah River, use caution, as the descent is windy and abruptly leads you onto a one-lane bridge. Because this is approximately halfway through your ride, take this opportunity to enjoy a break and a swim. The south side is shallow and safe for wading in the cool, serene river.

The second half of the ramble follows the Shenandoah back to the northeast. The ride back is relatively flat, but, unfortunately, river views are limited. About 4 miles past the river crossing, you'll come to a small cafe and convenience store on your right. This is your only opportunity on the ride to stock up.

Start: From the Burwell-Morgan Mill parking lot in Millwood.

Length: 26 miles

Terrain: Gently rolling, with a few climbs. Suitable for beginners.

Traffic and hazards: Exercise caution on the descent to the Shenandoah River. Watch out for fast traffic on the short stretch of Route 17/50.

Getting there: From I-81 near Winchester, go east about 10 miles on Route 17. Make a left on Route 255, then go 0.6 mile to Route 723. Go left 0.1 mile to the mill on the left. Some street parking also available.

You will have to cycle a short distance on Route 17/50. Although the traffic is fast, there is an adequate shoulder on the road and on the bridge. Use caution here. As you leave the highway, you'll climb a little out of the riverbed and back up to Millwood. You'll pass even more stately manor houses and horse farms, for which Clarke County is noted. At the ride's end, be sure to visit the historic Burwell-Morgan Mill.

The Burwell-Morgan Mill dates to 1782 and is noted for its 20-foot diameter interior water wheel. This feature allowed for grinding of wheat and corn year-round. Having just gone through a second renova-

The meandering Shenandoah River.

tion, the mill is now restored to its original configuration and now offers week-ly grinding exhibitions.

LOCAL INFORMATION

♦ Berryville/Clarke County Chamber of Commerce, 101 East Main St., Berryville, VA 22611, 540–955–4200.

LOCAL EVENTS/ATTRACTIONS

♦ Shenandoah Valley Steam and Gas Engine Show and Antique Market, last full weekend in July, 540–955–4200.
♦ Spring (April) and Fall (October) Art at the Mill Show, Burwell-Morgan Mill, 540–955–2600 or 540–837–1799.

RESTAURANTS

♦ Battletown Inn, 102 W. Main St., Berryville, 540–955–4100. American and Virginia favorites.
♦ L'Auberge Provencale Country Inn and Restaurant, Route 340, White Post, 800–638–1702. Up-scale French.

ACCOMMODATIONS

♦ Battletown Inn, 102 W. Main St., Berryville, VA 22611, 800–282–4106. Elegant, antique-appointed guest rooms. High-end.
♦ The Lost Dog Bed and Breakfast, 211 S. Church St., Berryville, VA 22611, 540–955–1181. A 112-year-old B&B in Berryville's historic district. Mid-range.

BIKE SHOP

♦ Blue Ridge Schwinn, 2228-G Paper Mill Rd., Winchester, VA 22601, 540–662–1510.

REST ROOMS

♦ At the start, Burwell-Morgan Mill
♦ Mile 16.9: Shenandoah Farms Grocery and Snack Bar, Cafe

MAP

♦ DeLorme *Virginia Atlas and Gazetteer* maps 74, 75, 78, and 79

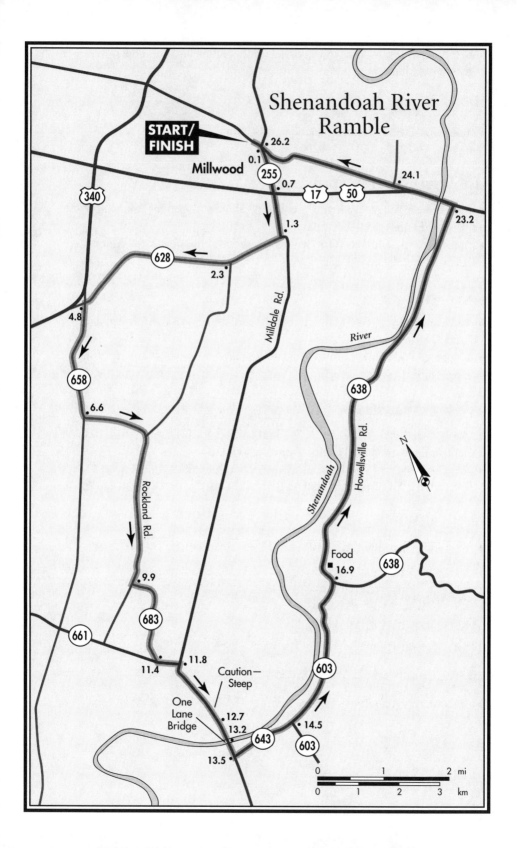

Shenandoah River Ramble

START/FINISH

Millwood

26.2

0.1

255

0.7

17 50

24.1

340

23.2

1.3

628

2.3

Milldale Rd.

4.8

River

658

638

6.6

Rockland Rd.

Shenandoah

Howellsville Rd.

N

Food
16.9

638

9.9

683

661

11.8

11.4

Caution—
Steep

603

One
Lane
Bridge

12.7

13.2

14.5

643

603

13.5

0   1   2 mi

0   1   2   3 km

0.0 Make a right out of the Burwell-Morgan Mill parking lot onto Rts. 255/723.

0.1 Turn right on Bishop Meade Rd./Rt. 255.

0.7 Go straight on Red Gate Rd./Rt. 624. Caution crossing highway.

1.3 Turn right on Nelson Rd./Rt. 626.

2.3 Turn right on Berry's Ferry Rd./Rt. 628.

4.8 Turn left at the stop sign on White Post Rd./Rt. 658.

6.6 Bear left to stay on Rt. 658.

9.9 Turn left on Bowling Green Rd./Rt. 683.

10.5 Pass the golf course.

11.4 Turn left on Fairground Rd./Rt. 661.

11.8 Turn right on Milldale Rd./Rt. 624.

12.7 Caution, steep downhill to river.

13.2 Go straight on one-lane bridge over the Shenandoah River.

13.5 Turn left on Howellsville Rd./Rt. 643.

14.5 Straight to stay on Howellsville Rd./Rt. 603.

16.9 Bear to the left to stay on Howellsville Rd./Rt. 638. Shenandoah Farms and Grocery and a cafe are on your right at this intersection.

23.2 Turn left on Rt. 17/50 at the T. Caution; fast traffic.

24.1 Bear right on Millwood Rd./Rt. 723.

26.2 Bear right to stay on Rt. 723/255.

26.4 End the ride at the Burwell-Morgan Mill on your left.

Piedmont Challenge

*J*ust west of bustling northern Virginia and east of the tranquil Blue Ridge foothills lies the lush, green rolling hills of Virginia's Northern Piedmont. Based in Warrenton, the Piedmont Challenge is a tour through preserved pre–Civil War villages and towns and through the famous horse-and-wine country for which Fauquier County is so well noted. At 54 miles, the challenge is constantly rolling but lacks any significant climbs. It can be completed in one day, with time left to explore Warrenton's unique shops and appealing restaurants.

There are a variety of places to pick up supplies in Warrenton before the ride, but you may want to consider planning lunch in Marshall about halfway into the ride. The visitor's center is open every day, so a stop is in order if you need water, a rest room, or some information on the area.

Although Warrenton is the crossroads of several main highways, getting out of town is still easy. Within 1¼ miles you will be out of town and rolling your way through the Piedmont. Cycling west, then northwest, you'll have some great panoramic views of the Blue Ridge, but you won't have to climb anything that even closely resembles it. The hills are frequent but manageable, and they are fairly evenly distributed throughout the challenge.

When you reach the village of Hume, you may consider a detour. Turning left instead of right will take you to the Oasis Winery. In addition to tours and tastings, Oasis offers an excellent lunch fare and picnic grounds with spectacular views of the Blue Ridge Mountains. The detour is 6 miles each way.

Some of the challenge's best descents await you after leaving Hume. They're fast and straight, so you won't have to worry about what's around the next bend. The route flattens a bit as it snakes around Big Cobbler Mountain on your left and brings you into Marshall. Founded as Salem in 1797, the village later changed its name to Marshall in honor of John Marshall, the first chief justice of the Supreme Court. Here you'll be able to make a pit stop at a 7-Eleven, deli, pizza shop, or supermarket.

Avoiding busy and boring Route 55, the challenge makes a loop to the north through some of the prettiest countryside in Virginia. It is in this area that numerous horse farms are concentrated and distinguished by split-rail fences and stone walls lining both sides of the roads. One cannot cease to marvel at the stately farmhouses, grazing animals, and bucolic countryside—and all on lightly traveled rural roads.

The Plains is your next village and stop. It dates back to the 1830s, with the Grace Episcopal Church being the village's highlight. Erected in 1852, the church was rebuilt in 1917 and remains one of the most beautiful in the area. Leaving The Plains, you must follow Route 55 fronting the interstate for about 3 miles. But you are rewarded with nearly 6 miles on Blantyre Road, another of Virginia's premier biking routes.

The route stays rural all the way past the Warrenton Reservoir on Blackwell Road. Then, out of nowhere, Warrenton pops right in front of you. It's less than 1½ miles to the ride's end,

THE BASICS

Start: From the Warrenton–Fauquier County Visitor Center in Warrenton.

Length: 54 miles

Terrain: Moderate hills. No major climbs, and some flat riding between hills. Though not for beginners, it is one of the easier challenges in the book.

Traffic and hazards: Use caution in traffic when leaving and reentering Warrenton. Traffic can be heavy on Route 55 in the vicinity of Marshall and The Plains. Be careful crossing the extremely rough railroad tracks when leaving Marshall.

Getting there: From the south, follow Route 17 Business north into Warrenton. The street name is East Shirley. Go straight through the stoplight at Culpeper Street, and make the next right on Keith Street. Go a few hundred yards to the visitor's center on the right. From the north, follow Route 17 Business south into town. You'll be on Broadway Avenue. When you see the Howard Johnson's on your right, continue straight through the stoplight at Waterloo on West Shirley. Go 0.6 mile, then turn left on Keith Street. The visitor's center will come up on the right. Free parking is available.

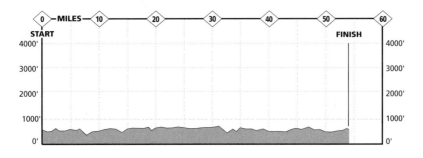

0.0 Turn right out of the Warrenton–Fauquier County Visitor Center on Keith St. Go 0.2 mile, then turn left on Lee St. Go 0.1 mile and bear right on Chestnut St. Go another 0.1 mile, then turn left on Waterloo St.

0.9 Continue straight at the stoplight on Waterloo St. Caution, busy intersection. In 0.1 mile, turn right on Rappahannock, then a quick left on Old Waterloo Rd.

4.9 Turn left on Old Waterloo Rd./Rt. 691.

7.0 Turn right on Leeds Manor Rd./Rt. 688.

12.6 Continue straight on Leeds Manor Rd./Rt. 688 in Orlean. Orlean Market is on the right.

18.8 Turn right on Hume Rd./Rt. 635. *Note:* If you want to visit the Oasis Winery, turn left here and go 6 miles for a 12-mile round trip.

22.1 Turn left on Ramey Rd./Rt. 732.

26.6 Turn right on Grove Lane/Rt. F185.

28.3 Enter Marshall. There are various stores and restaurants along the route.

28.7 Turn left on Rectortown Rd./Rt. 710. A 7-Eleven is on the left after turn.

29.5 Caution, very rough railroad crossing.

31.7 Turn right on Frogtown Rd./Rt. 702.

35.2 Turn right on Zulla Rd./Rt. 709.

36.4 Turn left on Milestone/Rt. 707.

37.6 Bear right on Whitewood Rd.

38.2 Turn left on John Marshall Hwy./Rt. 55. Caution, fast traffic.

38.9 Continue straight through the village of The Plains. Look for Grace Episcopal Church on the right. After the church, there is a cafe at the BP Station.

42.6 Turn right on Georgetown Rd./Rt. 674 just after underpass.

42.9 Continue straight on Blantyre Rd./Rt. 628.

49.1 Turn left on Airlie Rd./Rt. 605.

51.0 Turn right on Blackwell Rd./Rt. 672.

52.7 Continue straight at the stoplight on Blackwell Rd. Caution, busy intersection. Road name changes to Alexandria Pike.

53.7 Bear right on Main St. at the Old Courthouse. Make immediate left on Ashby St. The Old Jail Museum will be on your left.

53.8 Turn right at the stop sign on W. Lee St. Go 0.1 mile, then turn left on Keith St.

54.1 End the ride at the visitor's center on the left.

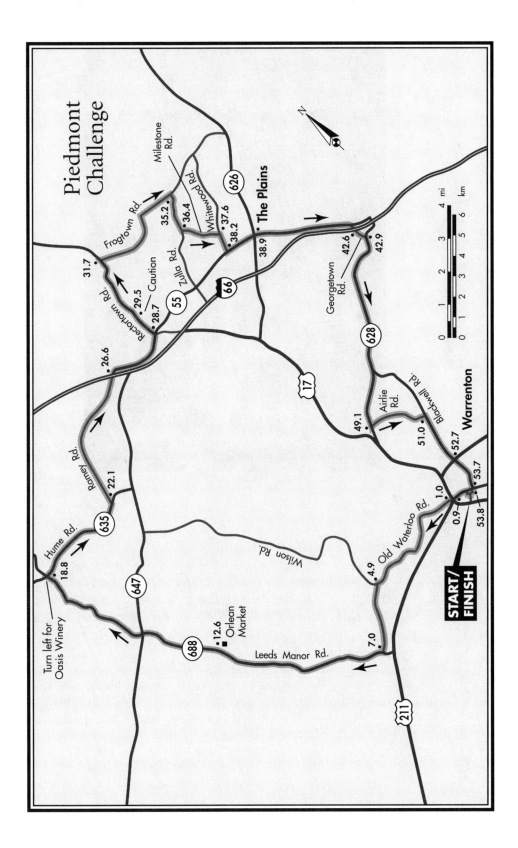

Cyclists begin a ride in front of the old courthouse in Warrenton. (Photo by Sandy Butler)

but cycle with caution on this final stretch into Warrenton's historic district. As you ride up Alexandria Pike, the Old Courthouse will come into view, along with the Old Jail. The courthouse is still in use, while the jail (one of the oldest in Virginia) is now a museum. Its two buildings (1808 and 1823) house Civil War, Indian, and Revolutionary War artifacts. The museum is open Tuesday to Sunday year-round and is free.

Warrenton offers a fine walking tour of its historic district and has an abundance of inns and restaurants, but I found the town to be a little snooty. The many attractions and events in Warrenton must attract so many visitors that no more are required—or desired. My advice is to do the ride, then head down the road to Culpeper for some real down-to-earth Virginia hospitality.

LOCAL INFORMATION

♦ Warrenton–Fauquier County Visitor Center, 183A Keith St., Warrenton, VA 20188, 800–820–1021. Open daily from 9:00 A.M. to 5:00 P.M.

LOCAL EVENTS/ATTRACTIONS

♦ Virginia Gold Cup, first Saturday in May, and International Gold Cup, third Saturday in October, Steeplechase Racing Classics, The Plains, VA, 540–347–2612.

RESTAURANTS

♦ Napoleon's Restaurant, 67 Waterloo St., Warrenton, 540–347–4300. Continental dining in small, cozy rooms.

ACCOMMODATIONS

♦ Hampton Inn, 501 Blackwell Rd., Warrenton, VA 20186, 540–349–4200. Mid-range.

BIKE SHOP

♦ Ashby Street Bicycles, 20 Ashby St., Warrenton, VA 20186, 540–347–9771.

REST ROOMS

♦ At the start in the visitor's center
♦ Mile 12.6: at Orlean Market
♦ Mile 28.3: at various locations in Marshall
♦ Mile 39.3: at Cafe at BP Station

MAP

♦ DeLorme *Virginia Atlas and Gazetteer* map 75

Culpeper Cruise

Nestled between the Rapidan and Rappahannock rivers in Virginia's Piedmont region, the town of Culpeper is the starting point for a tour of this picturesque and historic area. Although the first half is moderately hilly, the cruise is designed as an easy day ride for the intermediate cyclist. With numerous biking routes circling Culpeper County, this cruise is a delightful cross section, offering small towns and villages, woods and farms, and streams and rivers, Blue Ridge Mountain views, and Civil War battlefields. After taking it all in, spend time in Culpeper's architecturally rich and thriving downtown, and see why it was rated one of the ten best small towns in America.

Start your tour of Culpeper County at the visitor's center across Commerce Street. Besides a helpful staff, there are rest rooms, water, and additional area maps available if you need them. You'll also find many restaurants and stores along Davis and Main Streets for food and supplies.

The town of Culpeper was established in 1759 and is only one of two known towns to be planned by George Washington. Culpeper has maintained a thriving town center, and walking through it provides not only a study in American Colonial and Victorian architecture but also a sense of a real, down-to-earth identity. You'll find the town a warm and friendly kind of place—the kind that makes you want to go back and visit again.

Main Street is a great place to walk, but follow the route for West Street and you'll leave the town with considerably less traffic. When you turn off Route 229 for Chestnut Fork Road, you'll have several hills to climb but nothing too strenuous. The ridge that keeps coming into view on the left horizon is the Blue Ridge, of course. You won't be climbing that today. But the region you're in is the rolling Piedmont, and roll you will for the first 16 miles or so.

At about the ride's midpoint, the terrain eases up quite a bit. While cruising to the village of Remington, you'll pass miles of scenic cropland, livestock and horse farms, streams, woods, and orchards. Wow, and all before lunch. Speaking of lunch, if you need some, consider the Corner Deli in Remington. It's right on the route, and it's as local as you're going to find. It's open from 7:00 A.M. to 8:00 P.M. every day but Sunday. There's also a convenience store just across the street.

As you leave Remington and start heading west back to Culpeper, you'll cross the Rappahannock River and cycle through miles of flat pastures and cropland. It's a quiet and serene area, but wasn't always so. During the 1860s, these lands saw some of the most severe and significant battles of the Civil War. Culpeper's central location between Washington and Richmond, along with its two railroads and four major roads, made it strategically important. In fact, more than 160 skirmishes took place in and around Culpeper during the war, with occupation of the town changing on several occasions.

THE BASICS

Start: From the municipal parking lot adjacent to Culpeper Visitor Center.

Length: 40 miles

Terrain: First half is moderately hilly. Second half is flat to gently rolling.

Traffic and hazards: Route 229 exiting and reentering Culpeper can be busy. Use caution when crossing Route 15/29 Bypass before Remington and when on Route 15/29 Business in Remington. Entire route is paved and in good condition.

Getting there: Take Route 15 Business, Route 29 Business, or Route 522, which all lead to Main Street in Culpeper. From the south, follow Main Street, then make a right turn on Davis Street. Go 2 blocks to Commerce Street. Plenty of free public parking in the municipal lot on the left. Diagonally from parking lot is the Culpeper Visitor Center, located in the old train station.

The Battle of Kelly's Ford and the Battle of Brandy Station were both fought along these very same roads. At Brandy Station, about 18,000 mounted soldiers clashed in what was the largest cavalry battle ever fought on the North American continent. Be sure to pick up the brochure "The Civil War Battles Fought in Culpeper" at the visitor's center for a detailed map and deeper examination of these battles.

One good climb greets you as you make your way back to Route 229 and Culpeper. You'll backtrack on the same route on which you left town because it is by far the safest route. As you turn on Davis Street and head toward the finish, notice the small restaurant It's About Thyme on your left. I highly recommend this charming place for your end-of-ride celebration.

0.0 Head straight on Davis St. back to the center of town. Go straight through Main St.

0.2 Turn right on West St.

0.5 Continue straight across one-lane bridge. Turns into Old Rixeyville Rd.

1.3 Bear right and go to the light. Turn left on N. Main St. extension/Rt. 229.

2.9 Turn left on Chestnut Fork Rd./Rt. 685. Before you turn, look ahead on the right for Duke's General Store.

3.3 Bear right at the Y on Dutch Hollow Rd./Rt. 632.

6.2 Turn right on Alum Springs Rd./Rt. 633.

8.8 Turn left on Rixeyville Rd./Rt. 229. Caution, faster traffic.

9.5 Turn right on Ryland Chapel Rd./Rt. 640.

12.5 Continue straight on Ryland Chapel Rd./Rt. 625.

15.8 Turn right on Lakota Rd./Rt. 621.

18.2 Continue straight on Freemans Ford Rd./Rt. 651.

19.8 Turn left on Saint Pauls Rd./Rt. 660.

20.6 Turn right on Cemetery Rd./Rt. 658.

21.9 Bear right to stay on Cemetery Rd./Rt. 658.

23.1 Bear right to stay on Cemetery Rd./Rt. 658.

24.2 Turn left on Freemans Ford Rd./Rt. 651. Continue straight on West Main St. after crossing Rt. 15/29 Bypass. Caution when crossing.

24.7 Turn right on James Madison/Rt. 15/29 Business in Remington. At this corner, The Corner Deli is on the left, and a convenience store is across from it.

25.5 Turn left on Rt. 673 (unmarked Newby's Shop Rd.).

27.6 Turn right on Kelly's Ford Rd./Rt. 674.

29.2 Turn left just before railroad tracks on Elkwood Crossing/Rt. 678. Go 0.3 mile, then turn right on Rt. 676. Cross railroad tracks.

29.6 Go straight at the stop sign on Beverly Ford Rd. Caution while crossing Rt. 15/29.

29.8 Turn left on Fleetwood Heights Rd./Rt. 685.

32.1 Go straight on Rt. 685 at the stop sign in Brandy Station. Turns into Auburn Rd.

36.3 Turn left on Chestnut Fork Rd./Rt. 685.

37.6 Turn left on Rixeyville Rd./Rt. 229. Duke's General Store is on the right.

39.1 Bear right at the stoplight on unmarked Old Rixeyville Rd. When you reach the stop sign, continue straight on Old Rixeyville Rd.

39.9 Caution when crossing the one-lane bridge. Continue straight at the stoplight on West St.

40.2 Turn left on Davis St. Cross Main St., and note variety of shops and restaurants in town.

40.4 End the ride back at the municipal parking lot.

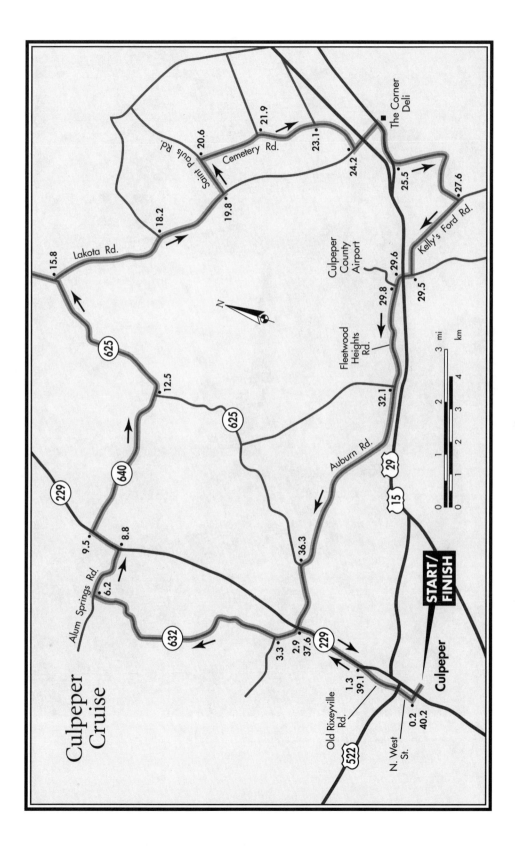

Culpeper Cruise

The Corner Deli

21.9
20.6
23.1
Cemetery Rd.
24.2
Saint Pauls Rd.
25.5
27.6
18.2
19.8
Kelly's Ford Rd.
15.8
Lakota Rd.
Culpeper County Airport
29.6
29.8
29.5
N
625
12.5
Fleetwood Heights Rd.
625
32.1
640
Auburn Rd.
229
29
9.5
8.8
15
6.2
36.3
Alum Springs Rd.
632
3.3
2.9
37.6
229
522
1.3
39.1
Old Rixeyville Rd.
N. West St.
0.2
40.2
START/FINISH
Culpeper

3 mi
km
2 3 4
0 1 2 3
0 1 2 3

Author's wife, Wendy, takes a breather alongside one of Virginia's many beautiful rivers.

LOCAL INFORMATION

♦ Culpeper Chamber of Commerce and Visitor Center, 109 S. Commerce St., Culpeper, VA 22701, 540–825–8628 or 888–285–7373.

LOCAL EVENTS/ATTRACTIONS

♦ Culpeper Train Days, sponsored by Culpeper Renaissance, Train Depot and E. Davis St., Culpeper, 540–825–4416, mid-September. Model train displays.

RESTAURANTS

♦ It's About Thyme, 128 East Davis St., Culpeper, 540–825–4264. Lunch and dinner.
♦ Jenner's Family Restaurant, 306 S. Main St., Culpeper, 540–825–4222. Breakfast.

ACCOMMODATIONS

♦ Fountain Hall B&B, 609 S. East St., Culpeper, VA 22701, 540–825–8300. An 1859 Colonial Revival mansion. Mid- to high-range.
♦ Holiday Inn of Culpeper, 791 James Madison Rd., Route 29 South, Culpeper, VA 22701, 540–825–1253. Mid-range.

BIKE SHOP

♦ The Bike Stop, 120 West Culpeper St., Culpeper, VA 22701, 540–825–2105.

REST ROOMS

♦ At the start in the visitor's center
♦ Mile 24.7: at the Corner Deli in Remington

MAP

♦ DeLorme *Virginia Atlas and Gazetteer* maps 69 and 75

Orange Ramble

T he Orange Ramble takes the cyclist on a scenic, gentle loop through historic Orange County. Starting in the county seat and town of Orange, the ramble first drops down to the village of Rapidan, nestled on both sides of the Rapidan River. This small village changed hands fifteen times during the Civil War. Continue through quiet countryside and past peaceful farmlands while gently rolling down to Lake Orange. Pack a picnic lunch and take a well-deserved break alongside this scenic 124-acre lake. After finishing this ramble, make the short drive to Montpelier and experience the world of James Madison, our fourth president and the father of the Constitution, and his effervescent wife, Dolley, who inspired the title First Lady.

Orange County was established in 1734 and named for William IV, Prince of Orange and husband of Anne, Princess Royal of England. Its original boundaries extended to the Mississippi River to the west and the Great Lakes to the north, giving it the distinction of being the largest county ever formed in Virginia. The county still packs a lot of history and scenic countryside in its now smaller package and makes for a delightful day of biking and exploring.

Turn right as you leave the visitor's center, and proceed to the next block. Here you will find Orange Grocery on your left and a 7-Eleven on your right. Pick up what you need here, as stores along the route are limited. A short climb will take you past a number of the town's stately homes and quickly out to the Orange County countryside.

After a few rollers and a gradual descent, you'll be on your way to Rapidan. Founded in 1772, this village changed hands fifteen times during the Civil War.

After fighting each other all day, soldiers of both armies would trade with each other at night, swimming across the river to do so. Take a breather at the photogenic train station in Rapidan before making your way back up to Waddell Memorial Church. This church, with its towering spires, is one of Virginia's finest examples of Gothic architecture.

A few rollers add some challenge to the ramble as you make your way south of Clarks Mountain. The terrain then levels for quite a while, and all you will see is more corn and cows. What a great stretch of road to relax and enjoy. Be sure to take the short turnoff to Lake Orange. Picnic tables are available overlooking this small, pretty lake, which makes for a perfect rest stop on this ramble. You might need to pack your own food, however, as soda machines are the only refreshment available at the lake site.

A few short rural miles later and you'll be back in Orange and ready to take in an exciting history lesson. Drive 4 miles west from Orange on Route 20 to Montpelier, the beautiful estate and lifelong home of James Madison. The fourth president of the United States, Madison was also a successful businessman, a member of the U.S. Congress, the secretary of state under Thomas Jefferson, and the primary author of the U.S. Constitution. Overlooking the beautiful Blue Ridge Mountains, Montpelier's exhibits bring to life the experiences and contributions of James and Dolley Madison, while the estate's outdoor interests include the formal gardens, the Madison cemetery, the old-growth Landmark Forest, and the historic tree walk. A Montpelier visit is a rich interweaving of history and scenic beauty. When combined with this delightful countryside ramble, it makes for a fulfilling and unforgettable day in the county of Orange.

THE BASICS

Start: From the Orange County Visitor Center at 122 East Main Street, Orange.

Length: 32 miles

Terrain: Gently rolling. Some long, flat stretches. Although there are no major climbs, cumulative climbing efforts will challenge beginners.

Traffic and hazards: All roads on this route are low traffic and rural. Use caution on the short stretch of Route 20 Business coming back into Orange.

Getting there: From I-64, take exit 136/ Route 15 north toward Gordonsville. Continue to Orange, then turn right on Main Street. Go about 300 yards to the train station on the right (Short Street). From I-95, take exit 130/ Route 3 West. Follow Route 3 West to Route 20 South. Follow Route 20 to Route 15, then go north. Follow Route 15, and turn right onto Main Street in Orange. Go about 300 yards to the train station on the right (Short Street). Free parking at the train station/visitor's center. Open daily from 9:00 A.M. to 5:00 P.M.

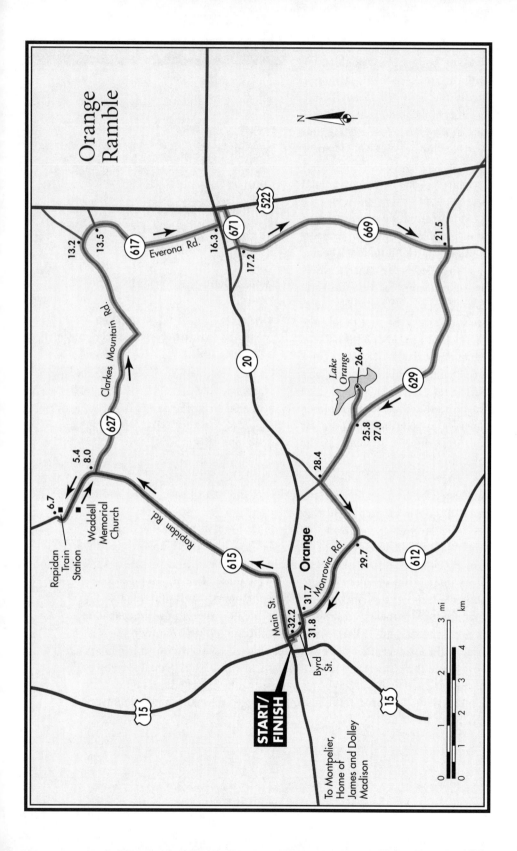

Orange Ramble

N

522

617 Everona Rd. 16.3
13.2
13.5
671
17.2

Clarkes Mountain Rd.

669
21.5

627

20

Lake
Orange 26.4
629

25.8
27.0

5.4
8.0

6.7

Rapidan
Train
Station

Waddell
Memorial
Church

28.4

Rapidan Rd.

615

Orange

Monrovia Rd.

29.7

612

Main St.

32.2
31.7

31.8
Byrd
St.

15

15

START/
FINISH

To Montpelier,
Home of
James and Dolley
Madison

3 mi

km

0   1   2   3

0   1   2   3   4

0.0 Turn right from the visitor's center on Main St. Continue to the stoplight, then go straight on Rt. 615. Orange Grocery is on the left and a 7-Eleven is on the right.

5.4 Go straight at junction with Rt. 627. (If you want to skip Rapidan, turn right here on Rt. 627. You'll shave off 2.6 miles from the ramble.)

6.5 Cross the Rapidan River. In 0.2 mile, you'll come to the old train station and an 1874 Episcopal church. After this photo op, turn around and head back up Rt. 615. In 0.4 mile, beautiful Waddell Memorial Church will be on your right.

8.0 Turn left on Clarks Mountain Rd./Rt. 627.

13.2 Go straight on Everona Rd./Rt. 617.

13.5 Continue straight on Everona Rd.

16.3 Turn left on Rt. 20. Go a few hundred yards to the stoplight, turn right on Rt. 522 South. Go a few hundred feet, and make a quick right on Rt. 671.

17.2 Turn left on Marquis Rd./Rt. 669.

21.5 Turn right on Rt. 629.

25.8 Turn right on Rt. 739. (If you want to skip the stop at Lake Orange, then continue straight here on Rt. 629 to shave off 1.2 miles from the ramble.)

26.4 Arrive at Lake Orange. Soda machines, rest rooms, and picnic areas are available. After your stop, turn around and head back to Rt. 629.

27.0 Turn right on Rt. 629.

28.4 Turn left on Brick Church Rd./Rt. 631.

29.7 Turn right on Monrovia Rd./Rt. 612.

31.7 Turn left on Constitution Hwy./Rt. 20. Rt. 20 Market is on the right.

31.8 Bear right on Byrd St./Rt. 20 Business.

32.2 Turn left on E. Church St. just before Hess Chiropractic Center. Then make a quick right on Short St. The train station/visitor's center and the end of ride are less than 0.1 mile on the left.

LOCAL INFORMATION

♦ Orange County Department of Tourism and Visitors Bureau, 122 East Main St., Orange, VA 22960, 877–222–8072 or 540–672–1653.

LOCAL EVENTS/ATTRACTIONS

♦ James Madison's Montpelier, 11407 Constitution Highway, Montpelier Station, VA 22957, 540–672–2728. Admission: $7.50 for adults, $2.50 for children. Call for hours.

◆ Annual Montpelier Hunt Races, equestrian flat track and steeplechase races located on the Montpelier Estate grounds, 540–672–0027. First Saturday in November.

RESTAURANTS

◆ Not the Same Old Grind, 110 East Church St., Orange, 540–672–3143. Stop here for something different.

ACCOMMODATIONS

◆ The Hidden Inn Bed and Breakfast, 249 Caroline St., Orange, VA 22960, 540–672–3625. An 1880 Victorian inn. Mid- to high-range.
◆ Days Inn, 332 Caroline St., Orange, VA 22960, 540–672–4855 or 800–DAYSINN. Mid-range.

BIKE SHOP

◆ The Bike Stop, 120 West Culpeper St., Culpeper, VA 22701, 540–825–2105.

REST ROOMS

◆ At the start in the visitor's center
◆ Mile 26.4: at Lake Orange

MAP

◆ DeLorme *Virginia Atlas and Gazetteer* maps 68 and 69

Luray Classic

The Luray Classic is one of the most scenic, spectacular, and thrilling rides in all of Virginia. While this classic is designed to be a one-day ride for advanced cyclists, the average rider will require two days to complete this loop ride. Starting in Front Royal, the classic takes the cyclist 30 miles down the Skyline Drive, one of the most scenic roads in America. Halfway through the ride is Luray, a small Shenandoah Valley town popular for its renowned caverns and as a base for exploring Shenandoah National Park. The second half of the classic requires a climb up Massanutten Mountain and a delightful spin through Fort Valley and the George Washington National Forest.

Front Royal is the starting and ending point for the Luray Classic. It's a popular base for bikers, hikers, canoeists, and rafters, as well as those exploring the caverns and the Shenandoah National Park. There are many hotels and restaurants from which to choose, and the visitor's center, which is open seven days a week, is a good place for information.

The first mile takes you through the town of Front Royal, and before you know it you're entering the Skyline Drive. If you aren't warmed up by now, the next few miles will certainly do it. Four miles of 6 percent grade is the price you must pay for some of the best views in the state. But don't think for a moment that once on top of the ridge, the going gets any easier. The Skyline Drive twists and turns and rises and falls, requiring all your energy and concentration. And it is all worth it.

The Skyline Drive runs more than 100 miles along the spine of the Blue Ridge Mountains from Front Royal to Waynesboro. The linear Shenandoah National Park encompasses the Skyline Drive and offers spectacular vistas of the Piedmont to the east and the Shenandoah Valley to the west. The Shenandoah

Start: From the Front Royal Visitor Center at 414 East Main Street.

Length: 83 miles

Terrain: Mountainous. Long, steep climbs and twisting descents. Gentle terrain after Massanutten Mountain. Advanced difficulty.

Traffic and hazards: Summer and particularly autumn weekends will find heavy traffic on the Skyline Drive. Use caution on the descent to Luray and off Massanutten Mountain (switchbacks). Expect heavy traffic on the Route 211 approach to Luray. The entire route is paved and in good condition.

Getting there: From I-66, take exit 6 to Route 340 South. Go 3.3 miles, then turn left on East Main Street. Go ¼ mile to the visitor's center on left. Free parking in adjacent lots.

River meanders in the valley below, with the North and South Forks separated by the 40-mile-long Massanutten Mountain. Within the park you'll find waterfalls, rock formations, lots of wildlife, and miles of horse and hiking trails, including the Appalachian Trail.

About 6 miles into the ride, you will want to stop at the visitor's center. It's the only one for this northern district and a good place to pick up maps, see a slide show, and recover from the climb. For the remainder of the Skyline, you will come across numerous overlooks, where you'll find yourself constantly taking pictures (and catching your breath). Another wayside at Elkwallow offers food service, rest rooms, and picnic facilities.

You will leave the Skyline Drive at Panorama (Route 211) and soon find yourself flying down the 9 miles to Luray. If you're attempting this classic in one day, you'll want to refuel here. There are quite a few restaurants in town, as well as a variety of accommodations. The visitor's center, which is right on the route, is a good source for information on eating, sleeping, and sightseeing. Luray's famous attraction is the Luray Caverns, located about 1¼ miles from town. These caverns are the largest and most visited underground attraction in the East, and, some say, the most entertaining, with the caverns' Great Stalacpipe Organ.

Now that your weary legs are rested, you should be ready for the ascent of Massanutten. This strenuous 3-mile climb starts at 5 percent and ends at 7 percent grade. You are rewarded once again with wonderful vistas of Luray, the Shenandoah River, and the Blue Ridge in the distance. You'll find the terrain easing up a bit as you pedal northeast through Fort Valley, which splits the northern portion of Massanutten in two. You will enter the George Washington National Forest, which protects this wonderful area from development. The ride through the Elizabeth Furnace Recreation Area is one of my personal favorites. The valley quickly narrows, and the steep canyonlike walls allow no more than the road and beautiful Passage Creek to flow through. Cherish the moment.

Upon leaving the National Forest, you'll turn onto Mountain Road and pass through the Virginia Fish Cultural Station. If the hatchery interests you, stop and talk to a Ranger, if one is on duty. If not, this still makes a pleasant rest stop. The next few miles are uneventful as you pedal back into Front Royal. The town offers a walking tour with some interesting sites, including the Warren Rifles Confederate Museum. After completing this classic, though, you may just want to walk next door to the Mill Restaurant and have a cold one.

LOCAL INFORMATION

♦ Front Royal Visitor Center, 414 E. Main St., Front Royal, VA 22630, 800–338–2576.
♦ Luray–Page County Chamber of Commerce, 46 East Main St., Luray, VA 22835, 540–743–3915.

LOCAL EVENTS/ATTRACTIONS

♦ Virginia Wine and Mushroom Festival, Front Royal, 540–635–3185. Mid-May.
♦ Warren Heritage Society Festival of Leaves, Front Royal, 540–636–1446. Mid-October.
♦ Luray Caverns, P.O. Box 748, Luray, VA 22835, 540–743–6551.
♦ Mayfest, Luray Annual Spring Street Festival, 540–743–3915. Third Saturday of May.

Touring cyclists take a breather on the Skyline Drive. (Photo by Tom King)

0.0 From the visitor's center, make a right on E. Main St.

0.2 Turn left on Royal Ave./Rt. 340.

0.6 Go straight at the light. Caution, busy intersection.

1.1 Turn left into the Shenandoah National Park/Skyline Drive entrance.

1.7 Stop and pay the park entrance fee at the gate ($5.00 for cyclists).

5.9 Dickey Ridge Visitor Center on right. Stop for information, food, the rest rooms.

25.1 Elkwallow Wayside on right. Food service, rest rooms, and picnic area.

32.5 Exit the Skyline Drive to the right. At the end of the ramp, turn right on Rt. 211 West toward Luray.

32.9 Begin descent. Caution, several switchbacks, faster traffic.

39.3 Turn left on Rt. 211 West Business.

41.0 Several stores and restaurants are in this area.

42.0 Luray Visitor Center is on your left.

42.1 Turn right at the light on N. Broad St./Rt. 340 North.

42.2 Turn left on Mechanic St./Rt. 675.

43.8 Continue straight to stay on Rt. 675. Road is now Bixlers Ferry Rd.

45.7 Turn left on Egypt Bend Rd./Rt. 675 just after crossing the river.

46.2 Turn right on Fort Valley Rd./Rt. 675 and begin climb up Massanutten.

49.0 Top of mountain. Caution, switchbacks on descent.

50.7 Bear right to stay on Rt. 675.

52.0 Bear right to stay on Rt. 675.

54.0 Go straight to stay on Fort Valley Rd./Rt. 678 in village of Kings Crossing. Rt. 675 goes to the left.

61.1 Fort Valley Country Store is on your left. Last chance for food.

69.4 Elizabeth Furnace campground is on your right. Picnic areas are nearby.

72.6 Turn right on Mountain Rd./Rt. 619.

72.9 Virginia Fish Cultural Station is on your left. Open weekdays from 8:00 A.M. to 3:30 P.M.

73.2 Continue straight to stay on Rt. 619.

77.0 Bear left on Rivermont Rd./Rt. 619.

81.3 Turn left on Rt. 340 North. Caution, faster traffic.

82.4 Go straight at the light on S. Royal Ave./Rt. 340 North.

82.8 Turn right on E. Main St.

83.0 End the ride at the visitor's center on your left.

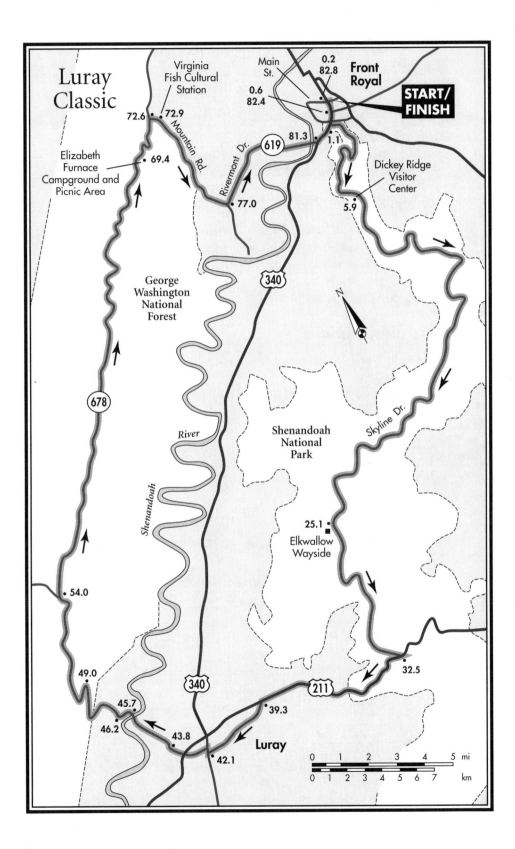

Luray Classic

Main St.
0.6
82.4

0.2
82.8
Front Royal

START/ FINISH

Virginia Fish Cultural Station

72.6 • 72.9

81.3

619

1.1

Dickey Ridge Visitor Center

69.4

Rivermont Dr.

Elizabeth Furnace Campground and Picnic Area

Mountain Rd.

5.9

77.0

George Washington National Forest

340

N

678

River

Shenandoah

Shenandoah National Park

Skyline Dr.

25.1
Elkwallow Wayside

54.0

49.0

45.7

46.2

340

43.8

42.1

39.3

Luray

211

32.5

0   1   2   3   4   5 mi
0 1 2 3 4 5 6 7 km

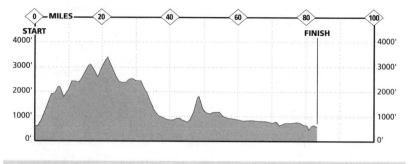

RESTAURANTS

♦ Main Street Mill Restaurant, 500 E. Main St., Front Royal, 540–636–3123. Housed in a remodeled 1800s feedmill, next door to the visitor's center.

♦ Big Meadows and Panorama Restaurants, Skyline Drive and Route 211, 540–743–5108.

♦ The Mimslyn Inn, 401 W. Main St., Luray, 540–743–5105. Southern cuisine.

ACCOMMODATIONS

♦ Quality Inn, 10 Commerce Ave., Front Royal, VA 22630, 800–821–4488. Mid-range.

♦ Budget Inn, 1122 N. Royal Ave., Front Royal, VA 22630, 800–766–6748. Low-end.

♦ Shenandoah River Inn, 201 Stagecoach Lane, Luray, VA 22835, 888–666–6760. Historic 1812 inn next to river. Cabins and chalets available.

♦ Cardinal Inn, 1005 E. Main St., Luray, VA 22835, 888–648–4633. Mid-range, on route in Luray.

BIKE SHOP

♦ Backyard Bikes, 518 Frederick Ave., Front Royal, VA 22630, 540–635–1225.

REST ROOMS

♦ At the start in the Front Royal Visitor Center
♦ Mile 5.9: Dickey Ridge Visitor Center
♦ Mile 25.1: Elkwallow Wayside
♦ Mile 41.0: many fast-food restaurants
♦ Mile 42.0: Luray Visitor Center
♦ Mile 61.1: at the Fort Valley Country Store
♦ Mile 69.4: Elizabeth Furnace campground and picnic area

MAP

♦ DeLorme *Virginia Atlas and Gazetteer* maps 73 and 74

Mount Jackson Cruise

The Mount Jackson Cruise takes the cyclist through the northern reaches of the magnificent Shenandoah Valley. Leaving Mount Jackson, the cruise starts out climbing the foothills of the Allegheny Mountains to the west. After cresting the small ridge, the cruise runs along its spine with spectacular mountain views in all directions. After a rewarding descent back into the valley, the cruise turns back to the north, following the North Fork of the Shenandoah River. Near the ride's end, cycle through historic Meems Bottom Bridge, the longest and one of the few remaining covered bridges left in Virginia.

Mount Jackson makes a good base for this tour of the northern Shenandoah Valley. Founded in 1812 as Mount Pleasant, it was changed to Mount Jackson in 1826 in honor of Andrew Jackson who would often visit here. During the Civil War, the town became a hospital center, and wounded would also fill Old Union Church (circa 1825), which still stands in the historic town center. Mount Jackson offers several restaurants, antiques stores, and boutiques, as well as some charming B&Bs close to town. In the heart of town is the town office which houses a small visitor's center where you can pick up information on the area.

The cruise leaves town and follows Mill Creek toward the mighty Allegheny Mountains to the west. Indeed, you'll be gaining elevation for a good 10 miles, but the gradients are mild (you only reach the foothills). Spectacular views of Massanutten Mountain greet you while you cruise along a low ridge. Massanutten Mountain is a 50-mile-long ridge that rises to nearly 3,000 feet and splits the Shenandoah Valley in two at its northern end. It provides the perfect backdrop to the scenic valley below, and you'll find yourself reaching for that camera.

Start: From the Mount Jackson First Virginia Bank, rear public parking lot.

Length: 32 miles

Terrain: First half is moderately hilly. Some long, flat stretches. Moderate difficulty.

Traffic and hazards: Use caution on the first 0.2-mile stretch and the last 1.9-mile stretch on Route 11, where traffic can be fast. Use caution on the short 0.2-mile stretch on Route 42 in Timberville. Entire route is paved and in good condition.

Getting there: From I-81, exit 273, take Mount Jackson Road east a short distance to Route 11. Turn right (south) and go 1.1 miles to First Virginia Bank on the right. Plenty of free parking behind the bank in the municipal lot. Plenty of stores along Route 11 to pick up supplies.

Once you leave the ridge, it's fairly easygoing the rest of the way. First, you fly down to the town of Timberville, where you can pick up some food and drink. You quickly leave town and drop to the rich farmlands flanking the banks of the North Fork of the Shenandoah River. One of the ride highlights is on Route 617, where cornfields line both sides of this rural, flat, well-paved, and low-traffic road with Massanutten Mountain soaring in the distance. It doesn't get much better than this.

Another highlight will come near the end of the ride, as you cycle through the covered Meems Bottom Bridge. The bridge was built in 1893 out of local materials and is 204 feet long, making it the longest in the state of Virginia. Meems Bottom was actually the third bridge at this site. Stonewall Jackson burned the first bridge as he pushed through the valley in 1862. In 1870 the second bridge was washed away in a flood. Meems Bottom was nearly lost in 1976, when Halloween arsonists attempted to burn it down. The single-span Burr arch truss was named after the Meems family, who owned the land west of the Shenandoah River. It is one of just eight covered bridges left in Virginia and one of five that are not located on private land. Enjoy cycling through the bridge, and be sure to stop on the far bank, where you can access the river for a pleasant break and a photo op.

Use caution on Route 11 through the last few miles into Mount Jackson, since the traffic can be fast and heavy. Back in town, pay a visit to the Mount Jackson Museum, which is dedicated to local and Shenandoah County history. Time your visit for a summer weekend when the Shenandoah Valley Music Festival is in full swing. Held in nearby Orkney Springs, the festival is in its fortieth season and features all types of music in a picnic-style setting under the stars.

LOCAL INFORMATION

♦ Mount Jackson Chamber of Commerce/Visitor Center, 5945 Main St., Mount Jackson, VA 22842, 540–477–3275.

Meems Bottom Bridge—the longest covered bridge in Virginia.

LOCAL EVENTS/ATTRACTIONS

♦ Shenandoah Valley Music Festival, most summer weekends, Orkney Springs, 800–459–3396.

♦ Old Union Church, next to the visitor's center, Mount Jackson. Built around 1825, this church also has a cemetery where Daniel Gray, a Revolutionary War soldier, is buried.

RESTAURANTS

♦ Kitt's Kafe, 5935 Main St., Mount Jackson, 540–477–2323. Local breakfast and lunch favorite.

ACCOMMODATIONS

♦ The Widow Kip's, 355 Orchard Drive, Mount Jackson, VA 22842, 800–478–8714. An 1830 B&B. Mid- to high-range.

♦ Strathmore House, 658 Wissler Rd., Quicksburg, VA 22847, 888–921–6139. Mid- to high-range B&B overlooking the Meems Bottom Bridge.

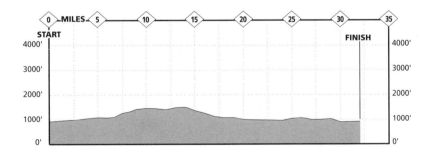

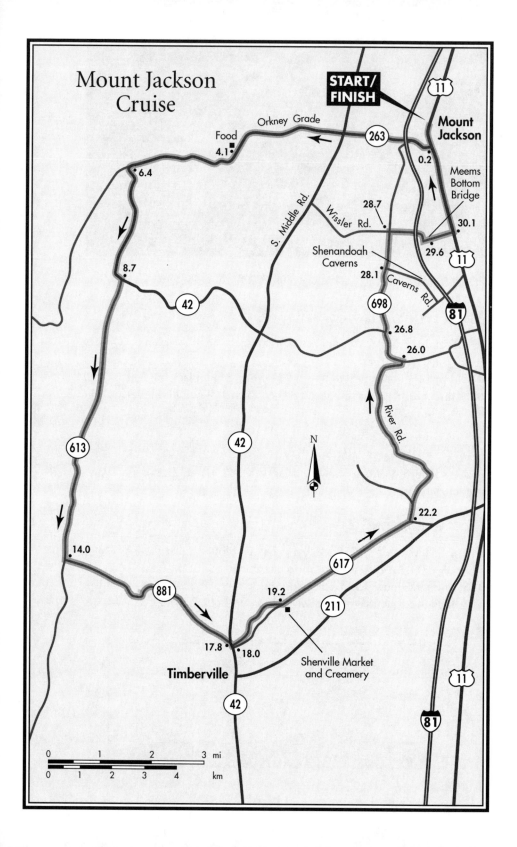

Mount Jackson Cruise

START/FINISH

11

Mount Jackson

Orkney Grade

263

Food
4.1

6.4

Meems Bottom Bridge

S. Middle Rd.

Wissler Rd.

28.7

30.1

0.2

29.6

11

Shenandoah Caverns

28.1

Caverns Rd.

26.8

698

81

8.7

42

26.0

River Rd.

613

42

N

22.2

14.0

617

881

19.2

211

17.8

18.0

Timberville

Shenville Market and Creamery

42

11

81

0   1   2   3 mi
0   1   2   3   4 km

0.0 Turn right out of bank and head south on Rt. 11.

0.2 Turn right on Rt. 263 West.

4.1 Bowers Grocery is on the right.

6.4 Turn left on Senedo Rd./Rt. 42 South.

8.7 Turn right on North Mountain Rd./Rt. 613.

14.0 Turn left on Orchard Dr./Rt. 881.

17.8 Turn right on Rt. 42 South in Timberville. Caution, traffic.

18.0 Turn left on Church St./Rt. 617 just after Rocking Hardware. *Note:* Food is available at the Chevron Food Mart if you continue on Rt. 42 South for 0.1 mile.

19.2 Bear to the left after crossing the railroad tracks. On the right is the Shenville Market and Creamery. Open Monday through Saturday, the market also has farm tours. Road name eventually changes to Evergreen Valley Rd.

22.2 Turn left on River Rd./Rt. 728 and 617. Then bear right on River Rd./Rt. 617 as Rt. 728 goes left.

26.0 Turn left on Ridge Rd./Rt. 616 in the village of Quicksburg. Within 0.1 mile, turn left on Quicksburg Rd./Rt. 767.

26.8 Turn right on Turkey Knob Rd./Rt. 698

28.1 Continue straight on Turkey Knob Rd. Shenandoah Caverns are located 1 mile to the right on Cavern Rd. should you want to tour them. Tired legs? No problem; these are the only caverns in Virginia with an elevator.

28.7 Turn right on Wissler Rd./Rt. 720. Within ½ mile, you'll cross railroad tracks and I–81.

29.5 Strathmore House B&B is on the left.

29.6 Cycle through Meems Bottom Bridge, the longest covered bridge in Virginia.

30.1 Turn left on Old Valley Pike/Rt. 11 North. Caution, faster traffic.

32.0 End the ride back at the First Virginia Bank.

BIKE SHOP

♦ Closest is in Harrisonburg: Blue Ridge Cycleworks, 774 E. Market St., Harrisonburg, VA 22801, 540–432–0280.

REST ROOMS

♦ Mile 4.1: Bowers Grocery
♦ Mile 18.0: Chevron Food Mart
♦ Mile 19.2: Shenville Market and Creamery

MAP

♦ DeLorme *Virginia Atlas and Gazetteer* map 73

Harrisonburg Cruise

The Harrisonburg Cruise is a short but fairly challenging ride that begins and ends in the heart of Harrisonburg. It is a perfect getaway for those sightseeing the city or visiting family and friends at James Madison University. Considering how busy this city can be, the cruise offers an easy and safe departure from and reentry into Harrisonburg. The surrounding Rockingham County offers many wonderful vistas, typical of any ride in this region of the Shenandoah Valley. Cyclists should be prepared, however, for constant roller-coaster terrain, making this cruise an excellent training ride.

Harrisonburg makes an excellent base for exploring the Shenandoah Valley. Not only does it have a wide variety of hotels and restaurants, but it is also convenient to many natural attractions, historical sites, and museums. Be sure to pick up a walking tour map of Harrisonburg's historic area at the visitor's center. The center is open every day and has an extremely helpful staff.

If you need to pick up water or food, do so while still within the city limits, as there are no stores on the route. The ride out of the city is via Chicago Avenue, a wide road that runs parallel to the busier city streets. Before you realize it, you will have crossed the city limits and will quickly find yourself in the Rockingham countryside. Don't let loose on your first downhill, however, since you need to make a right turn on Route 910 before you reach the bottom. It may be wise to ride the hill out, coast to a stop, then turn around and turn left on Route 910.

The terrain around Harrisonburg is moderately hilly. Although there are no major climbs, this route will challenge beginners, as there are numerous ups and downs that will eventually take their toll. You'll find a mix of woods and farmlands throughout this cruise, making for pleasant, peaceful, and sometimes shady cycling.

One peculiar feature of the area's landscape is the many fields of limestone outcroppings. This feature actually led to the city of Harrisonburg's original name—Rocktown. It was changed in 1849 in honor of its founder, Thomas Harrison. Another interesting feature of the Rockingham County countryside is the large number of poultry farms. Much of the county's industry is associated with poultry production, in which it leads the state. Do try to time your visit to coincide with the Rockingham County Fair, Virginia's number one agricultural fair held in mid-August.

About halfway through the cruise, you'll turn on to Indian Trail Road. After a short climb, you'll enjoy the next 7 miles—this is the Shenandoah Valley at its finest. With Massanutten Mountain looming on your left, you'll cruise along this lightly traveled country road, past small churches and large farms, where your only companions are horses and cows. This isn't the stretch of road on which to train—it's the kind that you should take slowly and savor. Enjoy its peacefulness and quietness. It's all yours, and it's truly special.

The last couple of miles on the ride back are rather nondescript. The route will take you through residential areas to avoid the busier main roads. Several stores and restaurants are available in the last 2 miles as you enter the city, but you may want to wait it out and get back to the visitor's center. Ask for directions to the L&S Diner, a Harrisonburg institution noted for its pan-fried chicken. Locally raised, of course.

THE BASICS

Start: From the Harrisonburg–Rockingham Convention and Visitors Bureau, 10 East Gay Street, Harrisonburg (corner of East Gay and North Main Streets).

Length: 26 miles

Terrain: Moderately hilly. Few flat stretches. No major climbs.

Traffic and hazards: Use caution on the first 1½ miles leaving the city. Right turn onto Route 910 from Route 763 is on a downhill. Maintain a safe speed. Traffic can be fast on the 0.3 mile you are on Route 11. Watch for railroad tracks at mile 24.6—bad angle. Slow down and try to cross at a 90-degree angle. Caution on last 1½ miles back into city. Entire route is paved and in good condition.

Getting there: From I–81, exit 247, follow Route 33 (East Market Street) for 1½ miles toward Harrisonburg. At North Main Street, turn right and go 4 blocks. Turn right on East Gay Street; the visitor's center is immediately on your left. Plenty of free parking.

LOCAL INFORMATION

♦ Harrisonburg–Rockingham Convention and Visitors Bureau, 10 East Gay Street, Harrisonburg, VA 22801, 540–434–2319.

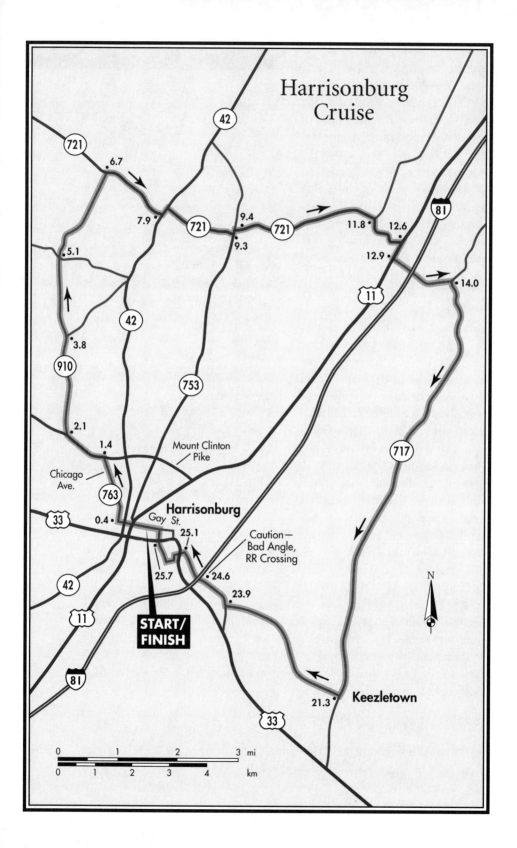

Harrisonburg Cruise

721

42

721

6.7

7.9

721   721

9.4

9.3

11.8   12.6

81

12.9

14.0

11

5.1

42

3.8

910

753

717

2.1

1.4

Mount Clinton
Pike

Chicago
Ave.

763

33

Harrisonburg

0.4   Gay St.

25.1

Caution—
Bad Angle,
RR Crossing

42

25.7

24.6

11

23.9

81

START/
FINISH

N

21.3   Keezletown

33

| 0 | 1 | 2 | 3 mi |

| 0 | 1 | 2 | 3 | 4 km |

0.0 Leave the visitor's center parking lot toward Gay St. Turn right on Gay. Continue straight through four stoplights.

0.4 Turn right on Chicago Ave. at the fifth stoplight.

1.4 Turn left at the stop sign on Mount Clinton Pike. After a short climb, use extreme caution on the descent, as the next turn is halfway down the hill.

2.1 Turn right on Fort Lynne Rd./Rt. 910.

3.8 Bear left to stay on Fort Lynne Rd.

5.1 Go straight at the stop sign on Fort Lynne Rd./Rt. 910. Road name changes along this stretch to Grist Mill Rd.

6.7 Turn right on Green Hill Rd./Rt. 721.

7.9 Turn left on Rt. 42/Rt. 721, then a quick right on Linville Edom Rd./Rt. 721.

9.3 Turn left at the stop sign on Kratzer Rd./Rt. 721 .

9.4 Bear right to stay on Rt. 721.

11.8 Caution, sharp turn to the right to stay on Rt. 721.

12.6 Turn right on Rt. 11 South/Valley Pike. Caution, fast traffic.

12.9 Turn left on Fellowship Rd./Rt. 721.

14.0 Turn right on Indian Trail Rd./Rt. 717.

21.3 Turn right on Keezletown Rd./Rt. 925.

23.9 Turn right at the stop sign on Country Club Rd.

24.6 Caution, railroad track crossing at bad angle.

25.1 Turn left on Vine St. at the stoplight, and continue straight through the next stoplight on Hawkins St. (cross E. Market). Use caution, busy intersection. Just past intersection, turn left on Norwood St. Various food stores and restaurants on E. Market St. if you turn right.

25.5 Turn right on Reservoir St.

25.7 Go straight on Sterling St. (cross E. Market).

26.0 Turn left at the stop sign on E. Gay St.

26.4 Turn right into the visitor's center parking lot and end of ride.

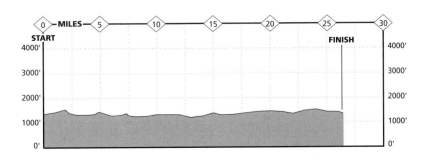

LOCAL EVENTS/ATTRACTIONS

♦ Rockingham County Fair, Harrisonburg, mid-August, 540–434–0005. Big-name entertainment, livestock shows, circus acts, food, games, and demolition derby.

♦ Virginia Mennonite Relief Sale, first Saturday in October, 540–434–0005 or 540–433–1265. Food, crafts, quilts, artwork, and furniture auctions.

♦ Virginia Quilt Museum, 301 S. Main St., Harrisonburg, VA 22801, 540–433–3818. Admission: $4.00 for adults, $3.00 for seniors and students, $2.00 for children six to twelve, and free for children younger than six.

RESTAURANTS

♦ L&S Diner, 255 North Liberty Ave., Harrisonburg, 540–434–5572.

♦ Jess' Lunch, 22 South Main St., Harrisonburg, 540–434–8282. Casual, local favorite.

ACCOMMODATIONS

♦ The Village Inn, 4979 S. Valley Pike Harrisonburg, VA 22801, 800–736–7355. Mid-range.

♦ Days Inn Harrisonburg, 1131 Forest Hills Rd., Harrisonburg, VA 22801, 540–433–9353. Mid-range.

BIKE SHOP

♦ Blue Ridge Cycleworks, 774 E. Market St., Harrisonburg, VA 22801, 540–432–0280.

REST ROOMS

♦ At the start in the visitor's center
♦ Mile 25.1: Various restaurants on right on E. Market

MAP

♦ DeLorme *Virginia Atlas and Gazetteer* maps 67 and 73

Mole Hill Ramble

Despite its name, the Mole Hill Ramble is a delightful and relatively easy spin through Rockingham County countryside.
The ramble takes the cyclist through miles of flat Mennonite country,
where on Sundays you're likely to encounter a horse-drawn carriage.
Then it's on to Mole Hill, a remnant of a fifty million-year-old volcano,
where spectacular views can be enjoyed from the top. The route passes
an 1822 mill at beautiful Silver Lake, then winds through the historic
town of Dayton on the way back to Bridgewater.

———————————

The ramble starts and ends in Bridgewater at Wildwood Park. Offering free
parking, this public park also has rest rooms and picnic areas alongside the
North River. The first mile takes you through the town of Bridgewater, where
you can pick up some food at several stores and fast-food restaurants. After
another mile through a residential area, you'll soon be out among the many
livestock and poultry farms that dominate this region.

More than 4,000 Mennonites live in the Rockingham/Augusta area. There
are many different sects, but it is the Old Order Mennonites who travel by
horse and buggy, and sometimes by bicycle. You'll notice them—they're the
ones without the helmets and Spandex. The Mennonites began settling here in
the 1700s, migrating to the Shenandoah Valley from Lancaster, Pennsylvania.

The terrain remains flat for several miles while you pedal through farms of
all types. Although corn and dairy farms are common, you'll notice many
farms with long, narrow buildings nearly 1,000 feet long. These are the chick-
en and turkey brood houses that make this region one of the top ten poultry-
producing areas in the country. As the ride takes a short jog on Route 33, take
the opportunity to stop at the Hinton Market and Deli on the right, and make
sure you are hydrated for your upcoming climb.

Start: From Wildwood Park in Bridgewater.

Length: 24 miles

Terrain: Flat to gently rolling. One short, moderate climb up Mole Hill.

Traffic and hazards: All roads on this route are low traffic and rural. Use caution while cycling on Main Street in Bridgewater and while descending Mole Hill (tight turns at the top). Entire route is paved and in good condition.

Getting there: From I–81, exit 240, follow Route 257 to Bridgewater. At the stoplight in center of town, turn left on South Main Street/ Route 42. Go ¼ mile, then turn right on West Bank Street. Go 0.4 mile, then turn left on Bank Street at the stop sign. Go 0.2 mile to Wildwood Park. Plenty of free parking.

At the midpoint of the ride, you will come to Mole Hill. This small, circular mountain (let's not make a mountain out of a mole hill) is actually the remnant of an ancient volcano. It looks as if a giant mole has pushed it up from below; hence the name. The climb is about 0.6 mile and at a 6 percent grade, and will challenge the beginner. It's worth it, though, since the views from the top are spectacular. Exercise caution on the descent, particularly near the top, where there are a couple of twists.

After some pleasant, gentle rollers, you'll come to a picturesque lake on your right. At the end of the lake sits Silver Lake Mill, built in 1822. If you happen to bike by on a Thursday through Saturday, stop for a visit and catch a glimpse of its history, or stroll through its fine china and glassware store. The terrain is quite easy while you pedal into the small town of Dayton.

Of particular interest in Dayton is the Daniel Harrison House, also known as Fort Harrison. This solidly built stone house, with additions of a stockade and underground passageway to a spring, served as a fort against Indian attacks during the 1750s. The house has been meticulously preserved and is open to the public on weekend afternoons from May through October.

The last few miles of the ramble double back on the same road you took to avoid busy Route 42. There are opportunities to pick up some food in Dayton or Bridgewater before you arrive back at Wildwood Park. If you happen to be in the area on a Thursday through Saturday, consider taking in the Dayton Farmer's Market. Here you'll find fresh foods and locally produced goods, including homemade Mennonite treats.

LOCAL INFORMATION

♦ Harrisonburg–Rockingham Convention and Visitors Bureau, 10 East Gay Street, Harrisonburg, VA 22801, 540–434–2319.

LOCAL EVENTS/ATTRACTIONS

♦ Bridgewater Lawn Party, sponsored by the Bridgewater Fire Department, third week in July, 540–828–3121. Food, games, tractor pull, and antique car show.

♦ Annual Dayton Autumn Celebration, early October, 540–879–9538. More than 200 arts and crafts exhibitors, food, games, and entertainment.

♦ Shenandoah Valley Folk Art and Heritage Center, Dayton, 540–879–2616. Local history.

RESTAURANTS

♦ Thomas House Restaurant and Bakery, 222 Main St., Dayton, 540–879–2181.

♦ McDonald's, Hardee's, Subway, and Dairy Queen all on N. Main St., Bridgewater.

Countless farms dot the landscape of the Shenandoah.

0.0 Leave Wildwood Park on Bank St. Go 0.2 mile, then turn right on W. Bank St.

0.6 Turn left at the stop sign on S. Main St./Rt. 42. Use caution on Rt. 42.

0.9 Go straight at the stoplight. Several stores and restaurants in the next ¼ mile.

1.2 Turn left on N. River Rd. just before the McDonald's on the right.

1.4 Turn right on Dry River Rd.

2.9 Turn left on Ottobine Rd./Rts. 738 and 257W.

3.2 Turn right on W. Dry River Rd./Rt. 738.

5.0 Bear right to stay on W. Dry River Rd.

5.2 Turn left to stay on W. Dry River Rd.

7.9 Turn right on Clover Hill Rd./Rt. 613.

8.2 Dry River Store on left.

9.5 Go straight at intersection on Whitmore Shop Rd. Cross Rt. 33.

10.8 Turn right on Mount Clinton Pike/Rt. 726.

12.0 Turn right on Muddy Creek Rd./Rt. 752.

13.7 Turn right on Rawley Pike/Rts. 752 & 33W. Go 0.1 mile, then make the left on Hinton Rd./Rt. 752. Hinton Market and Deli on right. Go another 0.1 mile and make a quick left on Coakley Town Rd./Rt. 732. Easy turn to miss.

15.0 Bear left on Coakley Town Rd./Rt. 732.

15.4 Turn left at the stop sign on Coakley Town Rd./Rt. 732.

15.5 Turn left on Mole Hill Rd./Rt. 913, and begin climb. Some great views near the top.

17.1 Turn right at the stop sign on Swope Rd./Rt. 736. Go 0.1 mile, then make a left on Silling Rd./Rt. 913.

17.6 Turn right on Silver Lake Rd./Rt. 701.

18.1 Silver Lake and Mill are on the right.

18.4 Turn left on Eberly Rd./Rt. 732.

18.6 Turn right on Rt. 42 Business. Daniel Harrison House (Fort Harrison) will be the right.

18.9 Dayton Market is on the right. Thomas House Restaurant and Bakery is on left.

19.1 Turn right at the stop sign on W. Mason St./Rt. 257W.

21.1 Turn left on Dry River Rd./Rt. 738.

22.7 Turn left at the stop sign on N. River Rd.

22.9 Turn right at the stop sign on N. Main St./Rt. 42.

23.5 Turn right on W. Bank St.

23.9 Turn left on Bank St.

24.1 End ride at Wildwood Park.

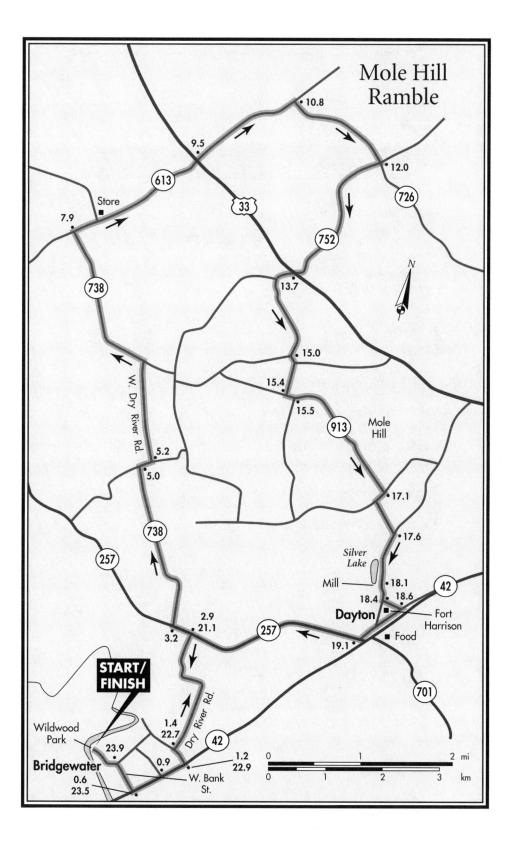

Mole Hill Ramble

10.8

9.5

12.0

613

33

726

Store

7.9

752

738

N

13.7

W. Dry River Rd.

15.0

15.4

15.5

913

Mole Hill

5.2

5.0

17.1

738

17.6

257

Silver Lake

Mill

18.1

18.4 **18.6**

42

2.9
21.1

Dayton

Fort Harrison

3.2

257

Food

19.1

START/ FINISH

701

Wildwood Park

1.4
22.7

Dry River Rd.

23.9

42

Bridgewater

0.9

1.2
22.9

0.6
23.5

W. Bank St.

0   1   2 mi

0   1   2   3 km

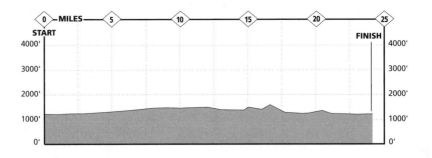

ACCOMMODATIONS

♦ The Village Inn, 4979 S. Valley Pike, Harrisonburg, VA 22801, 800–736–7355. Mid-range.
♦ Apple Orchard Farm Bed and Breakfast, 4478 Donnelley Dr., Bridgewater, VA 22812, 540–828–2126. Mid-range.

BIKE SHOP

♦ Mole Hill Bikes, 440 N. Main St., Dayton, VA 22821, 540–879–2011.

REST ROOMS

♦ At the start in Wildwood Park
♦ Mile 1.0: several fast-food restaurants in the area
♦ Mile 8.2: Dry River Store
♦ Mile 13.8: Hinton Market and Deli

MAP

♦ DeLorme *Virginia Atlas and Gazetteer* map 66

Shenandoah Valley Cruise

The Shenandoah Valley, extending north to south over 150 miles, is an area blessed with scenic beauty and rich in American history. The Shenandoah Valley Cruise takes the cyclist through the heart of the valley, past the farmlands that once served Robert E. Lee's armies and over hilltops providing unparalleled views of the valley and the Blue Ridge and Shenandoah mountains. This cruise features many of the same roads used by the Shenandoah Fall Foliage Festival held in Staunton in late October. Although designed to be a cruise, this ride can be made into a challenge by including the option of climbing to Todd Lake.

The cruise starts in Bridgewater, a small town that is home to the Church of the Brethren–affiliated Bridgewater College. You may want to stop at one of several restaurants and convenience stores in town prior to making your way to Wildwood Park. This peaceful park sits on the banks of the North River and offers plenty of free parking, rest rooms, and picnic sites.

The first mile is through a residential area, but you'll soon find yourself out of town and smack in the middle of the best countryside the Shenandoah Valley has to offer. After a couple of rollers, you'll be treated to miles of flat, lightly traveled country roads in the Sangerville area. When you reach Werner's Country Store on your right, be sure to turn left on Route 731 and make a stop at Natural Chimneys Regional Park.

Natural Chimneys consists of limestone structures towering to 120 feet. Their existence is proof that the Shenandoah Valley was once an inland sea. Forces of nature carved out these chimney-shaped towers when the sea receded. Because they also resemble medieval castle turrets, jousting tournaments

At peace in the Shenandoah Valley.

began at this site in 1821 and continue to this day. The tournament, held in late August, is the oldest continuously held sporting event in North America. Besides the Chimneys, the park offers camping, a camp store, playgrounds, hiking trails, and a swimming pool. If the Natural Chimneys Regional Park interests you, consider starting the cruise there and enjoy the swimming pool after the ride.

More flat riding awaits you after your visit to the Chimneys. When you reach Stokesville Road, however, you must decide if you want to cruise or be challenged. You are at the base of the Shenandoah Mountains, and the ride up to Todd Lake is 4.6 miles each way, with about 2½ miles of climbing on the way up. Todd Lake has swimming facilities but the park does charge for day use of the facilities. If you're not feeling very energetic, you should at least take the scenic Todd Lake option for 1 mile to the entrance of the George Washington National Forest. This is where the climbing begins and where you may want to turn around.

The terrain gets a little hillier as you make your way around Mount Solon.

Expect rural riding, lots of corn-fields, chicken farms, and hayfields. If you didn't take the Todd Lake option, expect to be challenged climbing Mount Solon Road up to Spring Hill. It's never steep, just long. Once on top, though, you are treated to some great views of the valley and a long gradual descent that you will wish would go on forever.

Once you reach Route 42 again, you may be tempted to take it all the way to Bridgewater. Instead, follow the cue and take Fadley Road. You'll have several short back-to-back climbs, but once again you'll be rewarded. There's a scenic pull-off at the top of Centerville Road, where you will want to stop for a great photo op. Then hang on for your thrilling descent back to Bridgewater.

THE BASICS

Start: From Wildwood Park in Bridgewater.

Length: 38-mile cruise or 47-mile challenge

Terrain: Rolling hills. Some long, flat stretches. Intermediate difficulty. Todd Lake option includes several miles of difficult climbing.

Traffic and hazards: All roads are paved and in good condition. Low traffic. Use caution on the short sections of Route 42 near Bridgewater. If doing Todd Lake option, use caution when descending (tight turns).

Getting there: From I-81, exit 240, follow Route 257 to Bridgewater. At the stoplight in the center of town, turn left on South Main Street/Route 42. Go ¼ mile, then turn right on West Bank Street. Go 0.4 mile, and turn left on Bank Street at the stop sign. Go 0.2 mile to Wildwood Park. Plenty of free parking.

LOCAL INFORMATION

♦ Harrisonburg–Rockingham Convention & Visitors Bureau, 10 East Gay Street, Harrisonburg, VA 22801, 540–434–2319.
♦ Staunton–Augusta Travel Information Center, located in the Frontier Culture Museum, off I–81, exit 222, 540– 332–3972. Take Route 250 West, then make left after ¼ mile. Open seven days.

LOCAL EVENTS/ATTRACTIONS

♦ Natural Chimneys Regional Park, Natural Chimneys Road, Mount Solon, 540–350–2510.
♦ Jousting Tournament, third Saturday in August, Natural Chimneys, 540–350–2510.
♦ Bridgewater Lawn Party, sponsored by the Bridgewater Fire Department, third week in July, 540–828–3121. Food, games, tractor pull, antique car show.

RESTAURANTS

♦ Sergio's Pizza, 425 N. Main St., Bridgewater, 540–828–6651.

0.0 Leave Wildwood Park on Bank St. Go 0.2 mile, then turn right on W. Bank St.

0.6 Turn right at the stop sign on S. Main St./Rt. 42. Use caution on Rt. 42.

0.8 Turn right on Springcreek Rd./Rt. 727.

4.1 Turn left at the stop sign on Sangerville Rd./Rt. 727.

6.6 Turn left at the stop sign on N. River Rd./ Rt. 730. Sangerville Country Store is on the left.

8.9 Turn left on Natural Chimneys Rd./Rt. 731 at Werners Country Store to go to Natural Chimneys Regional Park. The park is ½ mile down Rt. 731 on the left. Reverse direction when leaving the park to go back to Werners Store.

9.9 Turn left on N. River Rd./Rt. 730 at Werners Store.

13.2 Stokesville Market is on the right. Food, drink, and rest rooms.

13.4 Turn left at the stop sign on Stokesville Rd./Rt. 730. Option: Turn right if you want to go to Todd Lake for a 9.2-mile round trip (or 2-mile round trip flat option to the National Forest entrance). (To Todd Lake: Turn right at mile 13.4, then go 1.0 mile. Turn left at Forest Road 95, go 3.1 miles, then bear right to Todd Lake. Within ½ mile, you will enter the swimming and picnic facilities area just after you pass the camping area on the left.)

13.7 Bear right on Stokesville Rd./Rt. 730.

14.7 Go straight on Freemason Run Rd./Rt. 747.

15.7 Go straight at the stop sign to continue on Freemason Run Rd.

18.0 Turn right in Mount Solon on Natural Chimneys Rd./Rt. 731.

20.4 Continue straight on Rt. 607 where Rt. 731 bears right.

20.5 Go straight on Mount Solon Rd./Rt. 607. Caution when crossing Rt. 42.

24.9 Turn left on Spring Hill Rd./Rt. 613.

28.4 Bear right to stay on Spring Hill Rd./Rt. 613.

29.5 Bear left to stay on 613.

31.2 Top of hill. Caution, must stop at the stop sign 0.2 mile down the hill.

31.4 Turn right on Rt. 42 North.

31.8 Turn right on Fadley Rd./Rt. 646.

33.5 Turn left on Centerville Rd./699.

36.3 Turn right on Rt. 42 North.

37.2 Turn left on W. Bank St.

37.6 Turn left on Bank St.

37.8 End ride at Wildwood Park.

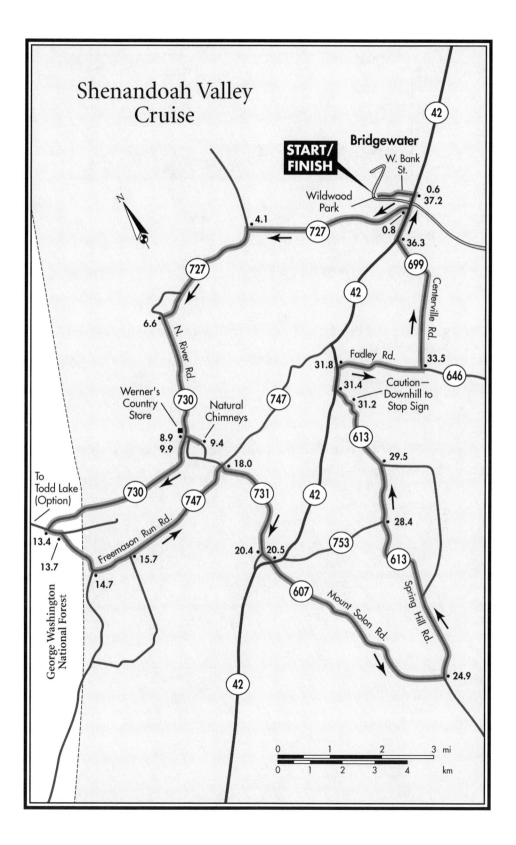

Shenandoah Valley Cruise

Bridgewater

START/ FINISH

W. Bank St.

Wildwood Park

0.6
37.2

0.8

36.3

42

727
4.1

727

699

6.6

N. River Rd.

Centerville Rd.

42

Fadley Rd.

31.8

33.5

31.4

646

Werner's Country Store

730

Natural Chimneys

31.2

Caution— Downhill to Stop Sign

8.9
9.9

9.4

613

29.5

18.0

747

To Todd Lake (Option)

730

747

731

42

28.4

753

13.4

20.4

20.5

613

13.7

15.7

Freemason Run Rd.

607

Mount Solon Rd.

Spring Hill Rd.

14.7

24.9

George Washington National Forest

42

N

0   1   2   3 mi
0   1   2   3   4 km

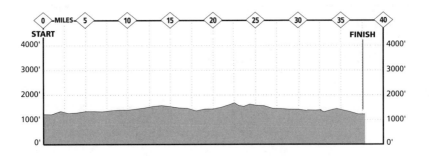

♦ McDonald's, Hardee's, Subway, and Dairy Queen all on N. Main St., Bridgewater.

ACCOMMODATIONS

♦ Apple Orchard Farm Bed and Breakfast, 4478 Donnelley Dr., Bridgewater, VA 22812, 540–828–2126. Mid-range.
♦ Hilltop House B&B, 1810 Springhill Road, Staunton, VA 24401, 540–886–0042. Mid-range.

BIKE SHOP

♦ Mole Hill Bikes, 440 North Main St., Dayton, VA 22821, 540–879–2011.

REST ROOMS

♦ At the start in Wildwood Park
♦ Mile 8.9: Werners Country Store
♦ Mile 9.4: Natural Chimneys Regional Park
♦ Mile 13.2: Stokesville Market

MAP

♦ DeLorme *Virginia Atlas and Gazetteer* map 66

Waynesboro Ramble

*T*he Waynesboro Ramble takes the cyclist through the far eastern reaches of the spectacular Shenandoah Valley. Starting in Waynesboro, whose motto is "Hospitality in the Valley," the route takes a long, gradual climb out of the city on its way to the base of Calf Mountain and the Blue Ridge. Circling around smaller Ramsey Mountain, the ramble rewards the cyclist with a beautiful and gradual run down to the South River. Circling through several small Augusta County villages, the ramble brings the cyclist back through the quaint and easily manageable downtown shopping district, where the city's hospitality can be experienced.

Nestled at the base of the Blue Ridge Mountains, Waynesboro is a picturesque city known for its fine neighborhoods and parks. Named for the dashing Revolutionary War hero "Mad" Anthony Wayne in 1797, Waynesboro has managed to retain its charm. It's also the southern terminus of Skyline Drive, just up Afton Mountain at Rockfish Gap. The area's scenic beauty combined with the city's many shopping and dining alternatives make for an enjoyable one- or two-day outing.

If you are looking for a grand breakfast to fuel you for the ride, walk through the park to Broad Street. Here you'll find Weasie's Kitchen, a local favorite and home of the valley's best omelets. You'll find a few convenience stores about ³⁄₁₀ mile into the ride.

Now that you're fueled, the ramble will take you on a very safe route out of the city. Unfortunately, you have one short, steep climb. Tackle that and you'll find yourself on beautiful Calf Mountain Road amid some fantastic country cycling. You really don't climb Calf Mountain; you basically just ride up the base a short way. The climb is long but gradual, and you'll actually be circling

Start: From The Pavilion at Constitution Park in downtown Waynesboro.

Length: 27 miles

Terrain: Gently rolling. One short, steep climb in the city, then one long, gradual climb to Calf Mountain, will challenge beginners.

Traffic and hazards: Use caution for the 0.2-mile stretch on busy Route 250. Watch for entering and exiting traffic on Tinkling Springs Rd. at the junction with I-64.

Getting there: From I-64, take exit 96 to Route 624 North (South Delphine Road) toward Waynesboro. Go 2 miles, then turn left on Route 340/250 (East Main Street). Go 0.2 mile, then continue straight on East Main Street/Route 340 where Broad Street/Route 250 goes to the right. Go 0.2 mile to the park on the right. Plenty of free parking.

smaller Ramsey Mountain on your left. Once you make your way around it, you'll follow a small mountain stream as it gradually drops down to the South River below. This is one of those moments that you wish would never end.

The ramble continues through the gentle Augusta County countryside. Hills pop up but are short. Great views of the Blue Ridge also abound, and you'll find yourself stopping to take it all in. You'll also pass several small villages, but mostly the route is rural all the way to Fishersville. In Fishersville, you'll find the Mossy Creek Cafe, Subway, and a food mart, making it a good rest stop. When you continue on Tinkling Springs Road, use caution at the junction with I-64. Just past the highway, don't miss the left turn onto Ladd Road. It's just across from McDonald's and is easy to miss.

When you cross Route 340 in a few miles, you may want to detour to take in the P. Buckley Moss Museum. Here you can enjoy the masterpieces of one of America's most celebrated living artists. The Shenandoah Valley scenery and the simple lifestyles of its many Amish and Mennonite peoples have always inspired Moss. The museum's exhibits and programs along with Moss's works send an important message to modern society about the cultural and environmental heritage of the "plain people."

The last few miles of the ramble take you through several of Waynesboro's pleasant residential neighborhoods. Again, use caution, as traffic will be heavier here than along the rest of the route. When you reach Main Street, turn right and continue through the heart of this small, quaint city. There's a lot of local specialty shops along Main Street, including my favorite, Cycle-Recycle Co. This large bike shop has numerous new and used bikes and biking gear and is a must stop after the ramble.

LOCAL INFORMATION

♦ Greater Augusta Regional Chamber of Commerce, 732 Tinkling Springs Road, P.O. Box 1107, Fishersville, VA 22939, 540–949–8203.

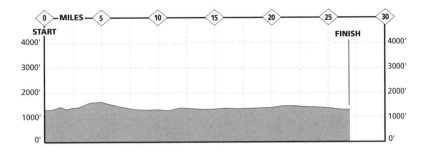

LOCAL EVENTS/ATTRACTIONS

◆ P. Buckley Moss Museum, 150 P. Buckley Moss Drive, Waynesboro, 540–949–6473. Free.
◆ Fall Foliage Festival Art Show, mid-October, downtown Waynesboro, 540–942–6705.

RESTAURANTS

◆ Weasie's Kitchen, 130 E. Broad St., Waynesboro, 540–943–0500. Local favorite.
◆ Pearl's Classic Lunch Counter, 412 W. Main St., Waynesboro, 540–943–7327.

ACCOMMODATIONS

◆ The Iris Inn B&B, 191 Chinquapin Drive, Waynesboro, VA 22980, 540–943–1991. Mid- to high-range mountainside retreat.
◆ Days Inn, 2060 Rosser Ave., Waynesboro, VA 22980, 540–943–1101. Mid-range.

BIKE SHOP

◆ Cycle-Recycle Co., 320 W. Main St., Waynesboro, VA 22980, 540–949–8973.

REST ROOMS

◆ At the start in Constitution Park
◆ Mile 17.9: Mossy Creek Cafe
◆ Mile 19.8: McDonald's
◆ Mile 26.7: various locations in Waynesboro

MAP

◆ DeLorme *Virginia Atlas and Gazetteer* maps 66 and 67

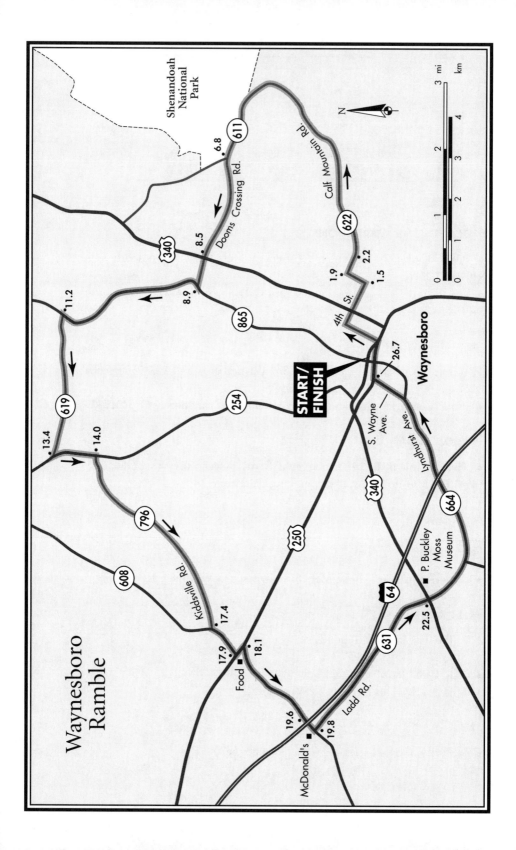

Waynesboro Ramble

Shenandoah National Park

START/FINISH

Waynesboro

Food

McDonald's

P. Buckley Moss Museum

Calf Mountain Rd.

Dooms Crossing Rd.

Kiddsville Rd.

Ladd Rd.

S. Wayne Ave.

Lyndhurst Ave.

4th St.

N

3 mi
km

611 · 6.8

· 8.5

340

865 · 8.9

622

· 1.9 · 2.2

· 1.5

11.2

619

· 13.4 · 14.0

254

796

608

· 17.4

· 17.9 · 18.1

· 19.6

· 19.8

631 · 22.5

64

664

250

340

26.7

0.0 From the Pavilion at Constitution Park, turn left on W. Main St.

0.2 Turn left on Charlotte Ave.

0.3 Go straight at this intersection with Broad St. Convenience stores are on both sides of the road.

0.8 Turn right on 4th St. Cross the wooden bridge over the railroad tracks.

1.1 Go straight at the light. Dave's Meats and Groceries is on the left.

1.5 Turn left on Jackson Ave.

1.9 Turn right at the stop sign on A St.

2.2 Turn left at the stop sign on Calf Mountain Rd./Rt. 622. The route number eventually changes to 611.

6.8 Go straight on Dooms Crossing Rd./Rt. 611. (Rt. 619 bears right.)

8.5 Continue straight on Dooms Crossing Rd./Rt. 611. Cross Rt. 340. Watch for rough railroad crossing.

8.9 Turn right on Rockfish Rd./Rt. 865.

11.2 Turn left on Hildebrand Rd./Rt. 619.

13.4 Turn left at the stop sign on Hermitage Rd./Rt. 254 East.

14.0 Turn right on Kiddsville Rd./Rt. 796.

17.4 Bear left on Long Meadow Rd./Rt. 608.

17.9 Go straight at the stop sign and continue to the stoplight at Rt. 250. Turn left at the light on Rt. 250 East. Mossy Creek Cafe is at this intersection. Caution, busy road.

18.1 Turn right at the light on Tinkling Springs Rd./Rt. 608. Subway restaurant and Exxon Food Market are located here.

19.6 Go straight at the stoplight on Tinkling Springs Rd. Caution, I–64 interchange here.

19.8 Turn left at the stoplight on Ladd Rd./ Rt. 631. McDonald's is on the right before the turn.

22.5 Go straight at the stoplight on Ladd Rd./Rt. 631. Cross Rt. 340. (If you want to visit the P. Buckley Moss Museum, go left here on Rt. 340 for 0.3 mile.)

23.7 Enter city limits. Road name changes to Lyndhurst. In a few more miles, you'll cross the South River, and the road name changes again to S. Wayne Ave.

26.7 Turn right at the stoplight on W. Main St.

26.9 Turn left into Constitution Park.

Charlottesville Challenge

T he Charlottesville Challenge is a scenic, moderately hilly ride through the Albemarle County countryside known locally as "Mr. Jefferson's Country." Based in Charlottesville, the challenge follows the National Bike Route 76 as it rolls west toward the Blue Ridge, offering fantastic vistas at the crest of each hill. Reaching but not climbing the Blue Ridge, the challenge takes a turn and explores the pastoral paradise south of Charlottesville. Several hundred years ago, this desirable region attracted the likes of Jefferson and Monroe. Today, it still draws the rich and famous, as a number of entertainers and authors now live here. The challenge then sneaks you in the back door to Charlottesville, directly through Thomas Jefferson's "academic village," the University of Virginia.

On your way in to Charlottesville, stop at the University of Virginia Visitor Center on the right side of Ivy Road/Route 250, as soon as you exit Route 29. Pick up a campus map, which will come in handy for exploring the university near the end of the challenge.

The starting point of the ride (plaza parking lot) is rather nondescript, but it serves the cyclist well. Most importantly, it offers a fairly easy ride out of and back into the city, avoiding much of the congestion that has begun to plague this fine university community. The Foods of All Nations grocery store located here has something for just about everyone. You'll also find a deli/bakery, a coffee shop, and a Chinese restaurant adjacent to the plaza. There are several stores along the route as well.

Within a mile of the start, you'll be out of the college rush and into rural Albemarle County. The challenge follows National Bike Route 76 (east to west) over rolling terrain for nearly 20 miles. I'm sure that when the route was developed some twenty-five years ago it didn't have the traffic and speeds that it has now. But the route is gorgeous, and you'll be rewarded with stunning Blue Ridge views on the horizon. Just be cautious on this stretch.

A few miles out of Charlottesville, you'll come to Oakencroft Vineyard and Winery. Home to many award-winning wines, Oakencroft is open every day from April through December for tours and tastings. It's also one of the prettiest wineries in the state, with its Blue Ridge views and serene lake fronting the complex. For information on the winery's many events, call 804–296–4188.

The challenge runs right up to the base of the Blue Ridge Mountains but, fortunately for the weary, does not climb it. Instead, you'll turn south and head through orchards, where in season, you can purchase peaches from roadside stands. When you cross Route 250

THE BASICS

Start: From the public lot of the shopping plaza on Ivy Road just west of the Ivy Road/Alderman Road intersection.

Length: 45 miles

Terrain: Moderately hilly. Designed for the stronger cyclist.

Traffic and hazards: Early on in the challenge, Routes 601 and 614 (Bike Route 76) can carry faster traffic and don't have much of a shoulder. Although these routes are popular with cyclists, only those experienced riding these types of roads should consider this challenge. Use caution while crossing Route 29 on Red Hill Road. Use caution on the short stretch of Ivy Road at the start and finish. All roads have good pavement.

Getting there: From I-64, take exit 118/Route 29 North. Go 2 miles, then exit at Route 250 Business (East)/Ivy Road. Go ¾ mile to the shopping plaza on the left. It is anchored by Foods of All Nations. If you go to the intersection with Alderman/Copeley Roads, you went too far. Parking is free.

and begin the southern segment of the challenge, you'll start noticing more of the mansions and stately homes for which this region is well noted. Occasionally, stone walls line both sides of the winding roads—either a way to keep others out or a symbol of their owners' wealth, I'm not sure. But with the walls and the tunneling effect of shade trees, it's as if you were transported back in time. Thomas Jefferson may not have been a cyclist, but it is easy to see why he was so attached to this land. This stretch south of Charlottesville ranks as one of the best biking regions in Virginia. Cherish it.

Before the challenge ends, you'll pass through one of the world's most beautiful college campuses, the University of Virginia. Founded by Thomas Jefferson in 1819, the campus is graced with spacious lawns, beautiful buildings, serpentine brick-walled gardens, and the signature landmark of the university, the Rotunda. Hopefully, you picked up a university map prior to the challenge. Take a few detours and explore one of Jefferson's proudest achievements.

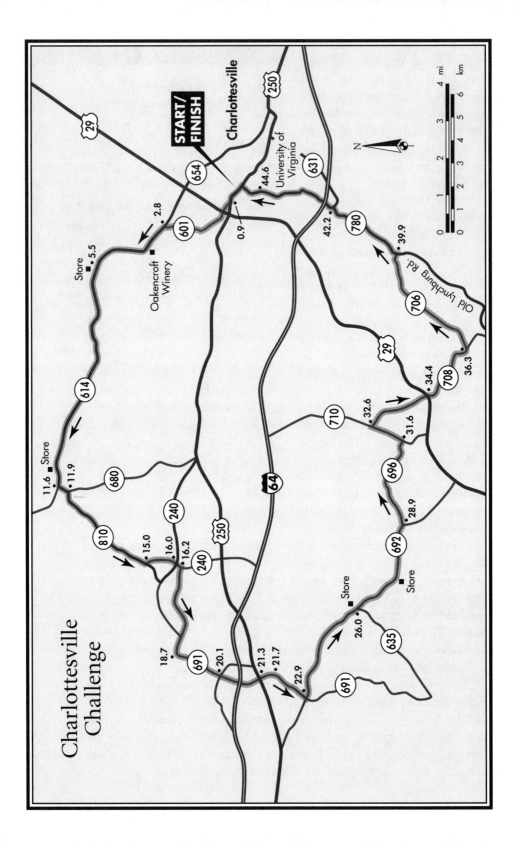

Charlottesville Challenge

START/FINISH

Charlottesville

University of Virginia

Oakencroft Winery

Old Lynchburg Rd.

Store

Store

Store

Store

Store

Store

29

250

654

601

631

780

706

708

29

710

696

692

691

691

635

680

614

810

240

240

250

64

2.8

5.5

0.9

44.6

42.2

39.9

36.3

34.4

32.6

31.6

28.9

26.0

22.9

21.7

21.3

20.1

18.7

16.2

16.0

15.0

11.9

11.6

N

0   1   2   3   4 mi

0 1 2 3 4 5 6 km

0.0 Turn right out of plaza parking lot on Ivy Rd./Rt. 250. Stay far to the right and in 0.1 mile, bear to the right on Old Ivy Rd.

0.9 Go straight at the stop sign on Rt. 601.

2.8 Turn left at the stop sign on Garth Rd./Rt. 601. Caution, fast traffic.

3.8 Oakencroft Winery is on the left.

5.5 Continue straight on Garth Rd./Rt. 614/676 where Rt. 601 bears right. Hunt Country Store is on the right at the intersection.

11.6 Turn left on Browns Gap Rd./Rt. 810 Wyant's Store is on the right at the turn.

11.9 Continue straight on Rt. 810 where Rt. 680 goes left.

15.0 Bear left on Crozet Ave./Rt. 810.

16.0 In Crozet, you'll pass a Dairy Queen on the right. In 0.1 mile, Crozet Country Club Restaurant will be on your right.

16.2 After passing through town and crossing the railroad tracks, turn right on Jarman Gap Rd./Rt. 691.

18.7 Bear left to stay on Jarman Gap Rd./Rt. 691.

20.1 At the stop sign, turn left and make a quick right to stay on Rt. 691. The road name changes to Greenwood.

21.3 Continue straight and cross Rt. 250. You will still be on Rt. 691, but the road name changes to Ortman. In 0.4 mile, bear right to stay on Ortman Rd.

22.9 Turn left at the stop sign on Plank Rd./Rt. 692 at Blue Ridge Farms.

26.0 Page's Store is on the left. In 0.1 mile, continue straight on Plank Rd./Rt. 692 in Batesville.

27.5 The Little Market is on the right.

28.9 Turn left on Edge Valley Rd./Rt. 696.

31.6 Turn left at the stop sign and the T on Rt. 710.

32.6 Turn right on Red Hill Rd./Rt. 708.

34.4 Go straight on Red Hill Rd./Rt. 708 Cross Rt. 29. Caution.

36.3 Turn left on Rt. 706 (Dudley Mountain Rd.—unmarked).

39.9 Turn left on Old Lynchburg Rd./Rt. 631.

42.2 Turn left on Old Lynchburg Rd./Rt. 780. Caution, easy turn to miss. If you go past the Wachovia Bank office, you've gone too far.

42.9 Continue straight at the stop sign on Old Lynchburg Rd.

43.3 Turn left at the stop sign on Jefferson Park Ave.

43.9 Continue straight at the stoplight on Maury Ave. Cycle through UVA campus.

44.6 Continue straight at the stoplight on Alderman.

45.1 Turn left at the stoplight on Ivy Rd. Caution, traffic.

45.2 Turn right into the plaza parking lot and end of the ride.

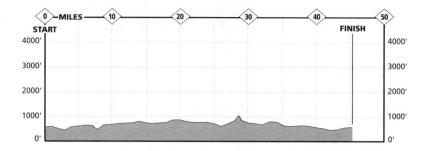

After the ride, Charlottesville has lots to offer. Consider heading to the historic Downtown Mall, a pedestrian-only street offering numerous restaurants and boutiques. Also, be sure to stop at Monticello, Thomas Jefferson's home and architectural masterpiece. A guided tour of the home and extensive gardens is a highlight of any visit to Virginia.

LOCAL INFORMATION

♦ Charlottesville/Albemarle Convention and Visitors Bureau, Route 20 South, Charlottesville, VA 22902, 804–977–1783. Open daily from 9:00 A.M. to 5:30 P.M.

LOCAL EVENTS/ATTRACTIONS

♦ Thomas Jefferson's Monticello, Charlottesville, 804–984–9822. Guided tours of one of Virginia's most impressive estates. Admission: $11.00 for adults, $6.00 for children. Open daily.
♦ Ash Lawn Highland Summer Festival, 804–979–0122. A variety of opera and contemporary music performances are performed throughout the summer at the home of our fifth president, James Monroe.

RESTAURANTS

♦ The Old Hardware Store Restaurant, 316 E. Main St. (Downtown Mall), Charlottesville, 804–977–1518. A fun, nostalgic, and casual restaurant housed in an 1895 hardware store.
♦ Historic Michie Tavern, 683 Thomas Jefferson Parkway, Charlottesville, 804–977–1234. Traditional Southern lunch and tour of a 200-year-old tavern and gristmill.

ACCOMMODATIONS

♦ The Inn at Monticello B&B, 1188 Scottsville Rd., Charlottesville, VA 22902, 804–979–3593. An 1850 manor home close to Monticello. Expensive.
♦ Red Roof Inn, 1309 W. Main St., Charlottesville, VA 22903, 800–843–7663. University location. Mid-range.

Pastoral paradise in Albemarle County.

BIKE SHOP

♦ Performance Bicycle Shop, 234 Zan Road, Charlottesville, VA 22901, 804–963–9161.

REST ROOMS

♦ At the start: in various restaurants
♦ Mile 5.5: at Hunt Country Store
♦ Mile 16.0: at the Crozet Dairy Queen
♦ Mile 26.0: at Page's Store

MAP

♦ DeLorme *Virginia Atlas and Gazetteer* maps 55 and 67

Farmville Cruise

The Farmville Classic is a long cruise around the gentle, rolling farmlands of Cumberland and Buckingham counties. This area is rich in history, for it was through this region that General Robert E. Lee and his armies retreated to Appomattox, the site of the last great drama of the Civil War. Take a short detour to Bear Creek Lake State Park, where an abundant variety of outdoor activities await the energetic—or a relaxing and refreshing swim for the weary. Cycle past numerous poultry farms on your way back to Farmville, where you can celebrate at Charley's Waterfront Cafe, housed in an old tobacco warehouse.

Before you head out for the cruise, stop in at the Chamber of Commerce on 116 North Main Street, just a few blocks from the start. Pick up some information on Lee's Retreat, Bear Creek Lake State Park, and, of course, Farmville. The C of C distributes a fine walking map of the town, part of which is listed on the Virginia Landmarks Registry and the National Register of Historic Places. Many of the buildings date to the mid-1800s and include a variety of architectural styles. Plenty of shops and restaurants make for an excellent start and finish to the cruise.

At 54 miles, this cruise could be categorized as a challenge. However, the route is not only rural but also very gentle. It is within the capability of any intermediate cyclist, especially when planning a rest stop at Bear Creek Lake. There are a number of stores along the route to refuel when needed.

Leaving Farmville, you'll follow River Road, one of the best cycling roads in this area. You'll parallel the Appomattox River most of the way, but, unfortunately, river views are scarce. About 5 miles into the ride, you'll come to an interesting historical marker on the right. It is one of many markers in the region commemorating Lee's Retreat.

Much of the area north of the North Carolina border and south of the James River was untouched by the Civil War. That changed in April 1865, when General Lee abandoned Petersburg. Union General Ulysses S. Grant pursued with vengeance. Lee's armies were weakened at Sailor's Creek, just 10 miles east of Farmville. They were finally pushed and cornered in Appomattox, where, out of options, Lee surrendered on April 9.

The historical marker mentioned above is located at High Bridge. Early on April 7, Confederate forces burned much of High Bridge, a 100-foot-high, ½-mile-long railroad bridge that spanned the Appomattox, in an effort to delay the advancing enemy. However, they failed to destroy a lower wagon bridge, thus enabling Union forces to continue their pursuit of Lee and his armies north of the river.

Although you can catch a glimpse of the bridge here, there is no access to it.

The cruise brings you into the small town of Cumberland, which offers several stores and restaurants. The 24 Hour Restaurant on Anderson Highway is your last chance for a sit-down meal. Otherwise, bike on to Bear Creek Lake State Park. If you do not plan on visiting the park, there is a market located at the entrance if you need food and drink.

There are a number of hiking trails located in the park as well as camping, a high-tech archery range, and lake swimming. The park is tranquil and features a deep hardwood forest. Numerous shelters and picnic areas make for a great rest stop and some peaceful, relaxing time off the bike. If you're really energetic, try the 14-mile multiuse Cumberland Trail for some additional off-road mileage. There is a $1.00 admission fee to the park.

The cruise remains gentle as it makes its way into Buckingham County. Many poultry farms as well as tobacco and cornfields dominate the landscape. At mile 42.5, stop at Grandma's General Store for a pleasant reminder that our country has not been completely overtaken by fast-food restaurants and convenience stores. You'll have some rollers, but the terrain is particularly easy on the way back to the Appomattox River and into Farmville. If you're feeling hun-

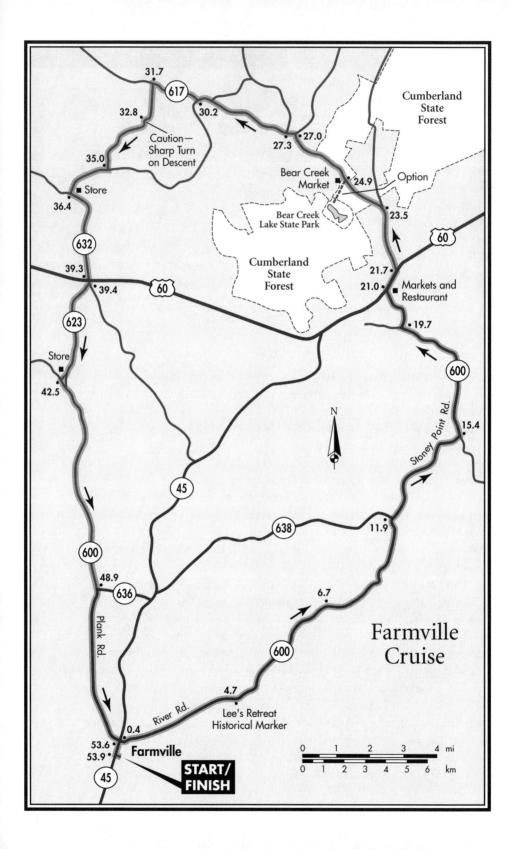

31.7

617

32.8

30.2

Caution—
Sharp Turn
on Descent

27.0

Cumberland
State
Forest

35.0

27.3

■ Store

Bear Creek
Market

24.9

Option

36.4

Bear Creek
Lake State Park

23.5

632

Cumberland
State
Forest

60

39.3

39.4

60

21.7

21.0

Markets and
Restaurant

623

19.7

Store ■

600

42.5

15.4

Stoney Point Rd.

N

45

638

11.9

600

6.7

48.9

636

Farmville
Cruise

Plank Rd.

600

4.7

Lee's Retreat
Historical Marker

River Rd.

0.4

53.6

53.9

Farmville

**START/
FINISH**

45

| 0 | 1 | 2 | 3 | 4 | mi |
| 0 | 1 | 2 | 3 | 4 | 5 | 6 | km |

0.0 Head left out of the parking lot on Second St. toward Main St. Turn right at the stoplight on Main St.

0.4 Turn right at the light on River Road/Rt. 600 after passing Green Front Furniture and crossing the Appomattox River.

4.7 Pull-off for Lee's Retreat High Bridge Historical Marker.

6.7 Continue straight on River Road/Rt. 600.

11.9 Turn right on Stoney Point Rd./Rt. 600.

15.4 Bear left to stay on Stoney Point Rd./Rt. 600.

19.7 Bear right to stay on Stoney Point Rd./Rt. 600.

21.0 Turn right on Anderson Hwy./Rt. 60 in Cumberland. Flippin's Food Store is at the intersection. Marion's Bi-Rite Market comes up on the right, and just after the market is the 24 Hour Restaurant. Caution, traffic is faster, but there is an adequate shoulder.

21.7 Turn left on Trents Mill Rd./Rt. 622.

23.5 Continue straight as Rt. 623 bears right.

24.9 Continue straight to stay on route. Bear Creek Market is at this intersection. *Note:* If you want to visit Bear Creek Lake State Park, turn left here on Oak Hill Rd./Rt. 629. In 0.8 mile, bear left at the Y on Rt. 666 to enter the park. There is a $1.00 admission charge to enter the park.

27.0 Bear left to stay on Trents Mill Rd./Rt. 622.

27.3 Go straight on Gravel Hill Rd./Rt. 617. Rt. 622 goes right.

30.2 Bear right to stay on Rt. 617.

31.7 Turn left on Rt. 668.

32.8 Caution, sharp bend to the left on descent.

35.0 Turn right at the stop sign on Rt. 650.

36.4 Turn left on Rt. 632. Chuck Stop Convenience Store is on the left after the turn.

39.3 Go straight on Rt. 632. Cross Rt. 60.

39.4 Turn right on Rt. 623.

42.5 Turn left at the stop sign and T on Rt. 600. Grandma's Country Store is on the right before the turn.

48.9 Continue straight on Plank Rd. at the intersection with Raines Tavern Rd./ Rt. 636.

53.6 Turn right at the stoplight on Main St.

53.9 Turn left at the stoplight on Second St.

54.0 End ride at the municipal parking lot.

Cyclists enjoy the incomparable Shenandoah Valley.

gry, head to Charley's Waterfront Cafe, housed in an old tobacco warehouse. In the mid-1800s, Farmville was the fourth-leading tobacco port in Virginia. Tobacco was stored in these very same warehouses and eventually shipped to Petersburg via the Appomattox River Canal. Enjoy the ride and your visit to historic Farmville.

LOCAL INFORMATION

♦ Farmville Area Chamber of Commerce, 116 N. Main St., Farmville, VA 23901, 804–392–3939.

LOCAL EVENTS/ATTRACTIONS

♦ Heart of Virginia Festival, downtown Farmville, early May, 804–392–3939. Fine arts show, crafts booths, festival foods, and entertainment.
♦ Bear Creek Lake State Park, 929 Oak Hill Road, Cumberland, 804–492–4410.

RESTAURANTS

♦ Charley's Waterfront Cafe, 201-B Mill St., Farmville, 804–392–1566. American cuisine in old tobacco warehouse.

◆ Macado's Restaurant, 200 E. Third St., Farmville, 804–392–8077. Overstuffed sandwiches; casual.

ACCOMMODATIONS

◆ The Longwood Inn, 408 High St., Farmville, VA 23901, 866–660–8149. An 1879 Victorian B&B. Mid- to high-range.
◆ Comfort Inn, Routes 460 and 15, Farmville, VA 23901, 804–392–8163. Mid-range.

BIKE SHOP

◆ Piedmont Bike Shop, 136 N. Main St., Farmville, VA 23901, 804–315–0066.

REST ROOMS

◆ Various locations at the start in Farmville
◆ Mile 21.0: various locations in Cumberland
◆ Mile 24.9: at the Bear Creek Market or at Bear Creek Lake State Park
◆ Mile 36.4: at Chuck Stop Convenience Store

MAP

◆ DeLorme *Virginia Atlas and Gazetteer* maps 46 and 56

Middlebrook Ramble

The Middlebrook Ramble takes cyclists through the rolling coun-tryside of southern Augusta County and the incomparable Shenandoah Valley. You won't find restaurants or souvenir shops along this route, nor will you find hotels, convenience stores, stoplights or traf-fic. That is why this ride is so special. This ride is well known as the Sunday Family route on Staunton's Shenandoah Fall Festival held in late October. Configured as a figure-eight, this ride can be done three ways: a very easy 9-mile beginner route, an 11-miler offering a few more hills, or by doing both loops for a fulfilling 20-mile ramble. Cyclists can pick up food and drink and do what is necessary in Staunton, just 10 miles to the north.

No doubt, you will want to start your day in Staunton, a Virginia Main Street Community. The city makes a convenient base for your adventures in the valley, as it offers a wide variety of accommodations, shops, and restaurants. There are no facilities on this ramble, and you'll want to fuel up in Staunton before your drive down to Middlebrook.

Although a short ride, the Middlebrook Ramble packs a lot of Shenandoah punch. Within a half mile, you'll be cycling past some of the valley's most pic-turesque farms, with the Allegheny Mountains looming in the distance. Quickly leaving Middlebrook, you're greeted with a pleasant, gradual downhill to Summerdean Road at the base of Little North Mountain. Here you will grad-ually climb for a few miles as you pedal by Middle River, which more resembles a creek. The climbing, however, is a mild 2 percent or less and will not challenge even the beginning cyclist.

Hay fields and livestock farms dominate the landscape as you make your way up to Middlebrook Road. An easy descent back into the village and to the ride's starting point is a pleasant end to the first half of the ramble.

The second half of the ramble is more challenging than the first but still within ramble standards because of its gradual ascents and short distance. You'll climb right at the start on Middlebrook Road, where you'll need to use some caution. Traffic is light but can be fast. But after a mile and a half, you'll be back on some of the area's nicest country roads. The scenery on the eastern part of the ramble is similar to the western half—beautiful.

Your last climb is on Stover School Road, where you'll be following Roaring Run. It's not a difficult climb, but it's a fairly long one that will make you earn your upcoming descent. And what a reward! You'll find yourself on top of the ridge with the village of Middlebrook nestled in the spectacular Shenandoah Valley below. With the Allegheny Mountains serving as the backdrop, you have nearly 2 miles of gradual downhill to end the ride—perhaps the greatest ride ending in the entire state. Enjoy it.

THE BASICS

Start: From gravel lot at intersection of Middlebrook Road/Route 252 and Cherry Grove Road/Route 670.

Length: 9, 11, or 20 miles

Terrain: Flat to gently rolling. The 11-mile loop has some hills that may challenge beginners.

Traffic and hazards: All roads on this route are low traffic and rural. Use caution on Middlebrook Road/Route 252 on both routes because traffic, although light, can be fast. Entire route is paved and in good condition. No hazards.

Getting there: From Staunton, take Route 252 South approximately 11 miles from downtown Staunton. The lot is just below Brubeck Hardware Store (the only store in the area) and the post office.

LOCAL INFORMATION

♦ Staunton Convention and Visitors Bureau, 116 W. Beverly, Staunton, VA 24401, 800–342–7982. Located in City Hall, second floor. Open Monday to Friday.

♦ Staunton–Augusta Travel Information Center, located in Frontier Culture Museum, off I–81, exit 222, 540–332–3972. Open daily.

LOCAL EVENTS/ATTRACTIONS

♦ Frontier Culture Museum, Frontier Drive off Richmond Rd./Route 250, Staunton, VA 24402, 540–332–7850. Focuses on the area's early settlers, with working farmsteads and demonstrations. Admission: $8.00 for adults, $4.00 for children.

0.0 Turn right out of the lot onto Middlebrook Rd./Rt. 252 North. Go about 100 yards, then turn left on Mish Barn Rd./Rt. 876.

3.2 Turn left at the stop sign on Summerdean Rd./Rt. 602.

5.8 Bear left at the Y on Shemariah Rd./Rt. 677.

6.5 Bear left to stay on Shemariah Rd.

8.0 Turn right on Cale's Springs Rd./Rt. 603.

8.5 Turn left on Middlebrook Rd./Rt. 252 North. Use caution—faster traffic.

9.3 Arrive back at the lot in Middlebrook. Soda machines can be found at the hardware store just past the lot.

9.3 Continue straight on Middlebrook Rd./Rt. 252 to begin the second half of the ramble. Use caution—faster traffic.

10.8 Turn right on Howardsville Rd./Rt. 701.

13.7 Turn right on McClures Mill Rd./Rt. 604.

14.8 Bear to the right to stay on McClures Mill Rd.

15.5 Turn right at the stop sign on Stover School Rd./Rt. 662.

18.2 Turn left on Cherry Grove Rd./Rt. 693. Road number soon changes to Rt. 670. Continue straight.

20.3 Turn right on Middlebrook Rd. and end the ride at the lot on the right.

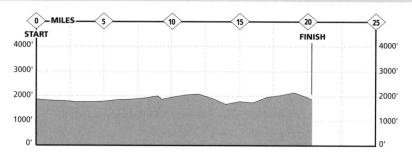

♦ Woodrow Wilson Birthplace, 24 N. Coalter St., Staunton, VA 24402, 888–496–6376. Beautiful home and museum depicts the life of our twenty-eighth president. Admission: $6.50 for adults, $4.00 for children.

♦ Shenandoah Fall Festival (Bicycling Weekend), usually the third weekend in October. Call the visitor's center for information.

RESTAURANTS

♦ Pullman Restaurant, 38 Middlebrook Ave., Staunton, 540–886–6612. Authentic train station restaurant and Victorian ice cream parlor.

♦ Wright's Dairy Rite, 348 Greenville Ave., Staunton, 540–886–1436. Historic curb-service restaurant.

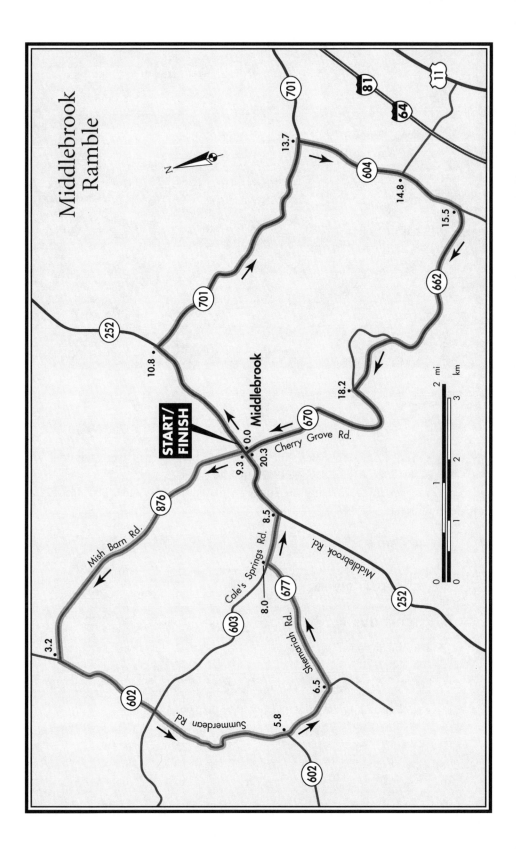

Middlebrook Ramble

Llama farm in the Shenandoah Valley.

ACCOMMODATIONS

♦ Thornrose House Bed and Breakfast, 531 Thornrose Ave., Staunton, VA 24401, 800–861–4338. Cozy 1912 inn. Mid-range.
♦ Sleep Inn, 222 Jefferson Highway, Staunton, VA 24401, 800–488–8750. Budget.

BIKE SHOP

♦ Closest is in Waynesboro: Cycle-Recycle Co., 320 W. Main St., Waynesboro, VA 22980, 540–949–8973.

REST ROOMS

♦ None on route.

MAP

♦ DeLorme *Virginia Atlas and Gazetteer* map 66

Goshen Ramble

T he Goshen Ramble is an out-and-back ride that follows the Maury River through magnificent Goshen Pass. Starting in the village of Rockbridge Baths, the cyclist will follow the boulder-strewn Maury River as it makes a cut through the rugged Alleghenies. Considered by many to be the most scenic area in Virginia, Goshen Pass is a 3-mile section of white water where rhododendrons, ferns, hemlocks, dogwoods, and pines blanket the riverbanks. The ramble turns around in the town of Goshen, then provides another opportunity to enjoy the Goshen Pass, this time from the opposite, and easier, direction. Although rather short, the Goshen Ramble is easily accessible from Lexington and is a must for your next trip there.

Normally, I try to avoid out-and-back rides. With some creativity, most out-and-backs can be made into a loop. In this case, doing so would result in a ride that would be considerably longer and more difficult. I wanted to present a Goshen ride that was within the capability of any cyclist. If there ever was a ride that you wouldn't mind doing twice, it is the Goshen Ramble.

The ride starts out in Rockbridge Baths, a small village that was home to a very popular resort in the 1800s. Many of Lexington's residents would visit the baths, including Robert E. Lee, during his presidency at Washington College (later Washington and Lee). The Olde Country Store is now closed, unfortunately, so you must pick up supplies before you begin your ride. If you forget, you'll have another chance in the town of Goshen halfway into the ride.

For the first several miles, the ramble follows the scenic Maury River upstream, where you'll slowly gain some elevation. Don't be alarmed; the gradient is slight, and beginners won't find themselves walking any hills. You'll soon come to Goshen Pass, a 3-mile-long gap that Native Americans, elk, and

Start: From the Rockbridge Baths Post Office.

Length: 20 miles

Terrain: Gentle terrain. Gradual climb as the route follows the Maury River upstream. Fairly level once through the pass. Suitable for beginners.

Traffic and hazards: Route 39 will be the primary road for the entire route. It is rural but can be fast through Rockbridge Baths and near Goshen. The route through Goshen Pass has a very low speed limit. Entire route is paved and in good condition.

Getting there: Take Route 11 North out of Lexington. Pass the junction for I–64, then turn left on Maury River Road/Route 39. Go 9.4 miles to the Rockbridge Baths Post Office on the left. Park on the east side of the building next to the closed Olde Country Store, which shares the building with the post office.

buffalo once used as they crossed the mountains in search of food.

The Maury River is named for Matthew Fontaine Maury, who was known as "the Pathfinder of the Seas" for his work and research in scientific navigation. A professor at the Virginia Military Institute, Maury requested, upon his death, to be carried by the VMI cadets through Goshen Pass, a place he so loved. At mile 4.0 of the ramble, a historical marker commemorates Maury.

Just after Maury's marker is a picnic area complete with shelter, rest rooms, water, and a safe wading area. This makes for a perfect break from cycling and a fantastic photo op. Be sure to stop.

The section through Goshen Pass is one of the most beautiful places in Virginia. As the Maury winds through the pass, its banks are draped with mosses, pines, rhododendron, and laurel and speckled with ferns and wildflowers. But what really makes the pass interesting is that it is actually a gorge. It cuts into the mountainside, revealing rocks and boulders the size of cars. The river is littered with them, creating hot spots for fishermen, obstacles for rafters, and stepping-stones for picnickers.

As you leave the pass, you'll still enjoy flat to gentle terrain while cruising along Calfpasture River. This river, along with the Little Calfpasture River, is what makes up the Maury. Soon, you'll be in Goshen, a small railroad town that makes an excellent place to stop for lunch, pick up supplies, and turn around for the return trip. There are several grocery stores and restaurants in town, and if your plans allow an overnight stay, consider the Hummingbird Inn. This 1853 Carpenter Gothic villa has wraparound verandas on the first and second floors and is furnished with antiques. There's even a wild trout stream bordering the property.

Your return ride to Rockbridge Baths will be even more delightful. Now you get to view the scenery from a different perspective, often taking in beautiful sights missed the first time through. Plus, the ride back follows the Maury downriver and is a relaxing and enjoyable descent. Here is your chance to stop at the picnic area at the pass in case you skipped it on the way up. Note that many other recreational activities are available at Goshen Pass. Besides cycling and picnicking, you can also swim, go tubing or canoeing, fish (rainbow trout, bass, and native brown trout), and hike several trails. So pack a swimsuit or a collapsible fishing rod and enjoy one of Virginia's scenic treasures.

LOCAL INFORMATION

♦ Lexington Visitor Center, 106 E. Washington St., Lexington, VA 24450, 540–463–3777. Open daily.

LOCAL EVENTS/ATTRACTIONS

♦ James River Basin Canoe Livery, 1870 E. Midland Trail, Lexington, VA 24450, 540–261–7334. Offers equipment rentals and white-water rafting and canoe excursions on the Maury River.
♦ The Virginia Horse Center, Route 39, Lexington, VA 24450, 540–463–2194. One of the largest facilities of its kind in the East, the center sponsors shows, sales, exhibitions, and competitions nearly every weekend. Also on the premises is the American Work Horse Museum.

RESTAURANTS

♦ Mill Creek Cafe, Routes 39 and 42, Goshen, 540–997–5228. Homestyle cooking.

ACCOMMODATIONS

♦ The Hummingbird Inn, 30 Wood Lane, Goshen, VA 24439, 800–397–3214. An 1853 B&B. Mid- to high-range.

The author and his wife, Wendy, enjoy a stop at gorgeous Goshen Pass.

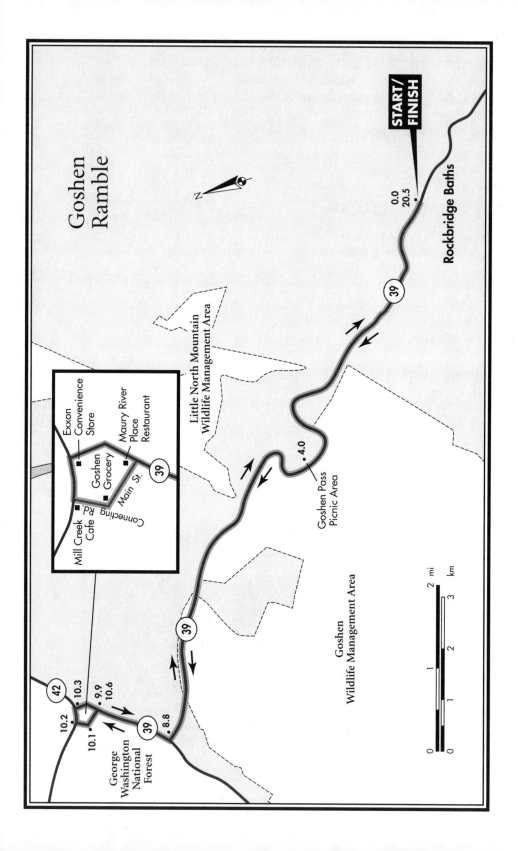

Goshen Ramble

MILES AND DIRECTIONS

0.0 Turn left out of the post office parking lot onto Maury River Rd./Rt. 39. Look for the swinging bridge across the Maury River just after the post office.

4.0 Matthew Fontaine Maury historical marker is on your right. Just past this is the Goshen Pass picnic area.

8.8 Bear to the right to stay on Rt. 39.

9.6 Little Food Mart is on the left.

9.9 Bear left on Main St. Maury River Place Restaurant is on the right.

10.1 Goshen Grocery is on the right just after the road bears right.

10.2 Turn right at the stop sign on Virginia Ave./Rt. 42 East. Just before the turn, Mill Creek Cafe is on the left.

10.3 Turn right on Maury River Rd. Just before the turn there is an Exxon and Edwards Convenience Store on the right.

10.5 Bear to the right to stay on Maury River Rd.

10.6 Continue straight on Maury River Rd./Rt. 39. You've just completed the loop around town, and the Maury River Place Restaurant is on your right. Continue the ramble by doubling back on Rt. 39 all the way to Rockbridge Baths.

20.5 End the ride at the Rockbridge Baths Post Office.

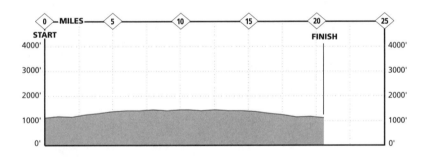

BIKE SHOP

♦ Lexington Bike Shop, 130 Main St., Lexington, VA 24450, 540–463–7969.

REST ROOMS

♦ Mile 4.0: at the Goshen Pass picnic area
♦ Mile 10.2: Mill Creek Cafe
♦ Mile 18.5: at the Goshen Pass picnic area

MAP

♦ DeLorme *Virginia Atlas and Gazetteer* map 53

Hot Springs Classic

The Hot Springs Classic is an extremely rural spin through the Allegheny Mountains of Virginia's Western Highlands. Although the classic can be completed in one day, it is designed as a two-day trip with back-to-back challenges and an overnight in the charming spa town of Hot Springs. Cycle through Highland County, the third least-populated county east of the Mississippi, whose rugged beauty led to its nickname, "Virginia's Switzerland." Then on to Bath County, where forests comprise 89 percent of the land and where not a single traffic light, billboard, or mosquito can be found. Pamper yourself in the world-famous Homestead Resort, and soak those tired muscles in the therapeutic waters. The classic ends with a bang, as a 6-mile climb up and over the Alleghenies brings you back to the maple syrup–producing hamlet of Monterey.

If you are doing this classic as a two-day ride, I suggest you start and end in Monterey and stay the night in Hot Springs or Warm Springs. With all the recreational activities and variety of accommodations in the Hot Springs area, it makes for a wonderful overnight stay. If you plan on completing the classic in one day, you may consider starting out in Hot Springs. You would have an interesting break and lunch in Monterey, then can take advantage of the hot baths at the end of a grueling ride.

Monterey is the county seat of Highland County, but don't expect much traffic here or the usual city pace. The turn-of-the-century village is charming, and a walk down its pleasant Main Street is a must. Consider a stay in the attractive Highland Inn, a grand Victorian built in 1904. Just outside town is the Little Highland Maple Museum. The museum's exhibits demonstrate the earliest known methods of making sugar and syrup as well as the latest techniques used today. Most of all, the museum provides a glimpse of a long-vanished way of American life.

You'll find the classic surprisingly easy as you wind your way along mountain streams and between Lantz and Back Creek mountains. Spectacular valley views greet you at every turn.

At about 20 miles into the ride you'll pass several large manmade lakes that comprise the Bath County Pumped Storage Project. The lakes, created by damming Big Back Creek and Little Back Creek, are restricted, as the water levels can rise or lower very quickly. The pumped storage facility is used not only for power generation but as a flood and drought prevention system. An area below the main lakes has been constructed for recreational use and includes picnicking, camping, and hiking areas, as well as a smaller lake for fishing and swimming. A small charge may apply for day use of the facilities.

Before your destination of Hot Springs, you'll pass through the quiet village of Bacova.

Bacova was established in the 1920s as a lumber mill company town and restored in the 1960s, with all its cottages painted in pastel colors. The Bacova Guild opened here in 1965 and made a variety of fiberglass products, including its popular cardinal-decorated mailbox. The Bacova Guild still operates several outlet stores and also offers its wares through various mail-order catalogs. To top it off, the pleasant, winding road through the small town is a delight to cycle.

People started visiting Bath County's springs around 1750 and numbered 6,000 annually in the early 1800s. Named for the English city of Bath, the county's warm, soothing waters have made the region a world-renowned resort attraction. There are numerous springs in the county, and every major community uses at least one for its source of water. Spring temperatures vary from

0.0 Head east on Main St./Rt. 250 to the junction with Rt. 220. There is a Texaco gas station with food and Ernie's Market at this intersection. Turn right on Rt. 220 South.

3.9 Turn right on Rt. 84 West.

14.3 Turn left on Rt. 600. Auction barn will be on your right at the turn.

17.2 Enter Bath County.

22.7 Bath County Pumped Storage Project facility is on the right.

23.3 Recreation area and campground will be on your left.

30.3 Turn left on Rt. 39 East. Mountain Grove General Store is on the right before the turn.

36.6 Reach the top of Back Creek Mountain. Use caution on the winding descent.

40.0 Turn right on Jackson River Turnpike/Rt. 687.

41.2 Pass through the village of Bacova.

42.7 Bear left to stay on Rt. 687.

45.7 Turn left on Bacova Junction Highway/Rt. 615.

48.5 Arrive at the junction with Rt. 220 in the town of Hot Springs. There are many stores and eateries in town. The Homestead Resort is straight ahead. To continue the classic, turn left on Rt. 220 North.

53.0 There is a small convenience store on the left.

53.5 Continue straight on Rt. 220 North in Warm Springs where Rt. 39 joins from the west. In 0.1 mile, continue straight on Rt. 220 North where Rt. 39 goes off to the east.

57.0 Sportsman's Inn Restaurant is on the right.

57.7 Turn right on Muddy Run Rd./Rt. 614.

66.7 Turn left on Dry Run Rd./Rt. 609 in the village of Burnsville. There is a small store on the right after the turn.

72.6 Turn left at the stop sign on Rt. 678.

76.1 Pass through the village of Clover Creek.

82.0 Turn left on Rt. 250 West in McDowell. Within next ½ mile, there will be a Stonewall Grocery and a Gas N Go on the right.

89.7 Reach the top of the last climb. Caution—there is one switchback on the descent.

91.5 Continue straight at the junction with Rt. 220. The Chamber of Commerce and the end of the ride are a few hundred yards up Main St.

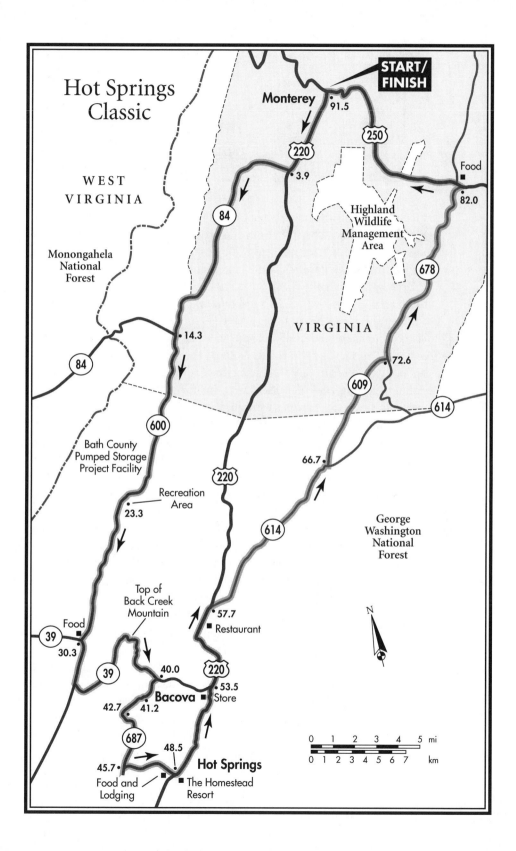

Hot Springs
Classic

START/
FINISH

Monterey
• 91.5

250

220

• 3.9

Food
■
• 82.0

WEST
VIRGINIA

84

Highland
Wildlife
Management
Area

678

Monongahela
National
Forest

VIRGINIA

• 14.3

84

• 72.6

609

614

600

Bath County
Pumped Storage
Project Facility

• 66.7

Recreation
Area
• 23.3

220

George
Washington
National
Forest

614

N

Top of
Back Creek
Mountain

• 57.7
■ Restaurant

Food
39 ■
• 30.3

39   40.0

220

Bacova ■ • 53.5
42.7 • 41.2   Store

687   • 48.5

45.7 •   Hot Springs

Food and
Lodging

■ The Homestead
Resort

| 0 | 1 | 2 | 3 | 4 | 5 | mi |

| 0 | 1 | 2 | 3 | 4 | 5 | 6 | 7 | km |

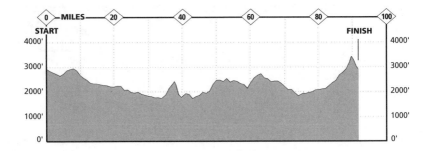

94 to 106 degrees Fahrenheit, while their flow rates range from 2,500 to 5,000 gallons per minute. The spring mineral water is so clear and healthful that some visitors drink it for its therapeutic properties. Whether you drink it or not, you must experience its curative and soothing powers after your ride.

Dominating the town of Hot Springs is The Homestead and its 15,000 acres of relaxation and recreation. This magnificent luxury resort and spa has hosted numerous presidents and the social elite. Its ballroom, dining rooms, and pillared colonnades reflect a grandeur on a par with the world's top resorts. Besides the springs for which it is famous, The Homestead offers three outstanding golf courses, downhill and cross-country skiing, lawn and indoor bowling, sporting clays and skeet trap, indoor and outdoor pools, tennis, mountain stream trout fishing, ice skating on an Olympic-size rink, and twenty-one boutique and specialty shops. Yes, it's pricey, but if you ever wanted to treat yourself to the best, here's your chance. Still can't handle the tariff? No problem; there are several hotels and B&Bs in the area, as well as a number of interesting shops and restaurants in town.

Leaving Hot Springs, you'll soon enter the village of Warm Springs and another chance to sample, at an affordable rate, the thermal springs at Jefferson Pools. Situated in a grove of trees at the intersection of Routes 220 and 39, the Jefferson Pools' crystal-clear waters are sure to relax those aching legs. One pool is for men, while the other is for women, so proper attire is not required. Reservations are not needed, and at about $12 per hour, your cures won't set you back nearly as much as at The Homestead.

The route back to Monterey is peaceful and pleasant, with considerable riding through the George Washington National Forest. When you arrive in the village of McDowell, be sure to fuel up for the upcoming climb. This is by far the most challenging climb on this classic, as you'll be ascending for about 6 miles. Close to the top, you'll negotiate a series of switchbacks while the grade increases to 5 or 6 percent. Once at the top, you're rewarded with some fine views of Monterey below and a descent that is easily manageable. Celebrate the end of the classic at High's Restaurant, Monterey's oldest, for home-cooked meals, homemade pies, and some good old southern hospitality.

LOCAL INFORMATION

◆ Highland County Chamber of Commerce, P.O. Box 223, Monterey, VA 24465, 540–468–2550.
◆ Bath County Chamber of Commerce, P.O. Box 718, Hot Springs, VA 24445, 800–628–8092 or 540–839–5409.

LOCAL EVENTS/ATTRACTIONS

◆ Highland Maple Festival, second and third full weekends in March, Monterey, 540–468–2550. One of Virginia's top annual events.
◆ Battle of Warm Springs, early August, 800–628–8092. Cavalry demonstrations, battle reenactments, period vendors, entertainment, and evening BBQ.

RESTAURANTS

◆ The Waterwheel Restaurant, located at The Inn at Gristmill Square, Warm Springs, 540–839–2231. Traditional American dinner in a historic gristmill built in 1900.
◆ The Homestead Dining Outlets. Include at least nine formal and informal dining establishments. For casual dining, try Sam Snead's Tavern, located directly across Route 220 from The Homestead, 540–839–7989.
◆ High's Restaurant, Main St., Monterey, 540–468–1600. Home-cooked meals.

ACCOMMODATIONS

◆ The Homestead, Hot Springs, VA 24445, 540–839–1766 or 800–838–1766. Upscale, luxurious resort spa with outstanding amenities.
◆ The Highland Inn, P.O. Box 40, Monterey, VA 24465, 540–468–2143. Midrange Victorian inn.

BIKE SHOP

◆ None available.

REST ROOMS

◆ At the start at the Texaco station and at various restaurants in Monterey
◆ Mile 23.3: at the Bath County Pumped Storage Project recreation area
◆ Mile 30.3: Mountain Grove General Store
◆ Mile 48.5: various locations in the town of Hot Springs
◆ Mile 57.0: Sportsman's Restaurant
◆ Mile 82.0: at the Gas N Go in McDowell

MAP

◆ DeLorme *Virginia Atlas and Gazetteer* maps 52, 64, 65

Rockbridge Challenge

S tarting in the historic college town of Lexington, the Rockbridge Challenge takes the cyclist on a scenic tour around Short Hills Mountain. Designed as an easier challenge, the route includes a few too many hills to classify as a cruise. The challenge follows many of Rockbridge County's fabulous biking roads with names like Possum Hollow, Toad Run, and Blue Grass Trail. Enjoy one of Virginia's greatest downhill runs as you gradually glide along South Buffalo Creek for 11 miles. After the ride, enjoy Lexington's hospitality and see why it is consistently ranked as one of America's best small towns.

Everyone seems to like Lexington; it's home to two great colleges; numerous country inns and B&Bs; a restored downtown that looks as though it hasn't changed in a hundred years; large, stately homes lining shady streets; and a variety of historic, recreational, and cultural pursuits. Even if you're in the area for just one day, the challenge should allow plenty of time for taking in some of the sights. Better yet, spend at least one night and bike the Goshen Ramble on the second day.

Start the challenge at the visitor's center, which is open daily and offers free parking, rest rooms, and a very helpful staff. Pick up your supplies in the city before you take off, since there are limited facilities on the loop.

Just after you start the ride, you'll pass the Stonewall Jackson House. Built in 1801, the house was the only one ever owned by the Confederate general. Jackson (whose actual name was Thomas; "Stonewall" was the nickname he acquired at the Battle of Bull Run) lived here for nearly a decade while teaching at the Virginia Military Institute. He is best known for his courageous and brilliant leadership in the 1862 Valley campaign. Jackson died in 1863 at the age of thirty-nine from wounds suffered in the Battle of Chancellorsville. A slide show, photos, and many of Jackson's own belongings tell the story of his life in Lexington. For information on the Stonewall Jackson House, call 540–463–2552.

Leaving Lexington, you'll follow fairly easy terrain while cruising along Possum Run and Buffalo Creek as you make your way down the east side of steep-sloped Short Hills Mountain. Traffic is extremely light and the scenery extraordinary in this area of Rockbridge County. Even when the terrain becomes more challenging, it's hard to notice or care. It's a beautiful spin—enjoy.

As you make your way around the southern end of Short Hills, you'll notice a constant gain in elevation. This isn't a mountain climb here, but a gradual and constant ascent that drops you off on Short Hills western slope and sets you up for a fantastic descent. As the challenge makes its way back to the north, you'll follow South Buffalo Creek downstream for about 11 miles. This won't be one of those thrilling white-knuckle descents, mind you, but one where you can relax, enjoy, and savor every moment. It ranks as one of Virginia's best biking roads.

Be sure to stop at Marshall's Grocery Store in Rapps Mill. It's the only store on the route outside Lexington. A few miles past Rapps Mill, notice the pair of mountains towering in the distance. Big House and Little House mountains reach 3,500 and 3,300 feet, respectively, and although they appear to be in your path, you won't have to climb them. But climbing is indeed in your plans as the most challenging segment of the ride occurs while crossing a succession of hills into Lexington. One last 2-mile descent is your reward as you coast all the way into the city and past the beautiful campus of Washington and Lee University. While on the campus, stop and visit the Robert E. Lee Chapel and Museum, built during Lee's university presidency. It's a fitting tribute to the heritage of George Washington, General Lee, and the university, the ninth oldest in the United States. If your legs are too sore at ride's end for a walking tour, call the Lexington Carriage Co. for a forty-five-minute carriage tour of the city and let the horses do the work.

THE BASICS

Start: From the Lexington Visitor Center.

Length: 44 miles

Terrain: Moderate to advanced difficulty. Several long, flat stretches along creek beds. Several good climbs.

Traffic and hazards: Use caution when cycling in Lexington. There are some tight turns while descending Enfield Road on the approach to Lexington at the end of the ride. Watch for 0.4 mile of unpaved road on South Sugar Creek Road.

Getting there: From I-81, take exit 188 to Route 60 West. Go 2½ miles to the Y, and bear right on East Washington Street. Go 0.3 mile to the visitor's center on the right at 106 East Washington. Or, when in town, take Main Street north, then turn right on East Washington Street to the visitor's center 1 block on the left.

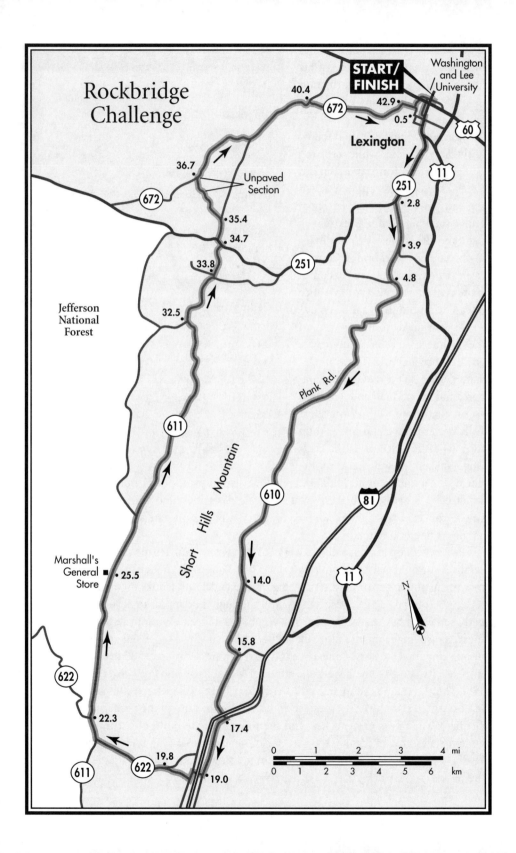

Rockbridge Challenge

START/FINISH

Washington and Lee University

Lexington

Jefferson National Forest

Marshall's General Store

Short Hills Mountain

Plank Rd.

Unpaved Section

672

672

251

251

611

610

622

611

622

60

11

11

81

40.4

42.9

0.5

2.8

3.9

4.8

36.7

35.4

34.7

33.8

32.5

25.5

22.3

19.8

19.0

17.4

14.0

15.8

N

| 0 | 1 | 2 | 3 | 4 mi |

| 0 | 1 | 2 | 3 | 4 | 5 | 6 km |

0.0 Turn right out of the visitor's center. Stonewall Jackson House is immediately on your right.

0.1 Go to the second stoplight, then turn left on Jefferson St.

0.5 Turn left on White St., then make an immediate right at the stop sign on Main St./Rt. 11.

1.0 Bear right on Thornhill Rd.

1.4 Turn right on Thornhill Rd. (turns into Rt. 251).

2.8 Turn left on Possum Hollow Rd./Rt. 764.

3.9 Turn right on Plank Rd./Rt. 610.

4.8 Bear left to stay on Plank Rd./Rt. 610.

14.0 Continue straight on Plank Rd./Rt. 610 at the junction with Rt. 692.

15.8 Bear right to stay on Plank Rd./Rt. 610.

16.8 Enter Botetourt County.

17.4 Turn right at the stop sign on Lee Hwy.

19.0 Turn right on Overpass Rd./Rt. 623. In 0.1 mile, turn left on Frontage Rd./ Rt. 623. In 0.1 mile, turn right on Buffalo Rd./Rt. 623.

19.8 Continue straight on Buffalo Rd. Route number changes to Rt. 622.

22.3 Bear to the right on Buffalo Rd. Route number changes to Rt. 611.

23.8 Enter Rockbridge County.

25.5 Marshall's Grocery Store is on the left.

32.5 Turn right on Blue Grass Trail/Rt. 612.

33.8 Turn left to stay on Blue Grass Trail/Rt. 612.

34.7 Turn left on Rt. 251 South. Continue past Effinger Fire Department, and turn right on Toad Run/Rt. 676.

35.4 Go straight on S. Sugar Creek Rd./Rt. 641. Toad Run bears right.

36.3 Road turns to dirt for 0.4 mile.

36.7 Immediately after the dirt section ends, turn right on Turnpike Rd./Rt. 672.

40.4 Turn right on Enfield Rd./Rt. 672 and begin climb. In 0.1 mile, continue straight on Enfield Rd. where Spring Valley Rd. heads right.

40.9 Crest the hill and use caution on the descent. Some tight turns.

42.9 Bear right on Lime Kiln Rd.

43.2 Turn left at the stop sign on McLaughlin St.

43.4 Turn left on Glasgow St.

43.5 Turn left on Nelson St., then an immediate right on Washington St. Pass through Washington and Lee University.

43.9 End the ride at the Lexington Visitor Center on the left.

Cyclist crosses a beautiful marsh in Tidewater Virginia.

LOCAL INFORMATION

♦ Lexington Visitor Center, 106 E. Washington St., Lexington, VA 24450, 540–463–3777. Open daily.

LOCAL EVENTS/ATTRACTIONS

♦ Virginia Military Institute, Lexington. For information on touring the nation's oldest state-supported military college, call 540–464–7207.
♦ Theater at Lime Kiln, 14 South Randolph St., Lexington, VA 24450, 540–463–3074. Theater and concerts presented in the ruins of a nineteenth-century lime kiln.

RESTAURANTS

♦ Wilson-Walker House, 30 N. Main St., Lexington, 540–463–3020. Fine dining in an 1820 Greek Revival town house.
♦ Spanky's, 110 S. Jefferson, Lexington, 540–463–3338. Casual, sandwiches, fun.

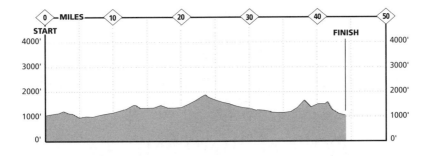

ACCOMMODATIONS

♦ McCampbell Inn, 11 N. Main St., Lexington, VA 24450, 877–463–2044. Historic 1809 country Inn. Mid- to high-range.
♦ Holiday Inn Express, P.O. Box 1108, Lexington, VA 24450, 800–480–3043. Mid-range.

BIKE SHOP

♦ Lexington Bike Shop, 130 Main St., Lexington, VA 24450, 540–463–7969.

REST ROOMS

♦ At the start in the visitor's center
♦ Mile 0.3: at various locations in Lexington
♦ Mile 43.7: at various locations in Lexington

MAP

♦ DeLorme *Virginia Atlas and Gazetteer* map 53

Peaks of Otter Challenge

The Peaks of Otter Challenge first rolls through Botetourt County's fertile valley and historic towns that lie between the majestic Allegheny and Blue Ridge mountains. After the 26-mile warmup, the challenge leaves the valley behind for a rigorous climb up the Blue Ridge at Bearwallow Gap. Stop for a rest or even the night at Peaks of Otter. The lodge, overlooking a scenic lake and with spectacular views of 3,875-foot Sharp Top Mountain, is in perfect harmony with nature and the only place one can stay right on the Blue Ridge Parkway System. After you reluctantly leave the Peaks of Otter, 20 more miles of fantastic Blue Ridge Parkway cycling await, affording extraordinary views on either side of the Blue Ridge. Finally, the descent back down to the valley is a just reward and a remarkable finish to the Peaks of Otter Challenge.

The challenge begins in the Troutville Town Park—a good starting point with its rest rooms and adjacent food market. Best of all, the challenge will end with a well-deserved descent from the Blue Ridge.

Head left (south) out of the park on Route 11. Don't be alarmed by the four lanes; traffic isn't heavy here, and you're on the highway for less than a mile. In a few miles, you'll cross busy Route 220 and have another chance to pick up food at a Getty Food Mart. Then it's a gentle, relaxing spin through Botetourt County on your way to Fincastle.

Fincastle was established in 1772 and serves as the county seat. During the 1800s, Fincastle was a popular summer resort and commercial center. Today, however, it's a quiet village of 325 residents and a virtual museum of American architecture. Pick up a walking tour guide at the visitor's center located in the

Court House Complex, and walk a few of its narrow streets. Marvel at the many wrought iron fences, gates, balconies, and varieties of architecture that have survived the last few centuries.

Leaving Fincastle, you'll gently roll for a few miles before cresting a small hill. For the next 6 miles or so, you'll gently descend through the beautiful Botetourt countryside on the way down to the James River. The road is steep enough to provide an enjoyable coast, yet not so steep as to necessitate caution. Add the fact that there is virtually no traffic and you have one of the premier biking roads in Virginia. Once you reach the James, the terrain is level all the way into Buchanan.

Nestled along the James River between steep Cove and Purgatory mountains, Buchanan was the principal river crossing via the "Great Valley Road" and later served as a Confederate supply line during the Civil War. The place works hard to maintain its small-town image and to preserve a high quality of life for its 1,200 residents. Indeed, it is an interesting town to shop, stroll, or take a needed break from the bike. Be sure to fuel up here, as there are no more facilities until you reach the Peaks of Otter. And standing ahead of you like Goliath is the formidable Blue Ridge.

This climb is by far the most difficult part of the challenge. Route 43 twists, turns, and climbs for about 4 miles, with grades up to 10 percent. You'll enter the Jefferson National Forest, where the scenery is indeed gorgeous—if you can appreciate such things under exertion. The climbing isn't over, unfortunately, when you reach the Blue Ridge Parkway. After a short descent, the parkway rises for several more miles to the Peaks of Otter. Whether you are staying the night or not, take a time-out here to enjoy and appreciate this blessing of nature.

The Peaks of Otter Lodge is extremely popular, and you must reserve far in advance in season. But the stay is well worth it. The lodge offers modest accommodations and amenities, but the entire complex is in perfect harmony with nature. Its picturesque lake, split-rail fences, balconies with splendid views, and rustic room decor invite relaxation. If you have the energy, you may want to hike to the top of appropriately named Sharp Top Mountain. At 3,875 feet, Sharp Top is one of Virginia's most popular mountains, and from which a stone was removed and contributed to the Washington Monument construc-

THE BASICS

Start: From the Troutville Town Park.

Length: 63 miles

Terrain: First half is gently rolling. The climb up the Blue Ridge is extremely challenging and not suitable for beginners or casual cyclists. Advanced difficulty.

Traffic and hazards: Use caution on Route 11. Blue Ridge Parkway can be busy at certain times of the year, particularly in autumn. Use caution for the 0.2-mile stretch of Route 460 when you exit the Blue Ridge Parkway. Entire route is paved and in good condition.

Getting there: From I-81, take exit 150B to Route 11 North. Go 2.2 miles to Troutville Town Park on the right. Plenty of free parking.

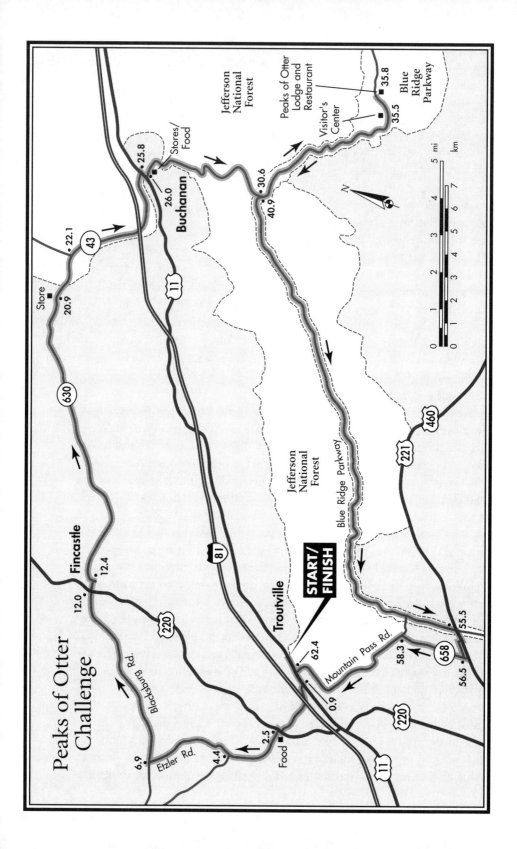

Peaks of Otter Challenge

0.0 Turn left on Rt. 11 South out of Troutville Town Park.

0.9 Turn right on Valley Rd./Rt. T779.

2.5 Turn right at the stop sign on Rt. 220, then make a quick left on Catawba Rd./ Rt. 779. Getty Food Mart is at this intersection.

4.4 Turn right on Etzler Rd./Rt. 672.

6.9 Turn right on Blacksburg Rd./Rt. 630.

12.0 Go straight at the stop sign on W. Main St. Cross Botetourt Rd.

12.1 On your left is the Courthouse Complex of Fincastle, visitor's center, Old Jail, and Botetourt County Museum. Continue straight to stay on the route.

12.4 Turn left on Hancock St./Rt. 630. In about ½ mile, the road name changes to Springwood Rd./Rt. 630.

20.9 Riverside Grocery is on the left. In ¼ mile, you'll cross the James River.

22.1 Turn right at the stop sign on Rt. 43. Caution, faster traffic.

25.8 Turn right at the stop sign on Rts. 11 and 43 South. Cross the James River again.

26.0 Turn left after bridge on Rt. 43. Burger King and an Exxon Food Store are at the turn. *Note:* If you want to ride through the town of Buchanan for its stores and restaurants, don't make the turn; instead, continue straight past Burger King on Rt. 11 South.

26.6 Begin ascending the Blue Ridge.

30.6 Turn left at the Blue Ridge Parkway Entrance. At the end of the ramp, turn left to enter the parkway and travel north.

35.5 Continue straight for the Peaks of Otter Lodge. On the left are the visitor's center and rest rooms; on the right are the campground, office, and camp store.

35.8 Turn right into the Peaks of Otter Lodge for its accommodations, restaurant, rest rooms, lake, etc. To continue the challenge, turn left when leaving the lodge and head south on the Blue Ridge Parkway.

40.9 Continue straight on the parkway at the Rt. 43 junction from Buchanan.

55.5 Turn right to exit the parkway. At the stop sign, turn right on Rt. 460 West toward Roanoke. Caution, faster traffic.

55.9 Turn right on Knoll Rd./Rt. 1430. Continue 0.1 mile to the stop sign, then turn left on Knollwood Dr./Rt. 1413.

56.5 Turn right on Laymantown Rd./Rt. 659. Just after the turn, continue straight on Rt. 658. Rt. 659 bears left.

58.3 Turn left at the stop sign on Mountain Pass Rd./Rt. 652.

62.3 Rough railroad tracks crossing.

62.4 Turn right at the stop sign on Lee Highway/Rt. 11 North.

62.9 Turn right into Troutville Town Park.

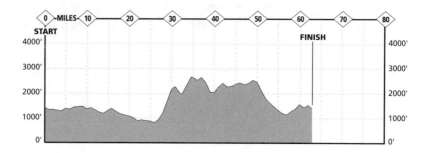

tion in 1852. Too tired to hike? There's a shuttle that will take you nearly to the top. Peaks of Otter also offers camping, a camp store, and a visitor's center with rest rooms, and a variety of nature exhibits.

Your ride down the Blue Ridge Parkway remains challenging as you traverse along the ridgeline but are constantly rewarded with magnificent vistas to the north and south. As you approach Roanoke, you begin losing elevation and finally receive the payback from all the earlier climbing. On Mountain Pass Road, you'll skirt the Jefferson National Forest and are treated to more great views of the Roanoke Valley. After more coasting, you're dropped off on Route 11 in Troutville, only ½ mile from the start. And, as amazingly rural as the challenge is, Roanoke, the "Capital of the Blue Ridge," lies just 10 miles to the southwest. Having something that appeals to everyone, Roanoke makes a wonderful base for further exploration of Botetourt County and the Blue Ridge.

LOCAL INFORMATION

♦ Botetourt County Chamber of Commerce, P.O. Box 81, Fincastle, VA 24090, 540–473–8280.

LOCAL EVENTS/ATTRACTIONS

♦ Botetourt County Museum, Courthouse Square, Fincastle, VA 24090, 540–473–8394 or 540–473–3713. Local history.
♦ Fincastle Festival, mid-September, 540–473–3077. Old-fashioned outdoor fair.

RESTAURANTS

♦ Peaks of Otter Lodge, on the Blue Ridge Parkway, 540–586–1081. Serves breakfast, lunch, and dinner.
♦ Kaleidoscope Cafe, Main St., Buchanan, 540–254–3019. Lunch and good coffees.

A peaceful moment at the Peaks of Otter Lodge.

ACCOMMODATIONS

♦ Peaks of Otter Lodge, on the Blue Ridge Parkway, P.O. Box 489, Bedford, VA 24523, 800–542–5927. Rustic hotel in beautiful, natural setting. Mid-range.
♦ Holiday Inn Express, Troutville, 3139 Lee Highway S., Troutville, VA 24175, 800–465–4329. Low-end.

BIKE SHOP

♦ Cardinal Bicycle, 2901 Orange Ave., N.E., Roanoke, VA 24012, 540–344–2453.

REST ROOMS

♦ At the start in Troutville Town Park
♦ Mile 2.5: at Getty Food Mart
♦ Mile 12.1: at several restaurants and museum in Fincastle
♦ Mile 26.0: at Burger King or various restaurants in Buchanan
♦ Mile 35.5: at Peaks of Otter Visitor Center
♦ Mile 35.8: at Peaks of Otter Lodge

MAP

♦ DeLorme *Virginia Atlas and Gazetteer* maps 42, 43, 52, 53

33

Chatham Cruise

The Chatham Cruise is a delightful rural tour through the tobacco-growing region of Virginia's largest county, Pittsylvania. Based in the tranquil town of Chatham, the Cruise's terrain is mild but offers several challenges as it winds its way through the rolling foothills just east of the Blue Ridge Mountains. Stop in Gretna for lunch and take in historic Yates Tavern, circa 1750. Finish the cruise in Chatham, then celebrate at the Streetcar Diner, an authentic streetcar eatery and one of only twenty left in the United States.

Founded in 1777, Chatham has a reputation as being the prettiest little town in Virginia's Southside. With only 1,300 residents, the town is indeed small but appealing. Lacking the attractions, shopping, and entertainment of typical tourist towns, Chatham offers a world of quiet pleasures and small delights. The favorite pastime here is to stroll the town's streets taking in the well-preserved architecture, many with a Victorian ambience. If you feel that you've somehow stepped back in time, well, consider that Chatham's modest prosperity, stability, and continuity of population and environment have existed for more than 200 years without interruption. If Chathamites have their way, and let's hope they do, the town will remain this way.

There are several stores around town if you need to pick up food and drink. The "57" Superette is on the route less than a mile from town. After that, there is nothing until Gretna, a little past the midpoint of the cruise.

You will be riding in the foothills of the Blue Ridge, but the terrain is actually quite mild. You'll enjoy some long, flat segments, some small roller-coaster hills, and several more challenging hills that will get the heart pumping.

Although the Blue Ridge Mountains come into view while cycling north, you won't have anything to climb that even resembles a mountain.

The Chatham Cruise is entirely in Pittsylvania County, the heart of the state's tobacco-growing region, a fact that will become clearly evident on this tour. Most of your riding will be on paved and low-traffic roads bordering the region's numerous tobacco farms, pastures, and hay fields. Indeed, the Pittsylvania countryside is synonymous with Chatham's quietness and charm.

In Gretna, you can stop at a Dairy Queen, pick up deli food at Food Lion, or have lunch at the Crossroads Restaurant as you're leaving town. When you're ready to turn left on Route 676 at mile 28.0, consider a detour to Yates Tavern. Built around 1750 and on the

THE BASICS

Start: From the Farmer's Market parking lot on Main Street in Chatham.

Length: 40 miles

Terrain: Gently rolling. Several long, flat stretches and a half dozen or so short, steep hills provide some challenge.

Traffic and hazards: All roads are paved and in good shape. Use caution when riding on Route 40 approaching Gretna. Just past mile 31.0, there is a narrow one-lane bridge at the bottom of a hill.

Getting there: Follow Route 29 Business into Chatham, where it becomes Main Street. The Farmer's Market is about 300 yards north of the intersection of Main Street and Depot Street/Route 57. The lot is directly across from Center Street/Route 1406. Free parking.

National Register of Historic Places, Yates Tavern is believed to be the only historic dwelling in the state to be constructed with overhangs. These 10-inch jetties on the second floor provided additional living space, as the tavern was once an "ordinary," a frontier bed-and-breakfast. The tavern is located 0.3 mile down Route 29 from the intersection. Cycle with caution, however, as Route 29 Business soon turns to a faster four-lane highway just before the tavern.

On your way back into Chatham, you'll cycle past many grand homes. If you're too tired for a walking tour, consider a continuation of the cruise down Main Street for a mile or two to take in more of Chatham's impressive houses and B&Bs. After your ride, be sure to stop in at the Streetcar Diner. With only about twenty such diners left in the country, the Chatham Streetcar Diner is a gem, serving up simple but delicious sandwiches at small-town prices. Throw in the streetcar charm, and your seemingly ordinary lunch will inevitably transform into a memorable dining experience.

LOCAL INFORMATION

♦ Pittsylvania County Chamber of Commerce, 38 North Main St., Chatham, VA 24531, 804–432–1650.

0.0 Turn left out of the Farmer's Market parking lot on Main St. Go 0.1 mile, then turn right on Depot St./Rt. 57 West. In about ½ mile, "57" Superette will be on the right. Depot St. becomes Callands Rd.

1.2 Turn left on Hunts Town Rd./Rt. 1425. In 0.2 mile, continue straight to stay on Hunts Town Rd.

1.6 Turn left on Hickory Rd./Rt. 612.

4.5 Continue straight on Mitchell Rd./Rt. 612.

5.8 Bear right on N. Flint Hill Rd./Rt. 829.

8.8 Turn right at the stop sign on Strawberry Rd./Rt. 750.

9.5 Go straight at the stop sign on Green Pond Rd./Rt. 750. Cross Rt. 57.

13.9 Turn right at the stop sign on Anderson Mill Rd./Rt. 649.

15.1 Go straight at the stop sign to stay on Anderson Mill Rd./Rt. 649. Cross Rt. 799. The Climax Mini-Mart is on the left at this intersection.

18.3 Turn left at the stop sign on Green Bay Rd./Rt. 797.

20.0 Turn right at the stop sign on Piney Rd./Rt. 790.

21.9 Turn right on Terry Rd./Rt. 791.

24.1 Turn right at the stop sign on Cotton Patch Rd./Rt. 672.

24.3 Turn left on Lotus Dr./Rt. 935.

26.2 Turn right on Gretna Rd./Rt. 40 East. Caution, there is a little more traffic here. There is a Citgo Mart, a One Stop Mart, and a Dairy Queen at this intersection. After you cross Highway 29, the road name changes to Vaden Dr.

27.4 On the left is a shopping plaza with a Subway and a Food Lion/Deli.

27.5 Turn right on Main St./Rt. 29 Business. Just down the road on the right is the (budget) Gretna Motel; on the left is the Crossroads Restaurant.

28.0 Turn left on Taylor's Mill Rd./Rt. 676. *Note:* If you want to see Yates Tavern, continue straight on Rt. 29 Business. The tavern is 0.3 mile on the right. Caution, traffic can be fast. There is a turnaround just after the tavern. The detour adds 0.6 mile to the cruise.

31.0 Caution, one-lane bridge at the bottom of the hill.

31.9 Continue straight on Taylor's Mill Rd./Rt. 689. The road name changes soon after to Strader Rd.

33.2 Turn right at the stop sign on Chalk Level Rd./Rt. 685. Take Rt. 685 all the way into Chatham, where its name changes to Hurt St.

39.8 Turn left at the stop sign on Main St.

40.2 Turn left into the Farmer's Market parking lot.

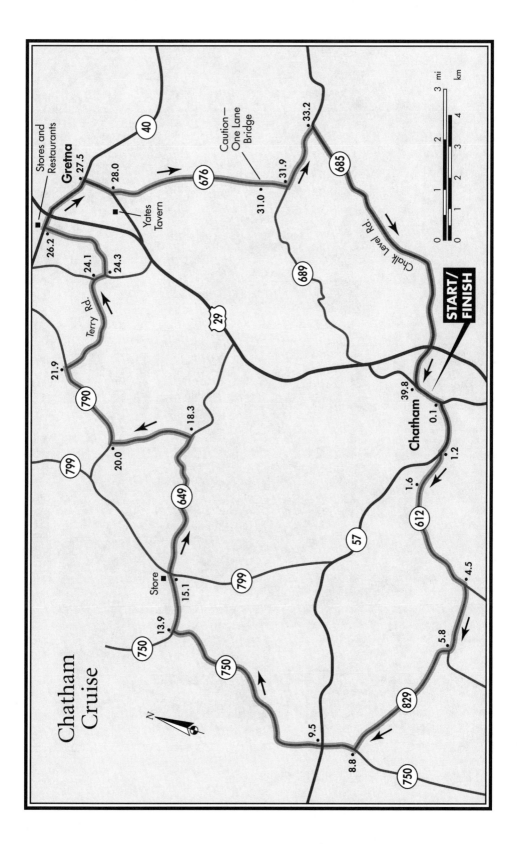

Chatham Cruise

The Streetcar Diner in Chatham is one of only twenty left in the United States.

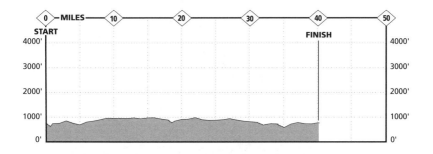

LOCAL EVENTS/ATTRACTIONS

♦ Yates Tavern, Route 29, Gretna, VA, 804–656–2958. Circa 1750 tavern on the National Register of Historic Places. Open by appointment only.
♦ Callands Festival, first Saturday in October, 804–432–1650. Celebration of the county's past with crafts, country music, fried pies, and longhunters. Free.

RESTAURANTS

♦ Chatham Streetcar Diner, 19 Main St., Chatham, 804–432–3150. Casual dining in an authentic streetcar. Open Monday to Saturday from 8:00 A.M. to 7:00 P.M.
♦ Pino's Restaurant, 14 S. Main St., Chatham, 804–432–2300. Casual pizza and Italian dishes. Open daily from 11:00 A.M. to 10:00 P.M.

ACCOMMODATIONS

♦ The Columns Guest House, 214 S. Main St., Chatham, VA 24531, 804–432–6122. Beautiful 1897 white-columned residence with curved porch. Mid-range.
♦ The Sims-Mitchell House, 242 Whittle St., Chatham, VA 24531, 800–967–2867. Civil War–era Italian villa. Mid-range.

BIKE SHOP

♦ None in the area.

REST ROOMS

♦ At the start in various places in Chatham
♦ Mile 26.2: at several convenience stores
♦ Mile 27.5: at the Crossroads Restaurant

MAP

♦ DeLorme *Virginia Atlas and Gazetteer* maps 27 and 28

Sevenmile Mountain Ramble

A ramble in the mountains? Yes, indeed. The Sevenmile Mountain Ramble, fortunately, goes around the mountain and not up it. One of the prettiest rides in the area, this ramble is also the most remote. Popular among Blacksburg cyclists, this ride rolls along scenic John's Creek for the first half of the short ride. A few hills will challenge beginners as the route swings around Sevenmile Mountain, then gradually slopes back down the valley to the village of Maggie. For those visiting Virginia Tech, this ramble makes a perfect getaway and is one of the easiest and most scenic rides in the area.

Sevenmile Mountain sits in Craig County, a rural, mountainous area tucked between Roanoke County and West Virginia. About a quarter of Craig County is agricultural, and the rest is pretty much comprised of the Jefferson National Forest. Be sure to pick up water and supplies in Blacksburg or Newport, since there are no facilities on this ramble. A Super Value grocery store is located in Newport at the junction of Routes 460 and 42. That is your last chance.

Once you drive over John's Creek Mountain, you will soon arrive at the old country store that serves as the ride's start. It will take just a few spins of your pedals to realize that the trek out here was worth the effort. Charming farmhouses dot the landscape along scenic John's Creek as it meanders through the valley. In between the hay, wheat, and cornfields graze numerous beef and dairy cattle, goats, and sheep. This is Virginia bicycling at its best. You'll even be following John's Creek downstream, making this stretch not only beautiful but also easy.

As you reach the far end of Sevenmile Mountain, you lose the farms but find yourself deeper in forest. You can still see and hear John's Creek, but you now have nature's canopy shielding you from the sun. Even though some hills now pop up, this remains a favorite segment of the ride. Once you make the turn around the mountain, you'll be gaining elevation for about 4 miles. The climbing isn't very difficult, however, as you get some relief from several plateaus and short descents. During this stretch, you'll pass Craig Springs Health Resort. The resort serves as a church camp and conference center and is more than a hundred years old. It supposedly is known for its healing cures from bathing in or drinking its mineral water. At various times throughout the year, it is open to the public for accommodations and food. Call 540–864–5768 for more information.

At about 15 miles into the ride, you'll reach its highest elevation. For the next 4 miles, you will enjoy this wonderful and gradual descent along Dick's Creek. There are no sharp turns or steep descents to worry about on your way to the bottom and the village of Maggie. Maggie does have a church and several houses, but that's it. As you cycle through Maggie and back the 1 mile to the start, you'll know that the ride's remoteness and lack of facilities are what make it so special. You will want to come back again.

THE BASICS

Start: From the parking lot of an old country store (closed) at the intersection of Routes 658 and 632.

Length: 20 miles

Terrain: First half is flat to gently rolling. Several hills starting at midpoint of ride may challenge beginners. Last 5 miles are downhill or flat.

Traffic and hazards: All roads on this route are extremely low traffic and rural. Entire route is paved and in good condition.

Getting there: From Blacksburg, take Route 460 West, then turn right on Route 42 in Newport. Go 9.7 miles, then turn left on Route 658. Go 4.2 miles to the intersection with Route 632. Park at the old store on the right.

LOCAL INFORMATION

♦ Blacksburg Regional Visitor Center, 1995 S. Main St., Suite 902, Blacksburg, VA 24060, 800–288–4061.

LOCAL EVENTS/ATTRACTIONS

♦ Newport Agricultural Fair, second weekend in August, 540–626–3186. Music, livestock and horse shows, and fireworks.

RESTAURANTS

♦ Bogen's Steakhouse and Bar, 622 N. Main St., Blacksburg, 540–953–2233. Steaks and nightly specials.

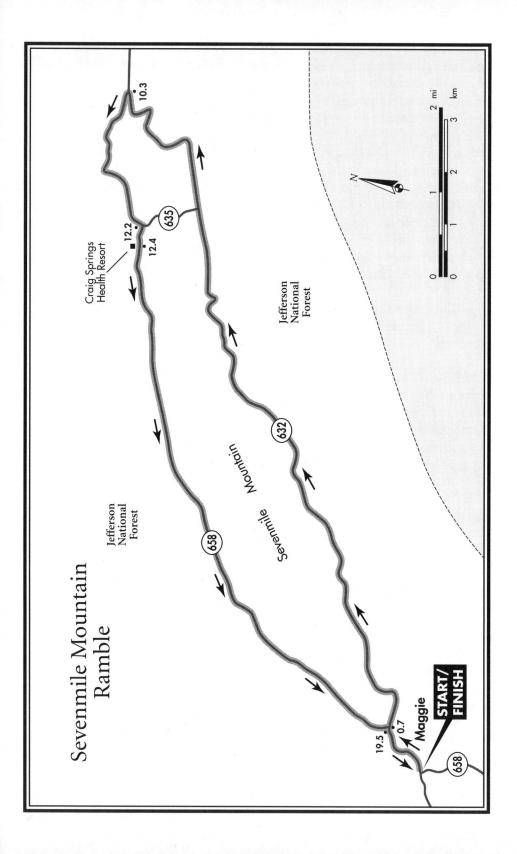

Sevenmile Mountain Ramble

Jefferson
National
Forest

Craig Springs
Health Resort

12.2
12.4

10.3

635

658

632

Sevenmile Mountain

Jefferson National Forest

658

Maggie

19.5

0.7

START/
FINISH

N

2 mi
1
km
3
2
1
1
0
0

0.0 Turn right out of the parking lot on Rt. 632.

0.7 Bear right to stay on Rt. 632 East.

10.3 Turn left at the stop sign on Rt. 658.

12.2 Bear right to stay on Rt. 658.

12.4 Craig Springs Health Resort is on the right.

19.5 Turn right on Rt. 632 in the village of Maggie.

20.2 End the ride at the parking lot on the left.

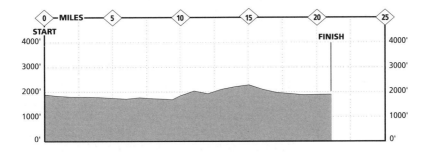

ACCOMMODATIONS

♦ Best Western Red Lion Inn, 900 Plantation Rd., Blacksburg, VA 24060. 540–552–7770. Mid-range.

BIKE SHOP

♦ East Coasters Cycling and Fitness, 1301 N. Main St., Blacksburg, 540–951–2369.

REST ROOMS

♦ None available

MAP

♦ DeLorme *Virginia Atlas and Gazetteer* map 41

Mountain Lake Challenge

D on't let the mileage for this ride fool you. *This Mountain Lake ride is a challenge. In fact, Tour de France champion Lance Armstrong used this very same climb to establish a strong lead in the 1996 Tour Dupont. This challenge, designed for the strong cyclist, offers a pleasant warm-up as the route follows Spruce Run on its way down to the New River. If you're not warmed up by this point, you'll surely be in the next 10 miles as you climb more than 3,200 feet up Salt Pond Mountain. You have a chance to rest those aching legs on top at beautiful Mountain Lake Resort. Overlooking one of only two natural lakes in Virginia, this charming resort built from native stone is popular as the site of the movie* Dirty Dancing. *It's unlikely, however, that after this climb you will be doing any dancing, dirty or otherwise.*

Popular with New River Valley cyclists, the Mountain Lake Challenge is often ridden in the opposite direction. But the challenge as presented, although requiring a more difficult ascent of Salt Pond Mountain, offers a welcome warm-up along Spruce Run and a fantastic finish down Clover Hollow Road. Whichever direction you choose, you're in for a good workout.

If you haven't stocked up on food and water, you'll get a chance early on. When you reach Route 460, a Super Value grocery store will be on your right. Be sure you have plenty of fluids for the climbs.

For the first 6 miles, you'll simply follow Route 605 as it winds its way down the valley between Gap and Spruce mountains. This is a very pleasant, low-traffic, and gradual-downhill spin along Spruce Run. After the creek empties in the New River, you'll follow the river a bit before beginning some moderate climbing at the base of Salt Pond Mountain. When you cross Highway 460, the terrain takes a short dip, then becomes increasingly difficult as you continue up the slope. Grades start out at 4 to 5 percent and gradually increase to 10 percent. (A 10 percent grade is equivalent to 100 feet of vertical gain over 1,000 feet of horizontal distance.) Usually, steep grades such as this are doable because they are seldom steep for very long. But once the grade reaches 5 percent on this challenge, there are more than 3 miles left to the top, with increasingly higher grades as you continue the climb. Don't say I didn't warn you.

Mountain Lake Resort sits atop

Salt Lake Mountain and overlooks one of just two natural lakes in the state of Virginia. The lake, which also is the highest lake in Virginia, at nearly 4,000 feet, was formed when a rock slide dammed the north end of the valley. Underground streams feed the lake, which keeps the water temperature from rarely exceeding 70 degrees Fahrenheit. There's something for everyone at Mountain Lake Resort: hiking, boating, fishing, bike rental, tennis, health club, carriage and pony rides, children's activities, and more. The Sunday brunch is legendary, but reservations are highly recommended. If the resort looks familiar, it's because the movie *Dirty Dancing* was filmed here in 1986. Personally, I would rather watch Lance Armstrong make the climb to the lake than Patrick Swayze strut his stuff around it. Enjoy your time here.

It might be wise to perform a little brake check prior to this descent. You'll be heading down Mountain Lake Road/Route 700, which, although not as steep as your ascent, twists and turns and attempts to distract you with extraordinary vistas. Take your time and enjoy the views from several of the scenic pull-offs. After your descent, you'll encounter some rollers as you make your way up a valley formed by Johns Creek Mountain on your left and Clover Hollow Mountain on your right. You'll then make the right turn onto Route 601 and begin the home stretch back to Newport. This pleasant country road is barely wide enough for one vehicle, which is the number of cars you can expect to see on this wonderful stretch. For 4 to 5 miles, you'll gently glide down the valley alongside Clover Hollow Creek. Perhaps this isn't a challenging ending to a beautiful ride, but it is a beautiful ending to a most challenging ride.

0.0 Head left out of the Newport Recreation Center on Rt. 42 West.

0.4 Bear left to stay on Rt. 42.

0.8 Go straight at the stop sign on Spruce Run Rd/.Rt. 605. Use caution when crossing Highway 460. Super Value grocery store is on the right at the intersection.

7.1 Turn right at the stop sign on Goodwins Ferry Rd./Rt. 625.

9.3 Continue straight. Route number changes to 682.

9.5 Turn left on Eggleston Rd./Rt. 730.

10.2 Turn right on Sinking Creek Rd./Rt. 772. Don't be confused by Rt. 612, which crosses Rt. 772 right after the turn. Just after you pass Rt. 612, there is an unnamed store on your right. After the store, you'll descend for about ¾ mile. Caution, tight turns at the bottom.

13.2 Turn left at the stop sign on Lebanon Rd./Rt. 771.

13.3 Bear right on the short connector road to Highway 460. Go straight on Doe Creek Rd./Rt. 613. Use caution while crossing Highway 460.

18.2 Turn left on Mountain Lake Rd./Rt. 613. In less than 0.1 mile, turn right on Hotel Circle to enter Mountain Lake Resort. Upon leaving, go back to Mountain Lake Rd. and turn left. When you reach Rt. 613, the route you just climbed, go straight on Rt. 700. Use caution on the descent—switchbacks.

23.0 Turn left on Rocky Sink Rd./Rt. 602.

24.6 Caution, sharp turn to the right after the descent.

25.1 Turn left at the stop sign on Rt. 602.

27.7 Turn right at the stop sign on Rt. 601.

32.0 Bear left on Clover Hollow Rd./Rt. 601.

32.8 Turn right on Blue Grass Trail/Rt. 42 West.

33.0 Turn left into the Newport Recreation Center parking lot.

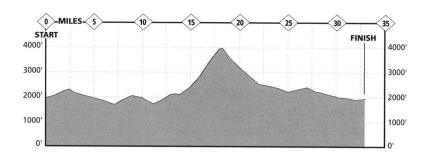

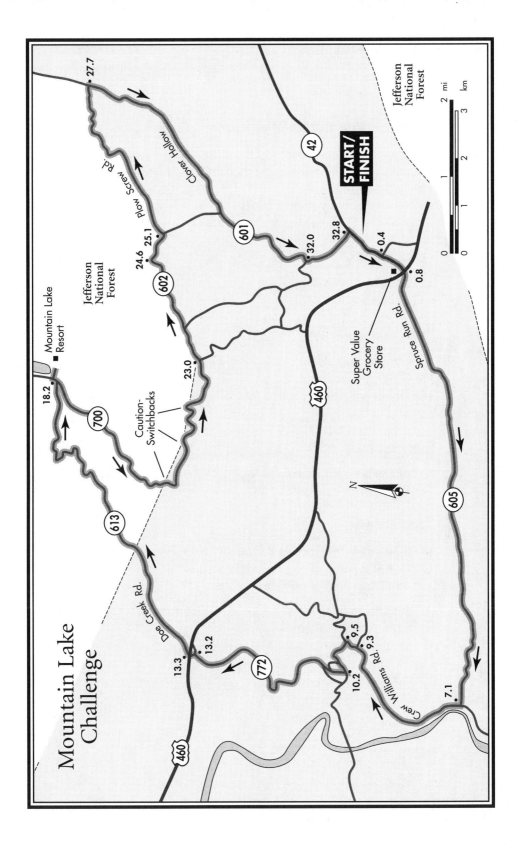

Mountain Lake Challenge

START/FINISH

Jefferson National Forest

Jefferson National Forest

Mountain Lake Resort

Super Value Grocery Store

Spruce Run Rd.

Plow Screw Rd.

Clover Hollow

Doe Creek Rd.

Crew Williams Rd.

Caution- Switchbacks

27.7
32.0
32.8
0.4
0.8
24.6
25.1
23.0
18.2
13.2
13.3
9.5
9.3
10.2
7.1

42
601
602
700
613
460
772
460
605

N

2 mi

km

3

2

1

1

0

0

LOCAL INFORMATION

♦ Blacksburg Regional Visitors Center, 1195 S. Main St., Suite 902, Blacksburg, VA 24060, 800–288–4061.

LOCAL EVENTS/ATTRACTIONS

♦ Mountain Lake and Pembroke Oktoberfest, last two Saturdays in September and every Friday and Saturday in October, at the Mountain Lake Resort, 800–346–3334.

♦ Cascades Recreation Area, Pembroke. Four-mile round-trip hiking trail to scenic 68-foot Cascades waterfall. Picnic areas.

RESTAURANTS

♦ Macado's, 922 University City Blvd., Blacksburg, 540–953–2700. Sandwiches, beer, and fun.

ACCOMMODATIONS

♦ Mountain Lake Resort, 115 Hotel Circle, Pembroke, VA 24136, 800–346–3334. Upscale.

♦ Comfort Inn, 3705 S. Main St., Blacksburg, VA 24060, 800–228–5150. Mid-range.

BIKE SHOP

♦ East Coasters Cycling and Fitness, 1301 N. Main St., Blacksburg, VA 24060, 540–951–2369.

REST ROOMS

♦ At the start in the Newport Recreation Center
♦ Mile 0.8: at Super Value grocery store on the right
♦ Mile 18.2: at the Mountain Lake Resort

MAP

♦ DeLorme *Virginia Atlas and Gazetteer* map 41

Blue Ridge Challenge

T he Blue Ridge Challenge offers the cyclist magnificent scenery, a sampling of its rich folk heritage, and some mean mountain climbing. Designed for the fit and strong cyclist, the challenge lets you experience the quiet Franklin County rural life as you roll through Ferrum, Callaway, and Algoma. Be prepared for the climb of your life on your way up Bent Mountain. Follow the spectacular Blue Ridge Parkway for 15 miles, and enjoy the thrilling descent down Five-Mile Mountain, as the Tour Dupont riders did several years ago. End your ride with a visit to the extraordinary Blue Ridge Institute and Museum to experience past and present Blue Ridge folklore.

The Blue Ridge Challenge is a variation of a ride submitted to me by Tom and Carol Bussey of the Franklin Freewheelers Bicycle Club. Their club ride begins and ends in Callaway, making it a little shorter and eliminating some climbing but still a fine challenge. I chose the tiny town of Ferrum for my start, simply because it is home to the Blue Ridge Institute and Museum at Ferrum College. For visitors coming into Franklin County to ride this challenge, your trip here isn't complete without a stop at this fine museum. More about it later.

Be sure to pick up some water and energy snacks in Ferrum, because you will need them for this ride. There is a convenience store early on as soon as you get on Route 40. You'll have just one more opportunity in Callaway. The challenge starts right after you pass Ferrum College. A good ¾-mile climb up Ferrum Mountain Road will get you warmed up. Control your descent, however, as there is a succession of tight turns.

You can expect flat to rolling terrain on your way to Callaway as well as your last opportunity to load up. The A&A Market at the intersection with

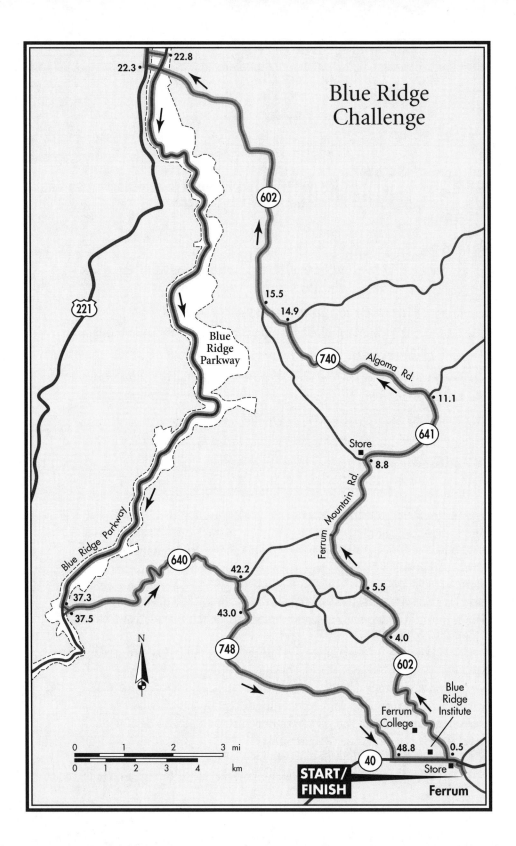

Blue Ridge
Challenge

221

602

740   Algoma Rd.

641

22.3 •   • 22.8

15.5 •
   • 14.9

Blue
Ridge
Parkway

• 11.1

Store
■
   • 8.8

Ferrum Mountain Rd.

Blue Ridge Parkway

640
   • 42.2

37.3 •
37.5 •

   • 5.5

43.0 •

   • 4.0

N

748

602

Blue
Ridge
Institute

Ferrum
College ■

0   1   2   3 mi
0   1   2   3   4 km

48.8 •
   ■
   • 0.5

START/
FINISH

40   Store ■

Ferrum

0.0 Turn right out of the Ferrum Post Office. Go across the railroad tracks, then bear right on Timberline Rd./Rt. 623. Pass "77" Restaurant on left.

0.2 Bear left at the Y onto Timberline. Go a short distance to the stop sign at Rt. 40. Turn left on Rt. 40 West. After 0.1 mile, look for Fuds Convenience Store on your left.

0.5 Turn right on Ferrum Mountain Rd./Rt. 602. Ferrum College is on the left.

1.8 Begin your descent. Caution, lots of twists and turns on this one.

4.0 Bear right to stay on Ferrum Mountain Rd./Rt. 602.

5.5 Bear right to stay on Ferrum Mountain Rd./Rt. 602.

8.8 Turn right at the stop sign on Callaway Rd./Rt. 641. A&A Market is at this intersection.

11.1 Bear left on Algoma Rd./Rt. 740.

14.9 Turn left at the stop sign on Rt. 739.

15.5 Turn right on Callaway Rd./Rt. 602. Start ascending Bent Mountain.

22.3 Turn right at the stop sign on Bent Mountain Rd./Rt. 221 North.

22.5 Turn right on Blue Ridge Parkway Entrance Rd.

22.8 Turn right at the stop sign on Blue Ridge Parkway South.

37.3 Turn left off the parkway on River Ridge Rd.

37.5 Turn left on Franklin Pike/Rt. 640. In about a mile, begin descent. Caution, switchbacks.

42.2 Turn right on Turners Creek Rd./Rt. 640.

43.0 Go straight on Turners Creek Rd./Rt. 748. (Rt. 640 bears left.) Phoebe Needles Retreat and Conference Center is on the right. Caution, steep descent ahead.

47.0 Go straight at the stop sign on Turners Creek Rd./Rt. 748.

48.8 Turn left at the stop sign on Franklin St./Rt. 40 East. Caution, faster traffic.

49.5 Blue Ridge Institute is on your left, and the Farm Museum is on your right.

50.0 Turn right on Timberline Rd. and continue through the town of Ferrum.

50.3 Bear left at the stop sign, then cross tracks to the Ferrum Post Office on your left.

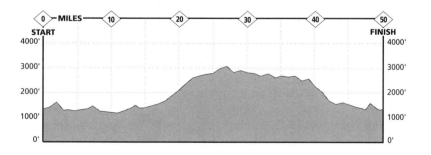

Start: From the Ferrum Post Office.

Length: 50 miles

Terrain: Mountainous. Advanced difficulty. Not suitable for beginners.

Traffic and hazards: All roads on this route are low traffic and rural. The exception is the Blue Ridge Parkway, which at certain times (particularly in autumn) can be heavily traveled. Use extreme caution when descending Ferrum Road/Route 602 and when descending Route 640 when leaving the Blue Ridge Parkway.

Getting there: From Route 220 Business in Rocky Mount, take Route 40 West approximately 10 miles to Route 623 (Timberline Road). Follow Timberline ¼ mile to a Y. Bear left and cross railroad tracks. The Ferrum Post Office is on the left. Park in the gravel auxiliary lot below the main building by the railroad tracks.

Route 641 should meet your needs. Last chance, folks. The real challenge lies just up the road.

The climb to Adney Gap and the Blue Ridge Parkway begins just after you return to Route 602. It starts off gradually, about a 2 percent grade, and remains that way for 2 miles or so. You'll then notice a slight increase in grade—to 3, then 4, then 5. . . . By the time you're nearing the parkway, the gradient is a difficult 7 percent, and you've been climbing for more than 6 miles.

You will feel relieved once you reach the Blue Ridge Parkway. However, don't get too relaxed, since the climbing continues for a while longer. Whether climbing or coasting, it's hard not to enjoy this fascinating "high" road. The parkway follows mountain crests for 470 miles from the Shenandoah National Park in Virginia to the Great Smoky Mountains National Park in North Carolina and Tennessee. The park is like a long museum corridor, with nature's most scenic treasures magnificently displayed at every turn. Expect to be challenged here, but also to be spiritually renewed by this wonderful escape from the pace of the modern world.

Leaving the parkway, you'll coast down Five-Mile Mountain on Franklin Pike, the same descent used by Tour Dupont a few years back. Remember, however, that you are not in that race. Some very tight turns must be negotiated, or your bike may end up in the scrap yard along with the other hundred or so junk cars you'll pass halfway down the mountain. After you turn on Turner's Creek Road, you'll crest a small hill and see Phoebe Needles Retreat and Conference Center on your right. Use caution on your descent after the retreat, as there is one more tight turn to negotiate.

Just before you get back to Ferrum, you'll pass Ferrum College on the left. Founded in 1913, Ferrum is a private college affiliated with the Methodist Church. On the Ferrum campus is the renowned Blue Ridge Institute and Museum. The gallery exhibits rotate each spring but always focus on regional folk traditions. When I visited, the history of the banjo was showcased.

Adjacent to the gallery is the Blue Ridge Farm Museum. Here, an 1800 Virginia-German farmstead has been re-created. Costumed interpreters perform hand spinning, open-hearth cooking, and other farm and household chores. Hands-on activities and lectures round out this unique opportunity to learn and experience Blue Ridge traditions.

LOCAL INFORMATION

♦ Franklin County Chamber of Commerce, 261 Franklin St., Rocky Mount, VA 24151, 540–483–9542.

LOCAL EVENTS/ATTRACTIONS:

♦ Blue Ridge Folklife Festival, fourth Saturday in October, 540–365–4416. Virginia's largest celebration of regional folklife. At the Blue Ridge Institute and Museum at Ferrum College.

RESTAURANTS

♦ "77" Restaurant, 4477 Timberline Rd., Ferrum, 540–365–7197.

ACCOMMODATIONS

♦ Old Spring Farm Bed and Breakfast, 7629 Charity Highway, Route 40, Ferrum, VA 24088, 540–930–3404. An 1883 working farm. Mid-range.

BIKE SHOP

♦ No local shops.

REST ROOMS

♦ Mile 0.4: Fuds Convenience Store
♦ Mile 8.8: A&A Market
♦ Mile 49.5: Blue Ridge Institute

MAP

♦ DeLorme *Virginia Atlas and Gazetteer* maps 26 and 42

Mabry Mill Challenge

The Mabry Mill Challenge takes the cyclist through scenic Patrick County, which is famous for its peach orchards. Some strenuous climbing is required to reach the Blue Ridge Parkway, where cyclists can stop at Chateau Morrisette, Virginia's largest winery. Cycle a few miles down one of America's most scenic roads and visit Mabry Mill, a gristmill built in the early 1900s. The mill and associated exhibits are one of the parkway's most popular attractions as well as one of the most photographed places on the East Coast. Hang on for a thrilling descent past the Pinnacles of Dan and along rhododendron-draped mountain streams back to the rural county seat of Stuart.

If you're attempting this challenge in one day, be sure to stop at the Farmers Food Market grocery store near the parking lot. Most of the climbing on this challenge is on the first half, so stock up with necessary water and food at the start.

You'll be riding Route 8/58 out of Stuart. Because both routes are funneled into one road, this segment can be busy. Don't expect traffic jams, however; there are only 18,000 residents in the entire county. Fortunately, the ride out is on a nice shoulder. After a few miles, Route 58 will veer left, and you'll stay on Route 8 all the way to the Blue Ridge Parkway. Traffic on Route 8 is fast but light, and an occasional shoulder makes it safe for experienced riders.

You'll soon pass many of the orchards for which Patrick County is well noted. In season, take the opportunity for refreshment at several roadside stands along the way. Another chance is at Orchard View Country Store just before Route 40 veers off to the right. Just past the Route 40 turnoff, the Dutchies View Bed & Breakfast will come up on your right. Located on a high grassy knob with terrific panoramic views, this B&B, run by Maarten and Hermien Ankersmit, is the perfect place for some warm Dutch hospitality.

The terrain now gets hilly and, in a few miles, mountainous. You'll have at least 4 miles of climbing at grades up to 7 percent on your way to Tuggle's Gap and the Blue Ridge Parkway. If it's any consolation, the climb is gorgeous. Mature trees blanket the route, offering shade any time of the day. It's one of the most beautiful areas of the ride and takes the bite out of the grueling climb.

The first few miles on the Blue Ridge Parkway are noted for more climbing and Rocky Knob, which rises like the cresting of a wave to overlook Rock Castle Gorge. In addition to a number of scenic overlooks that capture Rocky Knob, the next few miles will bring you to The Rocky Knob cabins and the information center. The cabins are a pleasant overnight stop if you plan on making the challenge a two-day affair.

After 6 miles on the parkway, look for Route 726 to the right. It leads to Chateau Morrisette, the largest winery in Virginia. Besides good wine, the winery offers tours, tastings, scenic views, a gourmet market, and elegant dining. It's open for lunch Wednesday to Sunday and for dinner on Friday and Saturday. Easy on the wine, though—there's still a lot of challenge left.

Farther down the parkway is the magnificent Mabry Mill. Born in Patrick County, Ed Mabry was one in a long line of Mabrys in this part of Virginia. He began construction of the mill in 1903 and first used it as a wheelwright and blacksmith shop, then a sawmill. From 1910 to 1935 he operated it as a gristmill while adding on a woodshop. During the summer, demonstrations are given, designed to reflect the hard work and self-sufficiency of our Appalachian ancestors. It's definitely worth a stop and a few pictures.

A few miles after the mill, there is an exit for Meadows of Dan. Just a few yards east and west on Route 58, you'll find a general store, several restaurants, a campground, and a hotel. You won't have many opportunities once you leave here, so stock up.

THE BASICS

Start: From the public parking lot behind the Virginian Hotel and adjacent to the police station in downtown Stuart.

Length: 64 miles

Terrain: Hilly to mountainous. Toughest challenge in the book. Only the strongest cyclists should consider completing the ride in one day.

Traffic and hazards: Route 8 out of Stuart is relatively low traffic but fast. Use caution. Most of the descents are technical. Maintain control, especially on Route 614, when leaving the parkway. Entire route is paved and in good condition.

Getting there: Come in to Stuart on either Route 8 or 58, which run together. In town Route 8/58 is called Blue Ridge Street. From the east, take Blue Ridge Street to Main Street. Go straight through the stoplight at Main Street, then make the next left on Slusher Street. Go ½ block to the public parking lot on the right. Parking is free and plentiful.

0.0 Turn left out of the parking lot on Blue Ridge St./Rts. 8 and 58. Farmers Food Market is located just below the lot.

1.3 Citgo Food Market is on the left.

3.1 Bear right on Woolwine Hwy./Rt. 8 North. Howell's Grocery is on the left after the turn.

11.8 Bear left to stay on Rt. 8. Rock Castle Cafe is located at the turn.

12.9 Orchard View Country Store is on the right.

13.3 Continue straight on Rt. 8. Rt. 40 bears right. Just past this intersection is Dutchies View B&B on the right.

19.6 Tuggle's Gap Restaurant is on the right.

19.8 Turn right to the Blue Ridge Parkway entrance. When you reach the Parkway, turn right at the stop sign to head south.

21.8 Camping available on right at Rocky Knob.

23.7 Rocky Knob Information Center is on the right.

26.3 Chateau Morrisette Winery is on the right. Exit at Rt. 726, then immediate left on Winery Rd./Rt. 777. The entrance is 300 yards down the road.

30.8 Mabry Mill is on the left. There is a small museum as well as rest rooms, short hiking trails, and a restaurant.

32.3 Continue straight on the parkway. Exit at Rt. 58 if you want to stop at stores or restaurants in Meadows of Dan.

38.5 Exit left off the parkway on the unmarked road. This is at mile marker 183.9. Go a short way to the stop sign. Turn right on Squirrel Spur Rd./Rt. 614.

38.9 Turn left on Squirrel Spur Rd./Rt. 614. Some great views of the Pinnacles of Dan on your left, then a steep, winding descent. Use caution.

45.0 Turn left at the stop sign on Ararat Hwy./Rt. 773.

49.6 Turn left at the stop sign on Claudville Hwy./Rt. 103. Sure Stop market is on the left.

50.2 Turn left on Little Dan River Rd./Rt. 647.

50.5 Turn right on Rt. 646.

54.2 Bear left on Rt. 647.

54.7 Bear left to stay on Rt. 647.

56.4 Continue straight to go on Rt. 631 just past Mary Horner Walker Church. Turns into Dobyns Rd.

63.6 Turn left at the stop sign on N. Main St. Short, steep climb into town.

63.7 Turn left on Rye Cove St., then a quick left on Slusher St. Continue on Slusher a short distance back to the parking lot.

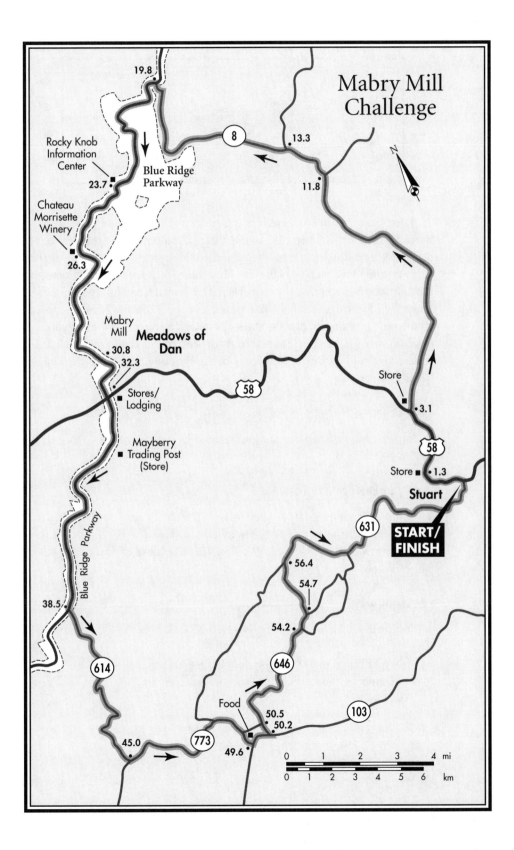

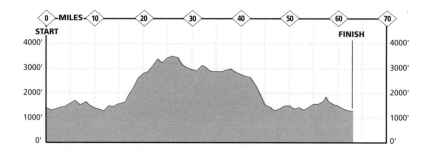

Keep your eye on your cyclocomputer for the turn off the parkway (it's unmarked and easy to miss). If you don't have a computer, try to keep track of the parkway's mileage markers. The turnoff is at mile marker 183.9. Leaving the parkway, you'll ride along a high ridge for a short while with fabulous views of the Pinnacles of Dan off to your left. Then it's a steep descent for a good 5 miles down the Blue Ridge. The hills aren't over, and you'll constantly roller coaster all the way in to Stuart, passing miles of mountain streams and more rhododendron than you've ever seen before. At the end of this challenge, you'll really deserve a cold one, or at least some of the Blushing Dog you picked up at Chateau Morrisette.

LOCAL INFORMATION

♦ Patrick County Chamber of Commerce, P.O. Box 577, Stuart, VA 24171, 540–694–6012.

LOCAL EVENTS/ATTRACTIONS

♦ Virginia Peach Festival, at the Rotary Field in Stuart, early in August, 540–694–6012. Arts and crafts, entertainment, and food.
♦ Chateau Morrisette Winery, P.O. Box 766, Meadows of Dan, VA 24120, 540–593–2865.

RESTAURANTS

♦ Coffee Break, Main St., Stuart, 540–694–4232. Where the locals start their day.
♦ Mabry Mill Restaurant, on the Blue Ridge Parkway, 540–952–2947. Open May to October.

ACCOMMODATIONS

♦ The Chocolate Moose Bed & Breakfast, P.O. Box 802, Stuart, VA 24171, 540–694–3745. This in-town B&B is run by a husband-and-wife team who are also massage therapists. Sessions can easily be arranged. They are also cyclists who have biked across the United States.

♦ Dutchies View B&B, 10448 Woolwine Highway, Woolwine, VA 24185, 540–930–3701. Dutch hosts. Mid-range.

BIKE SHOP

♦ Nothing in the county.

REST ROOMS

♦ At the start in the Farmers Food Market
♦ Mile 3.1: at Howell's Grocery
♦ Mile 11.8: at Red Castle Cafe
♦ Mile 19.6: at Tuggle's Gap Restaurant
♦ Mile 23.7: at Rocky Gap Information Center
♦ Mile 30.8: at Mabry Mill and at the Mabry Mill Restaurant
♦ Mile 32.3: at various locations at the Meadows of Dan exit off the Blue Ridge Parkway

MAP

♦ DeLorme *Virginia Atlas and Gazetteer* maps 25 and 26

New River Valley
Two-Day Challenge

T he New River Valley Challenge is a combination 43-mile hilly
road challenge and 49-mile relaxing cruise on the New River
Valley Trail. Although the challenge can be completed in one day by the
very fit cyclist, it is best when done as a two-day ride, with a night spent
in the delightful town of Galax. The first day of road riding is indeed a
challenge, taking the cyclist over the hilly terrain of Pulaski, Wythe, and
Carroll counties and past 4,500-acre Claytor Lake. Spend the night in
Galax, where you'll find several moderate hotels, a bike shop, and
numerous restaurants. Time your stay for mid-August and take in the
Old Timers Fiddlers' Convention, one of the oldest and largest such con-
ventions in the world. Enjoy your second day on the New River Trail
State Park rails-to-trail, nearly 50 miles of gorgeous trail, most of which
parallels the New River all the way back to the finish in Pulaski.

I'm not a real fan of out-and-back rides. So when I decided to include the
New River Valley Trail, I searched out a route that would create a doable loop
from Pulaski to Galax. Why include the New River Valley at all? Well, the New
River Trail is unique in that it is long for a rails-to-trail. Its 57 miles wind
through four counties, link numerous communities, and provide access to a
variety of landscapes, wildlife, and culture. The trail is a treasure.

The Xaloy access at the 2-mile marker of the trail is a good place to start the
ride. Parking, water, and rest rooms are available, and a busy section of highway
leading into Pulaski is avoided. If you need to pick up supplies before the ride,
continue north on Route 99, where you'll have plenty of options. Also, an Exxon

convenience store just 1.4 miles into the road ride has food and water.

Just a few miles into the ride, you'll cycle over Claytor Lake. Created in 1939 as a hydroelectric generating facility, the lake offers boating, swimming, camping, and fishing along its 100 miles of cove-studded shoreline. Claytor Lake dams the New River, and you'll cycle a few miles along its shores and pretty summer cottages. Enjoy this stretch of the ride, since it's one of the few flat miles on your way to Galax.

One of the tougher climbs will come when you reach Route 52. A good 3-mile ascent will bring you to the top of a ridge, where you'll glide for a while and enjoy some sweeping, panoramic views of rugged Carroll County. A slope greater than 20 percent characterizes approximately half of the county's land area. Hilly area, indeed! If you seem to be doing more climbing than coasting, well, you are. You actually gain more than 500 feet on your way to Galax, but you get it back on the trail to Pulaski.

Whether staying the night or just for lunch, Galax makes for a pleasant stop. Need a bike shop? There's one right at the Galax trailhead. Looking for something to eat or somewhere to sleep? Galax offers several choices with a lot of character. You'll pass a number of places on Route 58 on your way into town. For other services, continue past the Galax trailhead for 0.1 mile, then turn left at the light on Main Street. It's all there, packaged in a few charming town blocks.

The New River Trail is part of the rails-to-trails program and follows an abandoned railroad right-of-way. Norfolk Southern Railroad donated the land for this multiuse trail that winds through four counties. For most of its length, the trail follows the New River north. Despite its name, the New River is one of the oldest rivers in the world and one of only a handful in North America that flow north. From Galax, the trail follows Chestnut Creek for 12 miles and, later on, Claytor Lake for 1½ miles.

THE BASICS

Start: From the Pulaski–Xaloy access parking lot.

Length: 92.7 miles, 43.0 road, 49.7 rails-to-trail

Terrain: Ride is best described in two parts. First half is very hilly and suitable only for strong cyclists. Second half on the trail has flat to very mild grades. Trail is easier when cycling in the north direction, as this ride does.

Traffic and hazards: Most roads on this route are low traffic and rural. Use caution on the first mile with interstate traffic entering and exiting. The last ½ mile on Route 58 in Galax can be busy. There are several tight turns on descents. Rails-to-trail is unpaved. Hybrid and wider size tires (1¼ inches or greater) are recommended. Trail is crushed stone and can have some loose cinders or gravel in spots.

Getting there: From I–81, take exit 94 to Route 99 North toward Pulaski. Go 1.6 miles, then turn right on Xaloy Way. Go several hundred yards; trail parking is located on both sides of the road. Free parking. Rest rooms and water are available. Do not proceed on Xaloy Co. property.

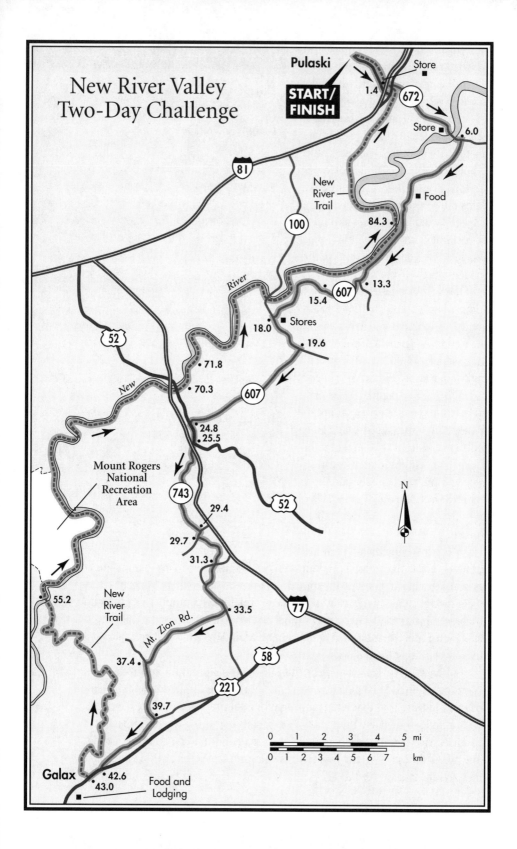

New River Valley
Two-Day Challenge

Pulaski

START/
FINISH

1.4

Store

672

Store   6.0

New
River
Trail

Food

84.3

81

100

River

15.4   607   13.3

Stores

18.0

19.6

52

71.8

New   70.3   607

24.8
25.5

Mount Rogers
National
Recreation
Area

743

29.4

52

29.7

N

31.3

55.2   New
River
Trail   33.5   77

Mt. Zion Rd.

37.4   58

221

39.7

0   1   2   3   4   5 mi
0 1 2 3 4 5 6 7 km

Galax   42.6
43.0   Food and
Lodging

0.0 Leave the parking area on Xaloy Way, then turn left on Rt. 99 South.

1.4 Exxon convenience store is on the left.

2.0 Turn left at the stop sign on unmarked F–047.

2.4 Turn right on Lowmans Ferry Rd./Rt. 672.

5.5 There is a Shop-Eez store on the right just before you cross the lake.

6.0 Turn right at the stop sign on Julia Simpkins Rd./Rt. 693. In about a mile, use caution on your descent—tight turn and narrow bridge.

9.5 There is a Stoney's Restaurant, a burger and pizza joint, on the left. Use caution again on upcoming descent back down to the New River—switchbacks.

13.3 Turn right on Boone Furnace Rd./Rt. 607.

15.4 Continue straight on Boone Furnace Rd. Changes to Rt. 608.

18.0 Turn left at the stop sign on Wysor Hwy./Rt. 100. There is a Denny's Stop & Go market across the street, and in 0.8 mile, a Shop-Eez will be on the left.

19.6 Turn right on Castleton Rd./Rt. 607.

24.8 Turn left at the stop sign on Chiswell Rd./Rt. 52.

25.5 Turn right on Pleasant View Rd./Rt. 743.

29.4 Turn right at the stop sign on Rescue Rd./Rt. 740.

29.7 Turn left at the stop sign on Oak Grove Rd./Rt. 743.

31.3 Bear right at the stop sign on Coulson Church Rd./Rt. 620.

33.5 Turn right on Mt. Zion Rd./Rt. 707.

37.4 Turn left at the stop sign on Hebron Rd./Rt. 635.

39.7 Turn right at the stop sign on Glendale Rd./Rt. 887.

42.6 Bear right at the light on E. Stuart Dr./Rt. 58. Use caution, busy stretch.

43.0 Turn right into New River Trail–Galax Access. End the road portion of the ride. New River Riders Bike Shoppe located on the left at trail access. *Note:* Some of the mile markers on the New River Trail are missing, while others are not exact. All you really need to know is that you must bear right toward Pulaski when you reach the Fries Junction. The trail, when coming from the north, splits at Fries Junction, one branch going to Fries, the other to Galax.

54.4 Enter Chestnut Creek Tunnel (193 feet long).

55.0 Begin crossing Fries Trestle (1,089 feet long).

55.2 Bear right to head north toward Pulaski.

67.2 Enter New River Tunnel (135 feet long).

70.3 Access to the Shot Tower Historical State Park.

71.8 Historic Fosters Falls Village.

84.3 Begin crossing Hiwassee Trestle across Claytor Lake (951 feet long).

92.7 End the ride at the Xaloy Way access near Pulaski.

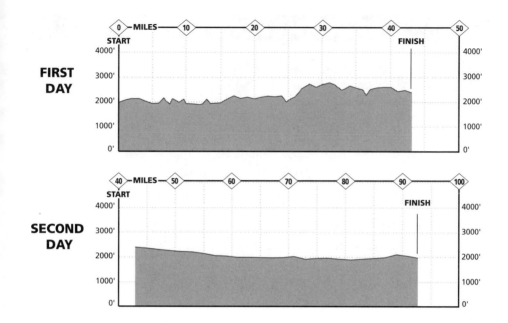

The route will pass through two tunnels, over three major bridges, and across nearly thirty other bridges and trestles on its way to Pulaski. Although the trail is flat, the surrounding landscape ranges from steep cliffs to rolling pasture and white water to lazy river. Although remote, the trail has a number of access points in case of emergencies. Nevertheless, play it safe and begin the trail ride prepared.

About halfway down the trail, you'll come to Shot Tower Historical State Park. The 75-foot-tall tower, built nearly 200 years ago, was the site of an ammunition, or lead shot, foundry. It's worth the small admission fee to climb the tower for some great views.

A little past the Shot Tower is Historic Fosters Falls Village. The village dates to the mid- to late 1800s and serves as the state park's headquarters. The village has both trail and river access and is fast becoming the recreational hub for the region. Bikes, canoes, inner tubes, and horses can be rented here. In addition, fishing, picnicking, and horseback riding are popular in this village, which has plans to preserve and protect its many historic buildings.

Although the trail is mostly on a downgrade in this direction, it does rise a little out of Claytor Lake. When you reach the "hump," it is just a few miles back to the northern trailhead. The trail is not completely finished at this time and stops at the Xaloy access, at about the 2-mile marker. Eventually, it will run 2 miles north to Pulaski Station.

Finally, a salute is due to the railroad companies that participate in the rails-to-trails program. Outstanding recreational opportunities abound because of them. Also, a salute to the communities that work so hard to make their land, history, and culture easily accessible to so many.

LOCAL INFORMATION

♦ Galax–Carroll–Grayson Chamber of Commerce, 405 N. Main St., Galax, VA 24333, 540–236–2184.
♦ Pulaski County Chamber of Commerce, 20 S. Washington Ave, Suite 1, Train Station, Pulaski, VA 24301, 540–980–1991.

LOCAL EVENTS/ATTRACTIONS

♦ Old Timers Fiddlers' Convention, Felts Park, Galax, second weekend in August, 540–236–8541. One of the oldest and largest in the world.
♦ New River Trail State Park, 176 Orphanage Drive, Fosters Falls, VA 24360, 540–699–6778.

RESTAURANTS

♦ Chubbies Cafe, Main Street, Galax, 540–236–4090. In-town spot for sandwiches and desserts.
♦ Aunt Bea's Restaurant, 526 E. Stuart, Galax, 540–236–8061.

ACCOMMODATIONS

♦ Knights Inn, 312 W. Stuart Dr., Galax, VA 24333, 540–236–5117. Low-end, in-town.
♦ Super 8, 303 N. Main St., Galax, VA 24333, 540–236–5127. Low-end, in-town.

BIKE SHOP

♦ New River Riders Bike Shoppe, 208 E. Stuart Dr., Galax, VA 24333, 540–236–5900. Located at Galax trailhead. Open Wednesday to Sunday.

REST ROOMS

♦ At the start: Xaloy Trail access
♦ Mile 1.4: at Exxon convenience store
♦ Mile 5.5: at the Shop-Eez
♦ Mile 9.5: at Stoney's Restaurant
♦ Mile 18.0: at Denny's Stop & Go
♦ Mile 42.6: at many locations in Galax
♦ Mile 45.3: at Cliffview access to trail
♦ Mile 55.8: primitive rest rooms after bridge
♦ Mile 70.3: at Shot Tower Historical State Park
♦ Mile 71.8: at Historic Fosters Falls Village
♦ Mile 88.5: at Draper Station

MAP

♦ DeLorme *Virginia Atlas and Gazetteer* maps 24, 25, 40, and 41

Burkes Garden Ramble

D*eep in the heart of Appalachia, there lies a valley that is the highest, greenest, and, some say, prettiest in the entire state of Virginia. The valley is geologically unique in that it is completely surrounded by one mountain. Nicknamed "God's Thumbprint," it indeed looks as if a large thumb made this indentation on Garden Mountain. Burkes Garden, as this valley is known, is a remote, unspoiled, pastoral paradise that is home to fewer than 300 people. And, after seeing some of those 300 residents driving horse and buggies, Burkes Garden is my choice for Virginia's best ramble.*

In 1748 a surveyor named James Burke discovered this valley while tracking elk. Burke was so impressed with his discovery and the abundant wildlife in it that he persuaded the survey team to return to this spectacular valley. When an early winter storm forced the team to halt its efforts and break camp, Burke covered some potato peels with dirt from the campsite. When the team returned the following year, a potato patch had grown, and Burkes Garden got its name.

The hardest part of this ramble is getting to the start. It is remote and requires driving up and over steep, switchback-laced Route 623. But as you drop more than 1,000 feet to the valley floor and enter this paradise, you'll forget all about the drive. Park at the general store, stop in to say hello, and pick up your water and food. There are no other facilities on the ride.

The terrain is gentle for southwestern Virginia. You'll find the western segment to be very easy, although the winds here can kick up a bit. About 260 people live in Burkes Garden now, most of them farmers. Several Amish families also make their home here. Look for their horse-drawn plows and buggies along Route 727. This peaceful community probably hasn't changed much in the last 200 years. The Lutheran Church on Route 623 has hand-chiseled German headstones dating to the 1700s. The Burkes Garden Post Office at the junction of Route 623 and 727 looks as if it hasn't even been painted since the 1700s. The entire Burkes Garden area has been designated a Historical District and National Landmark.

When you reach Route 625 and begin the eastern segment of the ramble, the terrain becomes a little more challenging. The valley floor rolls through here for about 4 miles until the sharp bend to the west on

THE BASICS

Start: From the bicycle-friendly Burkes Garden General Store.

Length: 19 miles

Terrain: Flat to gently rolling. Few hills on Route 625 will challenge beginners.

Traffic and hazards: All roads on this route are extremely low traffic and rural.

Getting there: From Route 460 Business in Tazewell, take Route 61 East for 4.8 miles. Turn right on Route 623, then go 6.4 miles to Burkes Garden General Store on the right. Cyclists are allowed to park here, although I recommend stopping in the store to offer thanks.

Burkes Garden Post Office.

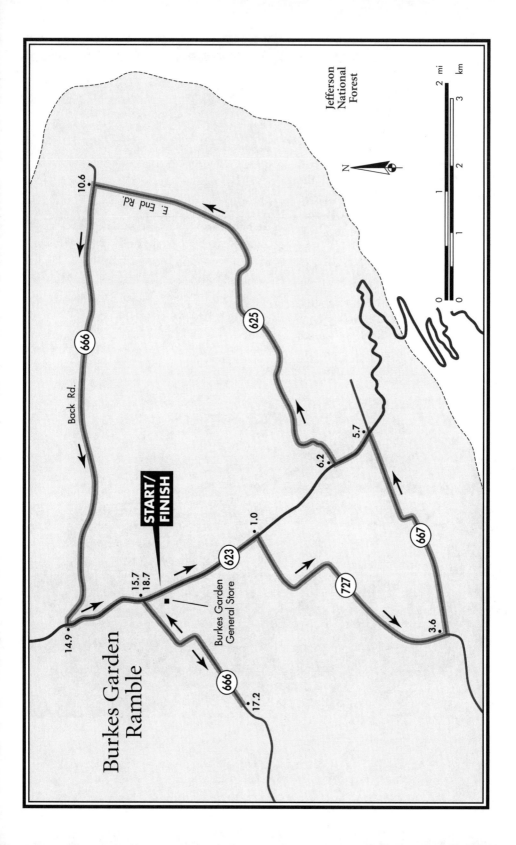

Burkes Garden Ramble

START/FINISH

Back Rd.

666

E. End Rd.

625

667

727

623

666

Burkes Garden
General Store

Jefferson
National
Forest

N

10.6

14.9

15.7
18.7

17.2

1.0

6.2

5.7

3.6

2 mi

km

0   1   2

0   1   2   3

0.0 From the Burkes Garden General Store, turn right on Burkes Garden Rd./ Rt. 623.

1.0 Turn right on West End Rd./Rt. 727.

3.6 Turn left on Medley Valley Rd./Rt. 667.

5.7 Turn left on Burkes Garden Rd./Rt. 623.

6.2 Turn right on Rt. 625.

10.6 Road bends to the left and changes to Back Rd./Rt. 666.

14.9 Turn left on Burkes Garden Rd./Rt. 623.

15.7 Turn right on Litz Lane/Rt. 666.

17.2 Turn around when road becomes gravel, return to Burkes Garden Rd.

18.7 Turn right on Burkes Garden Rd./Rt. 623.

18.9 End the ride back at the Burkes Garden General Store.

Back Road. You'll gradually lose some of that elevation in the next few miles and will be rewarded with some incredible views.

Most of Burkes Garden farmland is still owned by the same families that plowed the fields many generations ago. They are, as they have always been, reluctant to part with their land and their ways. Consider that in 1880, a wealthy railroad baron named George Washington Vanderbilt approached area landowners to purchase land in this fertile valley for his "dream home." Much to his surprise, the local farmers would not sell. Vanderbilt reluctantly moved on to his second choice and built his dream in Asheville, North Carolina, where Biltmore stands today.

There are only 20 or so miles of paved road in Burkes Garden. Since the ramble is only 19 miles, I wouldn't worry about getting lost. To make the ride any longer, you may have to double back on some of the roads. But it's not the distance that's important here. You don't do Burkes Garden for the miles. It's the valley's solitude and peacefulness that make cycling here such an experience. Perhaps the sign at the local post office expresses it best: GOD'S LAND.

LOCAL INFORMATION

♦ Tazewell Area Chamber of Commerce, Tazewell Mall, P.O. Box 6, Tazewell, VA 24651, 540–988–5091.

LOCAL EVENTS/ATTRACTIONS

♦ Burkes Garden Fall Festival, last Saturday of September, 800–588–9401.

• Tazewell County Fair, early in August, Tazewell Fairgrounds. One of Virginia's largest old-fashioned country fairs. Call the Chamber of Commerce for more information.

RESTAURANTS

• None in Burkes Garden.
• In Tazewell: Piggy Bank Cafe, 106 E. Main St., Tazewell, 540–988–2560.

ACCOMMODATIONS

• Fincastle Motor Inn, P.O. Box 855, Tazewell, VA 24651, 800–347–5647. Low-end.

BIKE SHOP

• None in the area.

REST ROOMS

• At the start in the Burkes Garden General Store

MAP

• DeLorme *Virginia Atlas and Gazetteer* map 39

Highlands Classic

Deep in the heart of Appalachia, the Highlands Classic offers the cyclist a splendid assortment of the Southwest Highland's history, nature, and culture. Starting in Abingdon, the classic can be completed in one day by fit cyclists, although an overnight stay at Hungry Mother State Park is recommended. Take time to explore historic and charming Abingdon, with its 20-block historic district and numerous shops and galleries, along with its renowned Barter Theatre. Spend a night at one of Hungry Mother State Park's cabins, and enjoy a swim in its cool 108-acre lake. In between, cycle through the rural, unspoiled countryside of Washington and Smyth counties, where Appalachian life unfolds at every turn.

Whether it's before or after your ride, be sure to spend some time in Abingdon. It's the perfect base for exploring the Southwest Highlands. Abingdon's roots go back to the mid-1700s and many of its earliest buildings still remain. The Barter Theatre was built as a church around 1832 and is now the centerpiece of a thriving arts culture. Theater tickets were often exchanged for produce and livestock; hence the name. The theater is now the longest running professional–residence theater in the country and is the state theater of Virginia. Pick up a walking tour map at the visitor's center and enjoy many of the cultural and historic offerings of one of Virginia's most charming small towns.

A few miles out of Abingdon, you will come to White's Mill. The mill is the oldest commercial waterpowered gristmill in southwestern Virginia. Built in 1790, the mill functioned until 1998. Attempts are under way to purchase and

Start: From the Abingdon Convention and Visitors Bureau.

Length: 83 miles

Terrain: Hilly, including one mountain crossing. Some long, flat to gently rolling stretches. Advanced difficulty.

Traffic and hazards: Use caution while riding through the towns of Abingdon and Marion. There are many switchbacks descending Walker Mountain on Route 16. All roads are paved.

Getting there: From I-81, take exit 17, and go north on Route 58 Business/Cummings Street for ½ mile to the visitor's center on left (335 Cummings Street). Free parking.

restore the mill, which is on the National Register of Historic Places. Although inoperable at the moment, this makes for an enjoyable rest stop and photo op.

For the next 10 miles or so, the classic follows Rich Valley Road as it parallels the mountains to the west for a rather easy and enjoyable spin to Saltville. It is during this stretch that you will encounter Appalachian life in its truest form. Numerous small farms dot the landscape, with tobacco being the most popular crop. But as serene as the countryside can be, the area is, unfortunately, distinguished by pockets of poverty with which Appalachian life is often associated. Some of the living conditions may even shock you. Keep in mind, however, that beneath the exterior lies a pioneering spirit that has endured centuries of sometimes harsh life to remain free, independent, and proud.

You'll find several places to eat and to pick up supplies in Saltville. The nation's first salt mine began here in the 1790s, providing the town the nickname "Salt Capital of the Confederacy." The operation was destroyed by Union troops in 1864, but some authentic equipment can be seen at Salt Park, along the classic route. Saltville is also known for its Ice Age Excavation Site, where well-preserved specimens are continually being discovered. Fuel up in Saltville, since a good ascent awaits you as soon as you leave town.

You'll next wind your way up the valley between Brushy Mountain to your left and Walker Mountain to the right. Keep a good eye on Walker Mountain, as you'll soon be climbing it. You'll gain elevation even before you reach Route 16, but you'll notice it even more after you get on the attractive two-lane highway. It's a good 3 miles to the top of Walker Mountain, making it the hardest climb of the classic by far. Take note of all the switchbacks on the way up, as the descent is similar. Maintain control.

At the end of your descent, you'll come to beautiful Hungry Mother State Park, an unspoiled 2,000-acre paradise. Here you'll find a sandy beach, a 108-acre lake, hiking trails, a campground, cabins for rent, and a popular restaurant. I highly recommend making the classic a two-day ride by staying overnight here and going for an evening swim. Be sure to stop at the visitor's center and take in some of the exhibits pertaining to the area's animals and nature.

White's Mill—the oldest waterpowered gristmill in southwestern Virginia.

Legend has it that Molly Marley and her young child were captured by Indians when their settlement was destroyed. Having escaped their captivity, Molly and her child wandered through the forest eating only berries. When Molly collapsed, the child followed a creek downstream until she found help. The child's only words were "Hungry mother." Later, Molly was found dead at the foot of the mountain, which today is called Molly's Knob. The creek was called Hungry Mother Creek, and when it was dammed in the 1930s, Hungry Mother Lake was created. Just in case you were curious.

Marion provides several choices for restaurants and food markets, especially if you venture off the route in town. You'll have a little climbing once you leave town, but after that the classic is remarkably gentle on its way back to Abingdon. The region is very rural, with corn and tobacco fields dominating the landscape. On one particular stretch, you'll follow Rivermont Drive and the Holston River as it meanders through a valley just north of the rugged Mount Rogers National Recreation Area. This is backroads Virginia at its best and one of the most pleasant segments of the classic. You'll actually be cycling in the shadow of the three highest mountains in Virginia (the highest being Mount Rogers, at 5,729 feet).

Once back in Abingdon, consider spending the night at the Martha

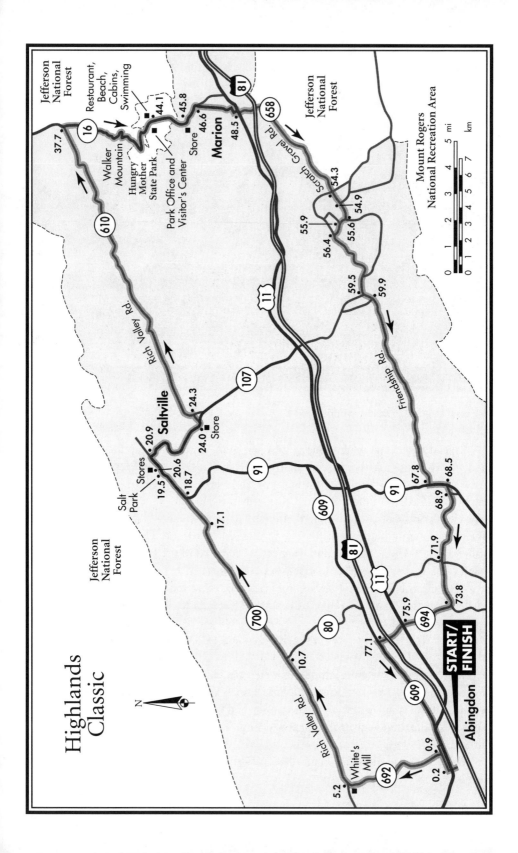

Highlands Classic

N

Jefferson National Forest

Jefferson National Forest

Restaurant, Beach, Cabins, Swimming

Walker Mountain

Hungry Mother State Park

Park Office and Visitor's Center

Store

Marion

Jefferson National Forest

Mount Rogers National Recreation Area

5 mi

km

44.1
45.8
46.6
48.5
37.7
16
610
54.3
54.9
55.6
55.9
56.4
59.5
59.9
658
81

Scratch Gravel Rd.

Rich Valley Rd.

Friendship Rd.

11

107

24.3

Saltville

24.0 Store

20.9
20.6
18.7
19.5
17.1
91
609
91
67.8
68.5
68.9
71.9
73.8

Salt Park Stores

Jefferson National Forest

81
11
75.9
694
77.1
700
80
10.7
609

Rich Valley Rd.

White's Mill

5.2
692
0.9
0.2
0.2

START/ FINISH

Abingdon

0.0 From the visitor's center, turn left on Rt. 58/Cummings St. Continue straight through the stoplight at Main St./Rt. 11.

0.2 Turn right on Valley St. NW.

0.9 Turn left on White's Mill Rd.

5.2 Turn right at the stop sign on Rich Valley Rd./Rt. 700. White's Mill is on the left before the turn.

10.7 Turn right on Rt. 80, then an immediate left back on Rich Valley Rd./Rt. 700.

17.1 Turn left on Old Saltworks Rd./Rt. 745.

18.7 Turn left at the stop sign on Rt. 91.

19.5 Salt Park is on the left. Road turns into Main St. in Saltville.

20.6 Saltbox Cafe and Grill is on the left. A Rite-Aid will soon come up on the left.

20.9 Turn right on Worthy Blvd./Rt. 107 South.

24.0 Turn left on Rt. 610. Big L's Convenience Store is on the right before the turn.

24.3 Turn left on Rich Valley Rd./Rt. 610.

37.7 Turn right at the stop sign on B. F. Buchanan Hwy./Rt. 16 South.

40.7 Nearing crest of Walker Mountain. Caution on descent—switchbacks.

44.1 Arrive at Hungry Mother State Park. Park office and visitor's center are on the right. To the left, Rt. 348 will take you through the park. No entrance fee for bicyclists. Restaurant, cabins, swimming, snack bar, etc., in the park. If not entering park, continue straight on Rt. 16 South.

45.8 Bear left to stay on Rt. 16. Hungry Mother Grocery is on the right.

46.6 Turn right at the top of hill on unmarked Prater Lane. Go 0.2 mile, then go straight at the stop sign.

47.9 Turn left at the stop sign on Chatham Hill Rd.

48.1 Make a sharp right on E. Lee St. Go 0.2 mile, then turn left at the stoplight on Broad St.

48.4 Turn right onto Main St. in downtown Marion. A few restaurants and markets are in town.

48.5 Turn left at the stoplight on S. Church St. In 0.3 mile, you'll bear to the right to stay on S. Church St. Road eventually becomes Scratch Gravel Rd./Rt. 658.

54.3 Go straight at the stop sign on Tilley's Bridge Rd./Rt. 658.

54.9 Turn right at the stop sign on South Fork Rd./Rt. 650.

55.6 Turn right at the stop sign on Red Stone Rd./Rt. 650.

55.9 Continue straight to stay on Red Stone Rd./Rt. 650.

56.4 Turn left at the stop sign on Riverside Rd./Rt. 660.

59.5 Turn left at the stop sign on Old Airport Rd./Rt. 600.

59.9 Go straight at the stop sign and flashing light on Loves Mill Rd./Rt. 762.

62.0 J. T. Wilkinson and Son Mill Store on the left.

(continued)

67.8 Turn left at the stop sign on Monroe Rd./Rt. 91.

68.5 Turn right on Liberty Hall Dr./Rt. 803.

68.9 Bear right on Rock Spring Rd./Rt. 803.

71.1 Bear right to stay on Rock Spring Rd./Rt. 803.

71.9 Turn left on Rivermont Dr./Rt. 706.

73.8 Turn right on Greenway Rd./Rt. 694.

75.9 Turn left on Lee Hwy./Rt. 11, then a quick right on Stoney Brook Rd./Rt. 694.

77.1 Turn left at the stop sign on Rt. 609.

81.2 Turn right at the stop sign on E. Main St./Rt. 11 South.

82.9 Turn left at the stoplight on Cummings St./Rt. 58. Caution, busy road.

83.1 Turn right into the visitor's center and end of ride.

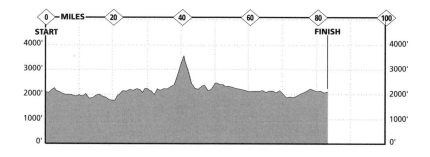

Washington Inn. Built in 1832, this gorgeous, upscale inn offers lavishly appointed rooms, many with museum-quality antiques and furnishings. With fine and casual southern-fare dining, the hotel also offers packages that include meals and Barter Theatre tickets. Need more cycling? Try the Virginia Creeper Trail, which begins in Abingdon and follows an old railroad bed for 34 miles to the North Carolina state line. Don't expect the usual flat rails-to-trail, however. The Virginia Creeper is through rugged countryside and includes grades uncharacteristic of most rail trails. If your legs are too sore from the Highlands Classic, search out the service in Abingdon that will transport you and your bike to the southern trailhead, and enjoy the easier ride back to town.

LOCAL INFORMATION

♦ Abingdon Convention and Visitors Bureau, 335 Cummings St., Abingdon, VA 24210, 800–435–3440 or 540–676–2282. Open daily from 9:00 A.M. to 5:00 P.M.

♦ Chamber of Commerce of Smyth County, 124 W. Main St., Marion, VA 24354, 540–783–3161.

LOCAL EVENTS/ATTRACTIONS

♦ Virginia Highlands Festival, Abingdon, first two weeks in August, 800–435–3440. One of the top tourist events in North America. Features crafts, antiques, and the performing arts.

♦ Hungry Mother Arts and Crafts Festival, at the Hungry Mother State Park, third weekend in July, 540–783–3161.

RESTAURANTS

♦ The Tavern, 222 E. Main St., Abingdon, 540–628–1118. Dine in Abingdon's oldest building, erected in 1779.

♦ Hungry Mother Restaurant, at the Hungry Mother State Park, 540–781–7420.

ACCOMMODATIONS

♦ Martha Washington Inn, 150 W. Main St., Abingdon, VA 24210, 540–628–3161 or 800–555–8000. Upscale historic hotel.

♦ Hungry Mother State Park, cabins and campground, 800–933–7275.

BIKE SHOP

♦ Dean's Bikes, 512 N. Main St., Marion, VA 24354, 540–783–5760.

REST ROOMS

♦ At the start in the Abingdon Convention and Visitor's Bureau
♦ Mile 20.6: Saltbox Grill and Cafe
♦ Mile 24.0: Big L's Convenience Store
♦ Mile 44.1: Hungry Mother State Park Office
♦ Mile 48.4: various stores and markets in downtown Marion
♦ Mile 81.2: various places in Abingdon

MAP

♦ DeLorme *Virginia Atlas and Gazetteer* maps 22 and 23

Appendix

SELECTED BICYCLING ORGANIZATIONS

National

Adventure Cycling Association
P.O. Box 8308
Missoula, MT 59807
800–755–2453
info@adv-cycling.org
www.adv-cycling.org
A nonprofit recreational cycling organization. Produces bicycle route maps and offers a variety of trips.

League of American Bicyclists
1612 K Street NW, Suite 401
Washington, DC 20006
202–822–1333
bikeleague@bikeleague.org
www.bikeleague.org
Works through advocacy and education for a bicycle-friendly America.

Rails to Trails Conservancy
1100 17th St., NW
Tenth Floor
Washington, DC 20036
202–331–9696
rtcmail@transact.org
www.railtrails.org
Connecting people and communities by creating a nationwide network of public trails, many from former rail lines.

Bike Virginia
P.O. Box 203
Williamsburg, VA 23187
757–229–0507
info@bikevirginia.org
www.bikevirginia.org
Conducts an annual five-day bike tour in various Virginia locations.
State Bicycle Coordinator

Virginia Department of Transportation
Ken Lantz
1401 E. Broad St.
Richmond, VA 23219
800–835–1203
vabiking@vdot.state.va.us
www.vdot.state.va.us
Works to integrate cycling into the state's transportation system. Produces the
Virginia Bicycling Guide.

Virginia Bicycling Federation
P.O. Box 5621
Arlington, VA 22205
703–696–4432
vabikefed@erols.com
www.vabike.org
Statewide advocacy alliance of bicyclists working to improve cycling conditions
throughout Virginia.

Virginia Department of Tourism
901 E. Byrd St.
Richmond, VA 23219
800–VISIT VA
804–786–4484
vainfo@vedp.state.va.us
www.virginia.org
State office for tourism, with excellent Web site.